From a Behavioral Point of View
A Psychological Primer

Jay Moore
University of Wisconsin at Milwaukee

2015
Sloan Publishing
Cornwall on Hudson, NY 12520

Library of Congress Cataloging-in-Publication Data

Moore, Jay (Professor)
From a behavioral point of view : a psychological primer / Jay Moore, University of Wisconsin at Milwaukee.
    pages cm
ISBN 978-1-59738-055-3 -- ISBN 1-59738-055-5
1. Behaviorism (Psychology) I. Title.
BF199.M663 2015
150.19'43--dc23
                                    2014042049

Cover design by Amy Rosen, K&M Design, Inc.

© 2015 by Sloan Publishing, LLC

Sloan Publishing, LLC
220 Maple Road
Cornwall-on-Hudson, NY 12520

All rights reserved. No portion of this book may be reproduced, in any form or by any means, without permission in writing from the Publisher.

Printed in the United States of America

10 9 8 7 6 5 4 3 2 1

ISBN 13: 978-1-59738-055-3
ISBN 10: 1-59738-055-5

The Cambridge Center—Sloan Century Series in Behavior Analysis

A. Charles Catania, *Series Advisor*

James M. Johnston & Dennis Reid, editors
The Promise of Behavioral Services for People with Intellectual Disabilities
(2016) (978-1-59738-065-2)

Rob Holdsambeck and Henry Pennypacker, editors
Behavioral Science: Tales of Inspiration, Discovery, and Service (2015)
(978-1-59738-048-5)

James M. Johnston
Radical Behaviorism for ABA Practitioners (2014)
(978-1-59738-043-0)

A. Charles Catania
Learning: 5th Edition (2013)
(978-1-59738-023-2)

Beth Sulzer-Azaroff, Kathleen Dyer, Susan Dupont, and Dianne Soucy
Applying Behavior Analysis Across the Autism Spectrum: A Field Guide for Practitioners, 2nd Edition (2013)
(978-1-59738-036-2)

G. Roy Mayer, Beth Sulzer-Azaroff, and Michele Wallace
Behavior Analysis for Lasting Change, 3rd Edition (2014)
(978-1-59738-050-8)

Erik Mayville and James A. Mulick, editors
Behavioral Foundations of Effective Autism Treatment (2011)
(978-1-59738-031-7)

Fred Keller
At My Own Pace (2008)
(978-1-59738-017-1)

Jay Moore
Conceptual Foundations of Radical Behaviorism (2007)
(978-1-59738-011-9)

For more information about these titles, visit our website at
http://www.sloanpublishing.com/behavior

Contents

Preface   xi

1. **Introduction**   1
   Why Study Behavior?   1
   What Is Behavior?   2
   Operant Behavior   4
   Operant Consequences: Reinforcers and Punishers   5
   The Development of Operant Behavior   6
   Operant Stimulus Control: Generalization and Discrimination   7
   The Generic Nature of Stimuli and Responses   8
   Unconditioned Respondent Behavior   9
   Conditioned Respondent Behavior   9
   Summary and Conclusions   10
   Key Terms and Concepts   10
   Study Questions   11

2. **What Is Inside?**   13
   Some Historical Background   13
   Mentalism   15
   Sometimes Mental Talk is Actually About Private, Covert Behavior   18
   Behavior as a Scientific Subject Matter in its Own Right   19
   Free-Will Objections to Behavior as a Scientific Subject Matter in its Own Right   19
   What Does "Free Will" Actually Mean?   20
   Summary and Conclusions   21
   Reference   22
   Key Terms and Concepts   22
   Study Questions   22

3. **Genes, Selection, and Physiology**   23
   Chromosomes   23
   Genes   24
   Genes as Causes of Behavior   26
   Selection   27
   The Selection of Behavior   28
   The Selection of Operant Behavior   30
   Summary and Conclusions   31
   Reference   32
   Key Terms and Concepts   32
   Study Questions   32

4. **The Nature of Verbal Behavior**   33
   The Evolution of Verbal Behavior   34
   Verbal Behavior, Language, and Communication   35
   The Functional Analysis of Verbal Behavior: Contingencies and Units   36
   The Mand Relation   37
   The Tact Relation   38
   The Intraverbal Relation   39
   Grammar and Syntax   39
   Higher-order Verbal Relations: Equivalence Relations   40
   Verbal Regulation   41
   Interpretation   42
   Verbal Behavior, Folk Psychology, and Mentalism   42
   Summary and Conclusions   43
   References   44
   Key Terms and Concepts   44
   Study Questions   44

5. **Self**   46
   Individuality   46
   Self as Agent   47
   What Does Agency or Freedom Mean?   48
   The Self in Behavior Analysis   50
   Summary and Conclusions   51
   References   52
   Key Terms and Concepts   52
   Study Questions   52

6. **Consciousness and Awareness   53**
   What Does Consciousness Mean?   53
   Private Behavioral Events   55
   Verbal Reports About Our Internal Sensations and Feelings   55
   The Influence of Covert Operant Behavior   57
   Consciousness From a Traditional Point of View   58
   Awareness   59
   Some Contemporary Issues   60
   Blindsight   60
   Phantom Limb Pain   61
   Consciousness in the Laboratory   61
   Summary and Conclusions   62
   References   62
   Key Terms and Concepts   62
   Study Questions   63

7. **Thinking, Cognition, and Memory   64**
   What is the Behavior of Thinking?   64
   Memory   66
   Traditional Views of Thinking, Cognition, and Memory   69
   Summary and Conclusions   71
   Reference   72
   Key Terms and Concepts   72
   Study questions   72

8. **Knowledge and Truth   73**
   Knowledge as Behavior   73
   Knowing How and Knowing That   74
   Knowledge From a Traditional Point of View   74
   Truth   75
   Verbal Processes, Truth, and Scientific Knowledge   76
   Summary and Conclusions   78
   References   79
   Key Terms and Concepts   79
   Study Questions   79

9. **Perceiving   80**
   Behavior Analysis and Perceiving   80
   Seeing as a Function of Environmental Circumstances   82

Some Representative Studies of Perceiving 83
Attention 85
Dreaming 86
A Traditional View of Perceiving 87
Summary and Conclusions 88
References 88
Key Terms and Concepts 89
Study Questions 89

10. **Purpose, Intention, and Belief** 90
Behavior Analysis and Purpose 90
Behavior Analysis and Intention 92
Behavior Analysis and Belief 93
Traditional Views of Purpose, Intention, and Belief 94
Summary and Conclusions 95
References 96
Key Terms and Concepts 96
Study Questions 96

11. **Personality and Individual Differences** 97
Personality 97
Behavior Analysis and Traits 99
Intelligence Testing 100
Creativity 103
Summary and Conclusions 105
References 106
Key Terms and Concepts 107
Study Questions 107

12. **Attitudes, Attributions, and Situations** 109
Behavior Analysis and Attitudes 109
Implicit Attitude Measurement 110
Behavior Analysis and Attribution 111
Attitudes From a Traditional Point of View 112
Internal Attributions and the Pernicious Social -isms 114
Summary and Conclusions 115
References 115
Key Terms and Concepts 116
Study Questions 116

13. **Feelings, Emotions, Moods, and Motives** 119
   Feelings From a Behavioral Point of View 119
   Traditional Accounts of Feelings 119
   Feelings and the Mind-Body Problem 120
   The Causal Status of Feelings and Emotions 120
   Other Minds 122
   Moods, Emotions, and Motives 122
   The Feelings of Reinforcers 124
   Summary and Conclusions 125
   References 125
   Key Terms and Concepts 125
   Study Questions 125

14. **Applied Behavior Analysis, Abnormal Behavior, and Therapy** 127
   Some Representative Behavior-Analytic Interventions 128
   Clinical Behavior Analysis 130
   Comparison to Traditional Views 132
   Why Do Forms of Traditional Therapy Work When They Do? 134
   Who Judges Improvement? 135
   Summary and Conclusions 136
   References 136
   Key Terms and Concepts 136
   Study Questions 137

15. **Ethics and Morality** 138
   What is Good Conduct? 138
   Social Impact as Another Consideration 140
   The "Good" 140
   The Temporal Context 142
   The Moral-Ethical Matrix 142
   Moral and Ethical Injunctions 143
   Summary and Conclusions 143
   References 144
   Key Terms and Concepts 144
   Study Questions 144

16. **Values, Rights, and Responsibilities** 146
   Values as Reinforcers 146
   Rights 147

Responsibility   147
Jurisprudence   148
Summary and Conclusions   150
References   150
Key Terms and Concepts   150
Study Questions   150

17. **Education   152**
A Behavior-Analytic View of the Educational Process   152
Contingencies and the Matter of Control   153
Verbal Knowledge   154
Tacts   154
Intraverbal Control   155
Some Traditional Assumptions About Students, the Educational Process, and the Role of the Instructor   156
Concepts, Collateral Responses, and Equivalence Classes   157
Behavior-Analytic Assessment   160
Summary and Conclusions   160
References   161
Key terms and concepts   161
Study questions   161

18. **Societies and Cultures   163**
Three Levels of Selection   163
Cultural Practices   164
Evolution of a Culture   166
Design of a Culture   167
Democracy   167
Summary and Conclusions   168
References   169
Study Questions   169

19. **Conclusion   170**

Name Index   173
Subject Index   175

Preface

In the late fall of 1995, Jim Johnston, Ed Morris, and I met in Milwaukee to discuss the possibility of a book on behavior analysis. We actually progressed as far as to decide on the general plan of the book. We decided on a list of chapters. Each chapter would then be devoted to the review of a single thematic topic, something like the chapters in Skinner's books Science and Human Behavior and About Behaviorism. A chapter would begin by introducing the central topic(s) for the chapter. Then it would compare how traditional psychology addresses that topic with how behavior analysis addresses it, including some conceptual extension to topics students will have likely heard about in other (psychology) courses. The chapters would be relatively circumscribed, to give instructors the option of selecting chapters to best suit their courses and supplementing the chapters as they saw fit. The chapters would not be the standard heavily sourced academic writing, with extensive citations and block quotes, but rather something more accessible to students, with minimal citations. The chapters would follow a path starting roughly with some fundamentals of behavior analysis, then leading to the individual, and finishing with society and culture.

Various events intervened in all our lives, and Jim and Ed both deferred to me when in 2009 I suggested returning to the project. The present book is the result. Any merit of the book can be attributed to their insights. I am especially grateful to Phil Hineline and to Ed Morris and his students for their heroic reading and comments on an earlier draft. Any liabilities of the book can be attributed to my shortcomings in executing it.

I dedicate the book to the contributions of Phil Hineline, Jim Johnston, and Ed Morris to behavior analysis.

J. Moore
Milwaukee, WI
Jan 1, 2015

Chapter 1

Introduction

This book is about *behavior analysis*. In simple terms, behavior analysis seeks to understand what individuals do and under what circumstances they typically do it. Behavior analysts believe that if we can better understand why behavior takes place, then we can better manage our own lives and more usefully contribute to the lives of others, so that we all can achieve our full potential as humans.

This book examines a series of important topics that are traditionally thought to belong to psychology, but treats them differently from a traditional viewpoint. By so doing, this book suggests that we can arrive at a new, different, and ultimately more helpful understanding of these topics. For instance, the discipline of psychology is traditionally defined as the science of behavior and the mental processes that cause behavior. A common misunderstanding that comes from this definition is that only psychology has anything important to say about the uniquely personal phenomena in our lives, such as language, the self, consciousness, knowledge, perception, purpose, belief, emotions, ethics, and values. These phenomena are regarded as belonging to the mental domain, rather than the behavioral domain. As a result, the analysis of these phenomena is thought to require a different approach than the analysis of behavior. In contrast to the traditional viewpoint, this book takes the position that such phenomena have always referred to behavioral matters. Accordingly, each chapter of this book reviews and analyzes one of these topics from a behavioral point of view, so that we may come to a new understanding of its relevance in our lives. Chapter 1 introduces some of the basic concepts in behavior analysis, to lay the foundation for the analyses that follow.

Why Study Behavior?

Behavior analysts consider behavior to be a scientific subject matter in its own right, to be investigated with the same empirical, observational methods as are used in the other natural sciences. This view is very important, as it distinguishes behavior analysis from more traditional views in psychology. As alluded to above, traditional views often assume the proper subject matter for psychology is some mental state, process, or entity in an individual's mind that underlies behavior. Thus, the study of behavior is relevant mainly to support inferences about the underlying phenomenon.

Behavior analysts have their own interpretation of how events going on inside a person contribute to an explanation of the person's behavior. We discuss the behavioral interpretation and contrast it with the traditional view in many of the chapters that follow. For now, suffice it to say that the behavioral interpretation is based on a thoroughgoing behavioral perspective that differs from that of traditional psychology in many important ways, especially involving appeals to the supposed causal properties of the mind. Taking a systematic and comprehensive behavioral point of view to such matters is what this book is all about.

We face many critical problems in the world today. For example, suppose we say we want to improve reading scores in children. Next, suppose we say the problem is that we don't know how children's brains change when they learn to read. Now, suppose we invent a new machine that allows us compare images of children's brains before and after they have learned to read. To be sure, children's brains do change when children learn to read. However, behavior analysts argue that we have not very meaningfully addressed our concerns unless we can identify how the children's behavioral experiences with respect their environments have caused their brains to change. After all, those experiences that have caused both the children's brains to change and their learning to read.

Similarly, suppose we say the problem is that the children don't read very well because they have low self-esteem, where self-esteem is theorized to be some underlying mental entity. We can even administer a paper-and-pencil test designed to measure self-esteem in children, and find that sure enough, children with high scores on such a test learn to read readily, and those with low scores learn to read only with some difficulty. Aside from the considerable question of how useful it is to say something mental like a self-esteem can cross a boundary and cause something behavioral like reading, behavior analysts believe we have not have not very meaningfully addressed our concerns unless we can identify how the children's behavioral experiences with respect to their environments have caused both (a) the behavior related to what we are calling self-esteem and (b) the behavior of reading. Indeed, how can we provide behavioral experiences that increase self-esteem and reading? As before, we can see that behavior is foremost among our concerns.

What Is Behavior?

What then is behavior? For behavior analysts, when we speak of behavior, we are speaking of a special kind of interaction or exchange between individuals and their environments. An instance of behavior is an event. Turning on a light when entering a dark room or typing the letter "A" on a keyboard are presumably uncontroversial instances of behavior. They involve movements and outcomes that are observable to others. What about standing at attention in a military formation? What about stifling a sneeze? What about weighing the pros and cons of playing a given card in a card game? What about teaching children to control their bodily processes through toilet training? These latter instances don't seem to involve any observable movement. For behavior analysts, all of the above instances are usefully considered behavior, even though some do not involve movement that is observable to others. Indeed, some seem to take place inside the skin. Nevertheless, we can consider all of these instances as behavior because there is a certain setting, or condition of the environment in which the behavior takes place, and what the individual is doing—even if just standing still, plays a certain role in an individual's life with respect to that environment. Standing at attention is obeying the command of the drill instructor, stifling a sneeze prevents the sneeze, weighing which card to play often contributes to winning the hand, and toilet training keeps our clothing dry and sanitary.

In addition, although our perceptual systems are not literally part of the systems that regulate our muscles and glands, our perceptual systems may be considered as an integral part of a behavioral event when they are influenced by prevailing circumstances in the environment. A common case is when we mistakenly reach for the phone just because we are waiting for an important phone call and have heard some sound that resembles the ringing of the phone. In an extension of the perceptual case, we may even close our eyes and imagine what we would see if we took a particular route from our home to a shopping center, for example, in a desire to avoid heavy traffic or road repairs. For behavior analysts such instances also constitute behavior, in the sense that the instances are causally related to how we live our lives, even though in some cases no one else may be able to detect what we are doing.

Behavior can be at any point along a continuum commonly labeled peripheral to central. At the peripheral end of the continuum, the behavior may well be observable to others because it is directed toward and operates on the surrounding observable environment. At the central end of the continuum, the behavior in question may not be observable to any other individual, for example, by being inside the skin, as in stifling a sneeze, deciding which card to play, or learning to control eliminative responses in toilet training. Behavior is then an event that occurs when many different variables come together. Our skills, actions, and capabilities are our possessions. We are what we do, even if others cannot observe what we are doing.

If instances of behavior fall on the continuum from peripheral to central, so also does the environment with respect to which the individual is behaving. Accessibility of behavior and environment are matters that pertain to the standpoint of an observer, rather than to an essential feature of either behavior or environment. Our responses to full bladders are in the same category as our responses to red and green traffic lights—it is just that the environment is peripheral and accessible to others in the case of traffic lights but central and inaccessible in the case of bladders.

An important feature of behavior analysis is its emphasis on the *functional characteristics of behavior*, as opposed to the *form of behavior*. We can consider some examples to illustrate this point. As one example, consider the case of typing. Here, the finger we use to strike a key on a keyboard doesn't matter—the keyboard registers the key that was struck regardless of whether we have used a finger from the left or right hand, index or ring finger. What matters are the functional properties of the response: that the response is sufficiently forceful and directed toward the location that results in the pressing down of the desired key, thereby contributing to the spelling of the desired word.

As another example, consider a motion-activated hand drier next to a sink. The hand drier has a sensor that reacts to movement immediately in front of it. For this sensor, the precise form of the movement doesn't matter—virtually any movement will do. Even the most casual observation will suggest that different people wave their wet hands in front of the hand drier in all sorts of different ways. There is not one and only one muscle movement that will activate the hand drier. Even though the precise topographies may well differ for different people or even for the same person at different times, all these topographies are equivalent in the sense they have the same function for the individual—their hands are wet, and motion in front of the hand drier will produce a stream of air that dries them.

Of course, in some instances a particular topography does matter. However, the topography matters because of the functional demands of the situation, rather than the structural definition of the behavior in question. Suppose someone stops us on the street and asks us how to get to the library.

We might point to the large building at the end of the block. Here, the particular topography is important—we would not want to point to just any building, or wave our hands in just any direction. We point explicitly to the library because doing so is what the situation demands—the person who has asked directions needs to know which building to go to. Nevertheless, the topography of pointing in a particular direction comes about because of the context in which it occurs, and may be understood in terms of its relation to that context. Sometimes the functional demands of a situation do require a particular topography, but sometimes they don't. Of course, we can point with our left or right hands, fingers extended or not, so even within the demands of this situation some variations are possible.

As we will see, some behavior is said to be innate, in the sense that through our genes we have inherited particular forms of responsiveness to particular forms of environmental stimulation. For example, we may salivate to food, or start to sweat when faced with an unpleasant or awkward situation. Other behavior is said to be learned in the sense that it is acquired as a result of various events we experience during our lifetimes. Turning on the light when we enter the room or typing the letter "A" on a keyboard are things we learn to do because they have consequences—the room is illuminated and we don't stub our toes, or we can spell a desired word. An older term that was used in connection with learned behavior was "habit." This term suggests that an individual possesses behavior as a result of some sort of mechanical or even unconscious inner essence or quality. Behavior analysts do not ordinarily use the term habit in any formal sense. Rather, for both innate and learned behavior, the important question is to what circumstances in the environment is the behavior functionally related, rather than to what inner essence or quality can we attribute the behavior.

Operant Behavior

For behavior analysts, probably the most important type of behavior is called *operant behavior*. In the case of operant behavior, the individual is said to emit a response in some particular setting. The response may then be followed by a consequence. The consequence determines whether the behavior occurs again in that setting. From this description we can see that the analysis of operant behavior involves three important elements: the setting, the response itself, and its consequence.

A systematic way of describing the relation among these three elements in operant behavior is called the *contingency of reinforcement*. In nontechnical language, the word contingency simply means "if–then." Recalling the three elements we identified above, we can express the notion of a contingency in terms of an "if–then" statement. For convenience, we describe the setting in terms of one specific feature, such as a light or a tone, even though the setting can be very complex, perhaps as a combination of many different features. Accordingly, in what follows we refer to the setting as a discriminative stimulus, symbolically represented as S^D. Thus, for operant behavior, the contingency may be schematically depicted as follows:

$$S^D : R \Rightarrow \text{consequence}$$

The simplest way to state this relation is to say that if a discriminative stimulus [S^D] is or has been present [:] and a response [R] is emitted, then [=>] a consequence will follow. Some behavior analysts refer to the three elements of operant behavior in a slightly different way, using an A : B => C relation. In this relation, A represents the *antecedent* setting that functions as a cue or signal that the response will have some consequence. In this way of describing the relation, A is the same as the discriminative stimulus or S^D. B represents the operant behavior itself, and is the same as R. C represents the consequence of the behavior.

We can see this three-term relation in many everyday cases. Suppose we need to meet someone at a specified time. When the clock reads the appropriate time, we leave, and we then keep the appointment. Suppose we want a cup of freshly brewed coffee. When the signal light comes on the percolator, we can help ourselves. Suppose we want to travel in our car from home to the market. When the light turns green at a traffic intersection, we can step on the accelerator and safely make our way to our destination. Suppose we have a pet dog we want to train to "Sit" on command. When we say "Sit" and the dog sits down, we give the dog a dog biscuit. In these cases, the time on the clock or the light on the percolator or the green traffic light or our verbal command of "Sit" functions as a discriminative stimulus to signal when the response will achieve some particular consequence.

In more complex cases, behavior is extended over longer periods of time. For example, when the clock shows the time to leave for an appointment, we may pick up our car keys, start the car, and drive to our destination by making a series of left and right turns at various landmarks or intersections. Here, the behavior is still operant behavior, but individual instances become organized in a sequence that is called a *chain*. The consequence occurs at the end of the chain, and we progress to that consequence by completing the intermediate stages, which are called links. Nevertheless, we are still talking about operant behavior.

In the case of humans, we note that the clock doesn't innately cause us to keep an appointment, the signal light doesn't innately cause us to pour a cup of coffee, the green light doesn't innately cause us to step on the accelerator, and the word "Sit" doesn't innately cause our pet dog to sit down. Rather, the response in question occurs because various conditions provide the occasion on which the response will have some consequence, in a contingency of reinforcement. As we will see throughout this book, the contingency of reinforcement is the fundamental unit for analyzing operant behavior.

Operant Consequences: Reinforcers and Punishers

Some consequences make behavior more likely. The term for these consequences is *reinforcer*. The term for delivering these consequences as well as for the effect of this procedure—the increase in behavior that results—is *reinforcement*. The source of "to reinforce" lies in the everyday sense of strengthening behavior, as observed when the behavior occurs more frequently. Reinforcers that are effective the first time they are encountered are called *unconditioned reinforcers*. Sometimes reinforcement involves presenting something. These instances are called *positive reinforcement*. Common examples are the presentation of life-maintaining substances like food when we are hungry or water when we are thirsty. Sometimes reinforcement involves terminating if not avoiding something altogether that would happen if a response was not made. These instances are called *negative reinforcement*. One example is escape from something, as when we escape from summer heat and humidity by turning on an air conditioner. Another example is avoiding something, as when we avoid a parking ticket by putting money in a parking meter.

Reinforcers that acquire their reinforcing effectiveness during the lifetime of an individual are called *conditioned reinforcers*. For instance, money is often a conditioned reinforcer in light of modern culture. Indeed, when it is an exceptionally strong reinforcer, such that it dominates a person's life, we may call the person materialistic. Awards for academic performance, plaques and awards for service on a committee, and medals for noteworthy achievements are other common conditioned reinforcers. Some conditioned reinforcers are very subtle but very powerful in our lives: eye contact, smiles, approval, peer recognition for a job well done.

Some consequences, however, make behavior less likely. The term for these consequences is *punisher*. The term for delivering these consequences as well as for the effect of this procedure—the decrease in behavior that results—is *punishment*. Punishers that are effective the first time they are encountered are called *unconditioned punishers*. Sometimes punishment involves presenting something, as when we are not paying sufficient attention and we hit our thumbs with a hammer when driving a nail. These instances are called *positive punishment*. Sometimes punishment involve taking something away, as when persons have their driver's licenses suspended because they have driven their cars too fast and received traffic tickets for speeding. These instances are called *negative punishment*. Punishers that acquire their punishing effectiveness are called *conditioned punishers*, as when someone frowns at us if we say something inappropriate. Everyday life is a complex and often subtle mix of reinforcers and punishers, both unconditioned and conditioned.

Most of the important forms of behavior in our lives as humans involve operant behavior: turning on a light when entering a dark room, typing the letter a on a keyboard, conversing with others, reading a book, attending school, working at a job, writing down a grocery list, driving a car, solving problems, and so on. As implied by some items in the above listing, an especially important form of operant behavior in our lives is verbal behavior. For present purposes, verbal behavior is operant behavior because it is functionally related to circumstances in the social environment: It achieves certain consequences through its effect on listeners. It can be analyzed in terms of the same contingencies of reinforcement we use to analyze other forms of operant behavior. We say a great deal more about the importance of verbal behavior in chapter 4.

In our everyday language, the term reinforcement is often said to involve receiving a pleasurable reward, and punishment is often said to involve inflicting pain. To be sure, we may well experience pleasure during reinforcement, and pain during punishment. Nevertheless, for behavior analysts, the terms reinforcement and punishment are more properly used in connection with their effect on behavior, rather than individuals. Thus, we say that responses are reinforced or punished, rather than individuals are rewarded or punished.

A further point regarding consequences concerns a concept called a *motivative operation*. A motivative operation is an environmental event, operation, or stimulus condition that affects the relevance of (a) discriminative stimuli and consequences for particular responses, and (b) the probability of responses that in the past were related to those consequences. For example, suppose we want to teach our dog to roll over on command. We start by depriving it of food for a short while. We can then teach our dog to roll over using the command of "Roll over" as the discriminative stimulus and a dog biscuit as a reinforcer. Here, the depriving of food is the motivative operation: It has established the dog biscuit as a reinforcer and the command as a discriminative stimulus. However, if our dog has just had a big meal, the dog biscuit will probably not function as a reinforcer. In addition, we can say "Roll over" as often as we want, but the command will probably not function as a discriminative stimulus. These two observations illustrate (a) above. Interestingly, after the dog has learned to roll over, we may find that just depriving it of food increases the probability that it will roll over, even when we have not commanded it to do so. All we have to do is stand silently in front of the hungry dog and it will roll over. This observation illustrates (b) above.

The Development of Operant Behavior

We said earlier that when operant behavior is emitted, it can be strengthened by its consequences. Readers may recognize that the behavior has to be emitted for some other reason first, before the behaving individual experiences the consequences that will ultimately maintain it. Behavior analysts commonly talk of two possible sources of operant behavior, singly or even in combination.

The first source is *random behavior*. Here, we may not be able to specify exactly the conditions that cause some form of behavior, beyond simply saying that at least on some occasions we observe individuals do move around and act nonselectively with respect to their environment. After all, individuals are living creatures, and one of the properties of living creatures is that they can move. In any event, once this form of behavior is emitted, it can be influenced by its consequences, even though we may not have been able to identify the conditions to which it was originally related. Individuals that have a large amount of this "uncommitted" behavior may have an advantage in adapting, as nature has more raw material with which to work in the process of adaptation.

The second source is called *shaping*. Shaping is a process in which an outside agent, say another human, delivers a consequence for responses that come progressively closer to some final, explicitly desired form. At the beginning, the behavior is often just random, but then the outside agent acts deliberately to alter it. A technical phrase often used in connection with shaping is *differential reinforcement of successive approximations*. At the end of the shaping process, the form of the response differs significantly from its form at the beginning. The terms "progressively closer" and "successive approximations" suggest that each response is reinforced as it gets closer and closer to satisfying the criteria for the final form of the behavior.

A useful metaphor follows from the word shaping. Consider a potter who is creating a vase from an undifferentiated lump of clay. The potter gradually applies pressure on the clay with hands or tools in a straightforward progression to shape the final, desired form of the vase. The undifferentiated lump of clay corresponds to the initial unfocused and random movement of the individual. Thus, a behavior analyst would apply pressure by making successive reinforcers contingent on forms of behavior that are progressively closer to the final, desired form of the response. Our teachers likely shaped our handwriting as we attended school when we were growing up.

A remaining point is that if the circumstances that caused the behavior in the first place are no longer in effect, the behavior will cease. We use the term *extinction* in connection with this state of affairs. Thus, it is useful to recognize that operants are a function of dynamic processes, reflecting the environmental circumstances that cause them. They are not static phenomena, such that once they are stamped in they do not change over time.

Operant Stimulus Control: Generalization and Discrimination

The concept of the operant contingency of reinforcement emphasizes the relation between the response and its consequence. However, as we noted earlier, it does not neglect the contribution of the prior stimulus. To recapitulate, the prior stimulus is called a discriminative stimulus and is abbreviated S^D. The relation called *stimulus control* is said to exist when the probability of a response varies with the properties of the discriminative stimulus. Let us now elaborate on this relation.

Two important terms relating to stimulus control are generalization and discrimination. These terms describe relations between antecedent features of the environment and behavior. More specifically, we speak of *generalization* when an individual responds similarly given similar discriminative stimuli. Thus, we speak of generalization when an individual responds in a particular way in the presence of one discriminative stimulus, and then responds in a similar way in the presence of a second discriminative stimulus, even though the individual may not have previously come in contact with the second discriminative stimulus. Why does the individual respond similarly? The answer is that the properties of the second stimulus are similar to those of the first. For example, suppose a pigeon's responses have been reinforced in the laboratory in the presence of a red light. If we then turn on an orange light, we will probably observe that the responses the pigeon makes to the orange light are similar to those the pigeon made to the original red light, based on the similarity between orange and red. In the world outside the laboratory, if we have learned to identify the make of a car based on its color or size or shape, we are likely to identify other cars as being that same make, based on similar color or size or shape, even though they might actually be different makes. Note that the term generalization describes a similarity between two instances of responding, based on a similarity between two discriminative stimuli. The generalizing is the name for the similar behavior. Thus, we do not say the behavior occurs because of generalization, but rather that it is an instance of generalization. In particular, we do not appeal to some hypothetical inner activity of the pigeon called generalizing to account for the similar responding.

We speak of *discrimination* when an individual responds differently given different discriminative stimuli. More specifically, we speak of discrimination when an individual responds in a particular way in the presence of one discriminative stimulus, and then responds in a different way in the presence of a second discriminative stimulus. Why does the individual respond differently? The answer is that the properties of the second stimulus differ from those of the first.

Further, in many cases, the behavior in the presence of the second stimulus differs because the second stimulus is associated with different experiences, such as different contingencies. For example, suppose a pigeon's responses have been reinforced in the laboratory in the presence of a red light, but not reinforced in the presence of a green light. The pigeon will then tend to respond to red but not to green, based on the difference between red and green lights and the contingencies with which each color is correlated. In the world outside the laboratory, we see these relations at work when we step on the brake at a traffic intersection when the traffic light is red but not green, and when we step on the accelerator at a traffic intersection when the traffic light is green but not red. We would then say a discrimination exists, based on our differential responses in the presence of green and red traffic lights. Note that the term discrimination describes a difference between two instances of responding, based on a difference between two discriminative stimuli and any contingencies with which they may be correlated. As with generalization, the discrimination is the name for the differential behavior. Thus, we do not say the behavior occurs because of discrimination, but rather that it is an instance of discrimination. In particular, we do not appeal to some hypothetical inner activity of the pigeon called discriminating to account for the differential responding.

The Generic Nature of Stimuli and Responses

A final important feature of analyzing behavior is the generic nature of stimuli and responses. By generic nature of stimuli we mean that individuals are influenced by classes of stimulus events, rather than simply isolated, unconnected stimuli. To take one example, we are often able to name a particular piece of music, even when it is played by a different instrument or sung by a different person and the auditory frequencies of the notes differ dramatically. To take another example, we are often able to recognize the letter A, even if it is handwritten or manually printed or printed in any number of computer fonts and the visual appearances of the letters differ dramatically. Our naming reflects that we recognize the instances of the music or letters are members of the same class, not necessarily two different pieces of music or letters. Thus, certain stimulus events are said to belong to the same class when they evoke the same response.

Just as stimuli belong to classes, so also do responses. We may turn on the light in a dark room using our left hand, our right hand, or even our elbow if our hands are full. These topographies differ, but they may usefully be regarded as part of the same class of responses because they are related to the same environmental circumstances: The room is dark, there is a light switch, and the outcome of operating the light switch, however we do so, is to illuminate the room so we can see where we are going. Thus, certain responses are said to belong to the same class when the same class of environmental circumstances evoke them.

Unconditioned Respondent Behavior

To be sure, behavior analysts recognize that there other forms of behavior than operant behavior. One form of behavior is simply innate and reflexive. This form occurs when an individual comes into contact with certain kinds of stimulation in the environment, and then responds in a relatively uniform way directly after this contact. Behavior analysts call this form *respondent behavior*. There are many examples of this relation: A puff of air to our eye causes us to blink, food in our mouth causes us to salivate, a tap on the patellar tendon causes our knee to jerk, or an unpleasantly loud noise causes our heart rate to increase or causes us to sweat more, as suggested by the everyday terms nervousness and anxiety.

The stimulation is said to *elicit* the behavior in question. The terms elicit and its cognate *elicitation* are used here to indicate that a response follows directly after an organism has come into contact with the stimulation. This form of behavior is relatively uniform within a given species of organisms, given the stimulation that elicits it, although the response that the stimulus elicits in one species may well differ from that which the same stimulus elicits in another species. As the term innate implies, these responses are part of an individual's genetic endowment, passed down through successive generations in the lifetime of the species. Although behavior analysts may well continue to use the term reflex in nontechnical situations, they have found it more useful to use a different term in technical situations: respondent behavior. We will use the term respondent here.

When the respondent occurs without any special history of interaction between the individual and environment, we speak of an *unconditioned respondent*. We further speak of the stimulation that elicits an unconditioned respondent as an *unconditioned stimulus*. Some respondents are linked to the autonomic nervous system and the smooth muscles of our internal organs. For example, consider food that causes our mouths to water. The food is an unconditioned stimulus that elicits the unconditioned respondent of salivation. Similarly, consider a loud, unpleasant noise that causes us to become anxious. The loud noise is an unconditioned stimulus that causes the unconditioned respondent of an increase in heart rate or sweating. Other respondents are linked to the somatic nervous system and the striped muscles of our skeletal muscle system. For example, consider a puff of air that causes our eye to blink. The puff is an unconditioned stimulus that elicits the unconditioned respondent of blinking. Similarly, consider a tap on the patellar tendon during a doctor's examination. The tap is an unconditioned stimulus that elicits the unconditioned respondent of leg flexion. Again, however, we label a response as a respondent because it is elicited by particular kinds of environmental circumstances, not because particular neural or motor structures are involved.

Conditioned Respondent Behavior

Some forms of respondent behavior are learned. The term "conditioned" is sometimes used in connection with this form of behavior, in the sense that the behavior depends on, or is conditional on, certain experiences during the lifetime of the individual. Behavior analysts call this form *conditioned respondent behavior*. A conditioned stimulus is one that acquires an ability to elicit a respondent through various learning experiences. Common synonyms for this form of learning are classical conditioning and Pavlovian conditioning.

A portion of the behavior in which humans engage is elicited, respondent behavior, both unconditioned and conditioned. As noted earlier, we may blink our eyes when we experience puffs of wind in our faces, salivate when we smell a delicious home-cooked meal, feel anxious when we approach a traffic intersection in which we almost had an accident the day before, feel apprehensive when we take a test for which we wish we had studied more, or feel excited when we near the time to be reunited with loved ones.

Summary and Conclusions

This chapter has introduced some of the basic concepts of behavior analysis. Behavior analysis is the science of behavior. Behavior may be defined as a special kind of interaction or exchange between an individual and the environment. Behavior is defined functionally, in terms of what causes it and how it contributes to the life of the individual, rather than structurally, in terms of its form. Why do behavior analysts study behavior? The answer is that we may usefully regard behavior as a scientific subject matter in its own right, rather than merely an indication of some underlying process supposedly taking place inside the individual. An important form of behavior, particularly for humans, is called operant behavior. Operant behavior is a function of a three term contingency, involving (a) an antecedent condition or discriminative stimulus, (b) the operant response itself, and (c) the consequence. Operant behavior is acquired during the lifetime of the individual organism. Some consequences make behavior more likely. These consequences are called reinforcers. Other consequences make behavior less likely. These consequences are called punishers. When a consequence has an effect that doesn't depend on particular experiences during our lifetimes, the consequences are called unconditioned. When a consequence has an effect that does depend on particular experiences during our lifetimes, the consequences are called conditioned. Motivative operations alter the effectiveness of discriminative stimuli and reinforcers for particular responses. Some forms of behavior are called respondent because they are elicited as a result of our coming into contact with particular stimuli in the environment. An everyday word for these forms of behavior is reflexive. These forms can appear as unconditioned respondents, when the response doesn't depend on particular experiences during our lifetimes, or as conditioned respondents, when the response does so depend. Our lives may be seen as a complex blend of operants and respondents, reinforcers and punishers, unconditioned and conditioned. For behavior analysts, an understanding of ourselves comes about when we understand how these factors play out in our lives. Just as the possibilities seem promising for improving the human condition through such other sciences as chemistry or physics, so also do the possibilities seem promising for improving the human condition through a science of behavior, and making ourselves genuinely free to achieve our full potential as humans.

Key Terms and Concepts

behavior analysis
functional characteristics of behavior
structural/topographical characteristics of behavior
emit/emission
operant behavior

three-term operant contingency
motivative operation
stimulus control
discriminative stimulus
unconditioned reinforcers
conditioned reinforcers
positive reinforcement
negative reinforcement
chain
unconditioned punishers
conditioned punishers
positive punishment
negative punishment
extinction
random behavior
shaping
differential reinforcement of successive approximations
stimulus control
generalization
discrimination
generic nature of stimuli and responses
elicit/elicitation
unconditioned respondent behavior
conditioned respondent behavior

Study Questions

1. Paraphrase what the chapter says about how standing still can sometimes be an instance of behavior.
2. Paraphrase what the chapter says about why behavior analysts emphasize functional rather than structural or topographical characteristics of behavior.
3. Paraphrase what the chapter says about why behavior can sometimes be unobservable and take place inside the skin, rather than why behavior must always be an observable movement.
4. Distinguish between the operant emission and the respondent elicitation of behavior in terms of the behavioral relations that are responsible for each.
5. Distinguish between conditioned respondent behavior and operant behavior as reflected in a three-term operant contingency. You may talk about the three-term operant contingency using either the more technical format of (S^D : R => consequence) or the informal A - B - C format.
6. Distinguish between a conditioned stimulus and a discriminative stimulus.
7. Distinguish between unconditioned and conditioned reinforcers.
8. Distinguish between unconditioned and conditioned punishers.
9. Distinguish between positive and negative reinforcement.

10. Distinguish between positive and negative punishment.
11. Describe an example of your own conditioned respondent behavior. Be sure to describe the conditioned stimulus, the response, and the unconditioned stimulus to which the response is ultimately related.
12. Describe an example of your own operant behavior under the influence of an contingency of positive reinforcement. Be sure to describe the discriminative stimulus, the response, and the reinforcer.
13. Describe two sources of operant behavior.
14. Distinguish between generalization and discrimination as forms of stimulus control.
15. Paraphrase what the chapter says about the generic nature of stimuli and responses.

Chapter 2

What Is Inside?

As we noted in Chapter 1, behavior analysts hold that behavior is a subject matter in its own right, and is to be studied according to the empirical, observational methods of the other natural sciences. The behavioral point of view differs from that of traditional psychology, which holds that the appropriate subject matter is some set of supposedly underlying mental states, processes, or entities, and the study of behavior is important primarily because it is evidence to support inferences about those mental phenomena. Chapter 2 examines some historical and conceptual background to the differences between these two views.

Some Historical Background

A common starting point for understanding the historical development of the study of behavior is that of *René Descartes* (1596-1650), the famous French philosopher, mathematician, scientist, and some would even say psychologist. A central feature of the Cartesian position is the distinction between the body, a physical entity, and the Mind or Soul, said to be a mental entity, not physically extended in space and time. However, even though Descartes took the mind and body to be distinct entities, he proposed that they still interacted in both directions, with events in the mind capable of influencing events in the body and vice versa. For example, sensory events impinging on a person's body would activate "animal spirits" in the person's nervous system. These events would ultimately register in the pineal gland of the person's brain, where they would then be viewed by the Mind or Soul. In the case of voluntary behavior, the process works in reverse. Here, Descartes argued that the Soul activates the pineal gland in the brain, which in turn activates "animal spirits" in the nervous system, which in turn causes muscles to contract and some portion of the body to move. Descartes' position is often called *interactionism*, in the sense that the mind and body are described as separate but interacting entities. Nevertheless, for Descartes the mind was the rational seat of ideas and deliberation. Simple reflexive action of the body didn't involve the mind. Voluntary or purposive action did. The mind, which was essentially a synonym for the Soul, was said to reflect on its ideas and cause the body to engage in voluntary behavior. The mind contained all the elements that defined the individual. The mind, not the body, was what was consciously aware. The mind, not the body, possessed essential ideas about perfection, unity, God, and the axioms of geometry. The mind, not the body, was also what conferred a person's identity. In short, the mind, not the body, should be the principal focus of psychology. According to a traditional view, then, the mind contains the faculties that allow us to know and understand anything, especially our identities as humans. We are innately able to apply these faculties and gain whatever knowledge is required, by virtue of being human.

Other points of view emerged over the next 250 years. Some of these views emphasized our experiences rather than innate faculties, but the underlying assumption of two domains—mental and physical—was not seriously challenged. Many historians argue that psychology emerged as a relatively independent discipline in the last quarter of the 19th century. The development of a laboratory by *Wilhelm Wundt* (1832-1920) in Leipzig, Germany, in 1879 is often cited. At this time, researchers tried to base their position on empirical considerations, instead of appealing solely to philosophical argument as had Descartes.

In the United States, the schools of psychology called structuralism and functionalism emerged in the late 1800s and continued to be influential into the early 1900s. These schools took for granted that the proper subject matter for psychology is mental life, as reflected in a person's consciousness. They further took for granted that the proper method for investigating this subject matter is *introspection*. Introspection may be understood as the process of asking subjects to look inward and then describe their sensations, images, or feelings. Their verbal reports were then presumed to give a clue as to the organization and structure of the mental phenomena in the conscious mind. An explanation of behavior was not of primary concern, but was presumed to follow from an account of the organization and structure of the mind.

A view of psychology that focused on mental life proved controversial. Its research results were often incoherent and unreliable. In addition, it failed to gain support in the culture at large, perhaps because of its mysterious language. The point of view called *classical S – R behaviorism* then emerged in the first quarter of the 20th century. Classical behaviorism, for example, as represented in the work of *John B. Watson* (1878-1958), rejected the focus that existed at the time on mental life, consciousness, and introspection. Instead, classical behaviorism emphasized the relations between observable stimuli and responses, hence the designation S – R psychology. In a famous article, Watson (1913) argued that the job of psychology is to predict the response, given the stimulus, and to identify the stimulus, given the response. Viewed as mental phenomena, introspection and consciousness played no part in Watson's conception of a science of behavior.

At the beginning of the second quarter of the 20th century, however, it was apparent that behavior was far more flexible than allowed by a formulation expressed exclusively in terms of observable S – R relations. As a result, many psychologists returned to adding unobservable phenomena to their explanations. Here, we abbreviate these phenomena with the letter O, to indicate they were states, processes, and entities hypothesized to be inside the organism. Their function was to mediate the observed relation between stimuli and responses. The result was an S – O – R formulation that was called *mediational neobehaviorism*. Some examples of these mediating phenomena inside the organism were attitudes, expectancies, moods, subjective perceptions, and so on. Variations in behavior could be attributed to variations in these mediating phenomena. The hypothesized mediating phenomena were not part of the behavioral domain, and in many ways were equivalent to the phenomena of mental life that had previously played such a large role in structuralism and functionalism.

Behavior analysts suggest that in large measure, the story of psychology ever since has been the steady proliferation of these mediating phenomena in the supposed mental domain. During the 1930s and 1940s, this position was solidified when operational definitions of the mediating mental phenomena in terms of publicly observable variables were taken to make them legitimate. The nature of the mediating phenomena has grown ever more sophisticated, but the appeal to phenomena in a mental domain to explain behavior is regrettably just as pervasive as it ever was. In contemporary psychology, the S - O - R account is evident in cognitive, information processing psychology, where cognitive processes, representations, and memories are assumed to be phenomena that mediate the relation between S and R, much as were earlier mediating phenomena.

Mentalism

Behavior analysts adopt a very different strategy than does traditional psychology with regard to explanations of behavior. As we have seen, traditional psychology often locates the causes of behavior inside the organism, in the mental domain, or sometimes with appeals to hypothetical or loosely-inferred physiology, but in any case a domain beyond the one in which behavior occurs. We have seen this practice beginning with Descartes and continuing with mediational neobehaviorism. A general term for this explanatory orientation is *mentalism*. In short, mentalism consists in explaining behavior by attributing its cause to phenomena from a domain that differs from the one in which behavior takes place. We speak of an explanation as mentalistic when it involves the following four inferences:

1. That an organism's psychological makeup includes a domain beyond the one in which behavior takes place, such as by being inside the organism in some sense. The domain of an explanation is at issue when its concepts are not expressed in the same terms and cannot be confirmed with the same methods of observation as the behavioral facts for which they are said to account. Representative descriptors that are used in connection with this other, nonbehavioral domain are mental, cognitive, subjective, spiritual, psychic, conceptual, hypothetical, mystical, and transcendental—in short, the domain of "mind." Different forms of mentalism emphasize different terms related to this inferred domain.

2. That this internal domain contains certain phenomena that cannot be characterized in the same terms as either behavior or environmental events, variables, and relations. These phenomena are inferred to be independent contributions of the organism that underlie behavior. They are unobservable. They are not influenced by events, variables, and relations experienced during the lifetime of the organism. As such, they are assumed to be innate. Often they are assumed to have or produce a content on which other structures or processes operate. Representative terms that are used in connection with these nonbehavioral phenomena are the acts, states, mechanisms, processes, entities, structures, faculties, and cognitions. Again, different forms of mentalism emphasize different terms related to these inferred phenomena.

3. That an explanation of behavior properly and necessarily consists in an appeal to these inferred, unobservable phenomena as causes of behavior, rather than to causes that are to be found in the same domain as behavior or environmental variables and relations. The way that these phenomena cause behavior differs in different versions of mentalism, and typically ranges from initiating to mediating. By initiating we mean that the phenomena themselves are the source of the behavior, such that no cause beyond the phenomena is necessary to explain the behavior. By mediating we mean that observable external stimuli activate or

trigger some unobservable intervening or mediating phenomena that are causally connected in some complex but systematic way to an ensuing observable response. Mentalism applies whether the domain and its causal phenomena are interpreted as dualistic or materialistic.

4. That the proper focus of psychology is the specification of the causal status of the inferred, internal, and underlying phenomena, rather than the functional relations between behavior and environmental variables, because the organism and its behavior are assumed to be in direct contact with only the inferred phenomena, rather than the environment. Observable behavior is important because it provides evidence to support inferences about the causal properties of mental phenomena, rather than because it is a subject matter in its own right.

Recognizing that different forms of mentalism conceive of the causal forces and entities in different ways, we can see that mentalism typically holds that a causal explanation of behavior is incomplete at best and defective at worst if it deploys only concepts from the observable behavioral domain. Rather, proper explanations must appeal to underlying, unobservable phenomena from a nonbehavioral, mental domain.

Behavior analysts oppose mentalism. Indeed, behavior analysts regard much of our Western culture as decidedly mentalistic, if not outright dualistic in the sense that Descartes proposed, largely because our culture embraces this traditional conception of the nature and causal status of internal events. Let us now examine an everyday instance of behavior to further illustrate what we mean by mentalism. Suppose we anticipate that it is going to rain, so we go to the hall closet to get an umbrella before we leave the house. A mentalistic explanation of this instance might proceed as follows. First, we name certain internal phenomena that we often experience. For example, we name our feelings or sensations—we have a feeling of fear that it will rain. To be sure, we may well experience an internal sensation called fear when the clouds darken and the wind increases, but as we shall see, what is at issue is the role of the internal sensation in a causal analysis. Second, we then accept those named internal phenomena as causes of behavior by virtue of their occurring at just the right time—prior to behavior. For example, we explain why we took an umbrella when we left the house by saying we did so because we "feared it would rain." Third, we then postulate other named but unobserved events as having causal properties in an analogous way. For example, we explain why we went to the hall closet before going outside by saying we believed it contained an umbrella. Note that in so doing, we attribute the cause of the behavior of going to the hall closet to a unobserved entity called a "belief." Fourth, we then assume that because these feelings and sensations and beliefs have been named but are unobservable, they must be from the mental domain, which differs from the domain in which behavior takes place. Fifth and finally, we accept the whole story as accurately providing a causal analysis of behavior. Even if traditional theorists try to correlate actually measured internal events with postulated events inside an individual—and they do not routinely do so, traditional theorists fail to assess the extent to which preceding environmental circumstances might be causing any internal events, in which case the internal events are not literally mental and from another domain after all.

Not widely recognized is that sometimes talk invoking physiology can be mentalistic. To be sure, physiological structures, pathways, and processes do participate in behavioral events. We would not be able to behave at all, much less even be alive, if we did not have underlying physiological structures, pathways, and processes. At issue is how these phenomena are to be investigated and then incorporated into a causal account of behavior. For behavior analysts, these phenomena are most usefully studied using the techniques and concepts of the discipline of neuroscience. Indeed, behavior will tell neuroscientists what structures, pathways, and processes to look for. We then need to take care that appealing to physiology does not lapse into mentalism in either of two ways.

In one way, we do not want to simply infer the existence of some physiological phenomenon on the basis of observed behavior and then cite the inferred phenomenon as a cause of that same behavior. For example, suppose we observe an individual acting in a way called depressed. We would not want to explain the behavior by automatically inferring that the individual's nervous system must be malfunctioning and operating in an abnormal manner. Indeed, to appeal to some physiological feature of our bodies as having some power or force to autonomously and independently cause behavior will lead us away from looking at any environmental circumstances of the individual's life that are responsible for the condition called depression.

In a second way, we would not want to cite some physiological phenomenon as a proxy for a mental cause, for instance, as some physiological mechanism that the mind operates. An example of this problem is when traditional psychology cites some physiological phenomenon as a "neural correlate" of a mental state. Again, suppose that we observe individuals acting in a way called depressed. We would not want to explain the depressed behavior by inferring that their minds have caused the low readings on various physiological measures we might make, such as heart rate or brain waves or brain images, and then cite the physiological measures as evidence of a malfunctioning mind. The causes of both (a) the states and activities of physiological structures and (b) the depressed behavior may well be found in the circumstances of the individuals' lives, rather than in another domain.

Overall, we can see that explanations of behavioral events of either the operant or respondent category are not to be "reduced" to physiology or activity of brain structures. Behavioral events are a function of the environmental circumstances in which they occur. The full analysis of behavioral events, whether observable to others or not, relates the behavior in question to those circumstances. To be sure, physiological events necessarily participate in every behavioral event, but not as a cause from another domain.

A closer analysis suggests that a great deal of mental talk is not about anything that actually exists in the standard dimensional system of space and time. Rather, the terms in such talk are just fanciful *explanatory fictions*. This talk reflects mischievous metaphors and the prevailing traditions of a culture and socially approved ways of offering an explanation of behavior. An example is depression. It is surely accurate to say that depression is the name for a condition that is very troublesome in contemporary culture. Often it is called the "common cold" of mental illness. Typical indicators are pervasive feelings of despair, inadequacy, personal worthlessness, as well as other forms of social and intellectual dysfunction. At issue is what causes depression, and how to remedy it. It is of little value to attribute the cause of depression to some internal state, without our being able to specify whether the circumstances of an individual's life as they exist in space and time have caused the internal state and the set of behaviors called depressed. If we do not so specify, we risk taking the name of the condition as a cause of the same condition. That is, we risk saying the individual has the pervasive feelings of despair, inadequacy, and so on *because* the individual has something from another domain called "depression." We have elevated "depression" to the status of an explanatory fiction. In contrast, if we recognize we have erroneously taken the name of some condition as the cause, we can then better look for what actually is the cause, and perhaps find a solution to the individual's problems.

Many sciences have fallen victim to this same trap. For example, chemists once explained combustion in terms of phlogiston, a fanciful chemical substance that had magical properties. When oxygen was discovered, explanations in terms of phlogiston were dismissed. Doctors once explained diseases in terms of mysterious spirits or vapors in the air. When bacteria were discovered, explanations in terms of spirits and vapors were dismissed. Physicists once explained the action at a distance produced by gravity or magnetism in terms of a hypothetical ether that provided the spatial continuity between the source and object of physical forces. Biologists once explained life in terms of mysterious vital spirits inside a living organism. In the final analysis, talk of other domains in psychology reveals that such talk is the product of mischievous and deceptive factors from which other sciences have ultimately freed themselves. As sciences progressed, the original fanciful explanatory fictions have fallen aside, to be replaced by useful and effective explanations in the terms of natural science. Traditional psychologists often assume that their talk accurately reflects actual causal events or entities in other, nonbehavioral domains. Sometimes the talk is justified as being "theoretical." However, for behavior analysts there are no other domains in the sense that traditional psychology envisions. According to behavior analysts mental talk interferes with an effective understanding of behavior, notwithstanding its theoretical pretensions, just as did talk of phlogiston, ether, and vital spirits.

As we have seen, behavior analysts do not assume, as traditional psychologists do, that behavior is caused by unobservable phenomena from a mental domain and therefore that those causes must be dealt with differently than are events, variables, and relations that are part of an individual's environment. Behavior analysts hold that even if some mental theory or intervention appears to be beneficial, its apparent validity should not be taken to mean that it has identified an actual cause of behavior from a mental domain, and that the mental talk is thereby validated. Rather, if a theory or intervention is effective, there are behavioral reasons for its effectiveness, not mental. A clarification and refinement in behavioral terms of those behavioral reasons can then provide a basis for further and presumably even more effective action. The particular problem is that the mentalism of traditional psychology advocates looking for particular kinds of causes that are believed to be inside a behaving organism in some sense and in a domain that differs from the one in which behavior takes place. If we accept the mentalism of traditional psychology as a general approach to understanding behavior, we fail to recognize and respect causes in the behavioral domain.

Sometimes Mental Talk is Actually About Private, Covert Behavior

Chapter 1 suggested that some aspects of both the environment and behavior are outside the skin and observable, but other aspects are inside the skin and unobservable. Nevertheless, we need not treat the aspects of the environment and behavior inside the skin as requiring a different kind of analysis from the aspects of environment and behavior outside the skin. As we have seen, traditional psychology does assume unobservable things inside the skin differ in both degree and kind from observable things outside the skin, such as by being in a mental domain.

For behavior analysts, some mental talk is actually about *private, covert behavioral events*, rather than phenomena that are literally mental and in another domain. This talk reflects the way we learn to talk about the sensations we call sharp or dull pains, as well as the way that covert operants like thinking influence subsequent behavior.

An important matter is that these events have been caused by environmental circumstances, even though these events are not accessible to more than the one person who hosts them. Talk of covert behavior is therefore concerned with behavioral events in the one domain. We analyze these kinds of events more extensively in Chapter 6. For now, suffice it to say that these events are critical to understanding behavior in all its complexity. Just as importantly, they need not be formulated in different terms and with different concepts than are publicly observable behavioral events.

Behavior as a Scientific Subject Matter in its Own Right

Behavior analysts focus on understanding how behavior is causally related to environmental events, variables, and relations. The environment consists of the sum total of objects, circumstances, and stimulus properties that constitute the occasion to which behavior is related. The environment can be past or present. It can be inside the skin, accessible to only the behaving individual, or outside the skin, accessible to others. When the environment is inside the skin, we make contact with it through our interoceptive and proprioceptive nervous systems. When the environment is outside the skin, we make contact with it through our exteroceptive nervous systems.

Roughly speaking, all sciences assume that they will be able to develop an orderly account of the events they study, where by orderly they assume they can identify how variables that exist in the current situation are functionally related to those events. They might recognize that the account they have at present may not be as accurate as they want, and tomorrow's might be more precise than today's, but that is why they conduct research. Behavior analysts suggest that much of our behavior today occurs because the environmental circumstances in which we find ourselves resemble the environmental circumstances of the past. If we can better understand such things as (a) the outcomes of our past behavior, (b) how closely today's circumstances resemble those of the past, and (c) how closely future circumstances are expected to resemble those of the past, we can better understand our present behavior and any behavior in which we might engage in the future.

For behavior analysts, the more knowledge we can gain about the circumstances accompanying our behavior, the better we can understand and explain our behavior, and when necessary, arrange relations to change it. We may want to provide certain kinds of consequences so that adaptive and useful behavior, like reading or being a good parent or a good citizen, is acquired more easily, and after being acquired, is more likely to occur in the future. We may want to provide certain kinds of consequences so that maladaptive behavior, such as biting one's fingernails or eating an unhealthy diet or polluting the environment, is less likely to occur in the future.

To be sure, it is impossible to have total knowledge of all the things that happened to us in the past. Similarly, it is impossible to have total knowledge of all the things that are currently present in our lives. We cannot possibly know all the things that will be present in our lives in the future. Nevertheless, the better we can identify what circumstances we experienced in the past, what we are currently experiencing, and what we are likely to experience in the future, the better off we will be. At the very least we can try to look for them.

Free-Will Objections to Behavior as a Scientific Subject Matter in its Own Right

A common objection to a science of human behavior is based on the doctrine of *free will*. A doctrine of free will assumes that human behavior is subject to the caprices of an ephemeral, autonomous internal agent, so human behavior is not even in principle a scientific subject matter. That is, free will assumes behavior of the present or future cannot be predicted or controlled, even probabilistically, by referring to past or current events, variables, and relations. For example, human behavior might be viewed as ultimately the outcome of some rational, free, and deliberative process or entity from another domain that is part of the psychological make-up behaving individuals. The entity within the individual is said to be the source or initiator of the behavior. Individuals may be viewed as agents who have conceptions about their status in the world, their relation to others, the purpose or intention of their behavior, and the means by which that intention may be realized. Humans are free to choose from among alternative courses of action. They may have reasons that inform their behavior, but in any event their behavior is not caused by events or sources outside their control. Free will is a mentalistic position, in that an explanation of behavior is held to reside in these phenomena from another domain.

One version of a free-will position, which we will call here the *strong position*, argues that *all* instances of human behavior show free will: *All* instances of behavior come about because an individual *always* chooses to behave in a particular way.

A second version, which we will call here the *weak position*, argues that only *some* instances of human behavior show free will: As before, these instances come about because an individual chooses to behave in a particular way. However, other instances come about because they are compelled by environmental circumstances. By this view, behavior needs to be examined on a case-by-case basis to identify which instances show free will and which are caused by environmental circumstances, and people might debate the percentages of free versus compelled behavior.

A third version holds that there are "underlying mechanisms" for human behavior. To be sure, these mechanisms operate in a thoroughly orderly fashion. They can therefore be investigated scientifically. However, humans still have the ability to choose in a free will sense whether to activate a given mechanism. By this view, the human ability to choose cannot be subjected to a scientific analysis. This version continues by saying that if psychology is to be a science, its mission is to work out the details of the underlying mechanism, even if the mechanism is assumed to be activated by phenomena from another domain.

These matters are extraordinarily complex, if only because the terms and concepts involved in discussing them have been so broadly construed over the years that they have developed many different meanings. Since the time of the Greeks, much of Western culture has assumed a non-deterministic stance toward human behavior. Indeed, such cultural institutions as religion and legal systems tend to assume free will.

What Does "Free Will" Actually Mean?

Behavior analysts question the usefulness of a doctrine of free will. If behavior was free, in the sense reviewed here, a scientific analysis of behavior would be impossible, just as a scientific analysis of any other subject matter would be impossible. For behavior analysts, the more relevant question is, What are the characteristics of behavior that we say shows free will? In an unadorned sense, let us suppose the notion of free is taken to mean that behavior is complex and flexible. Here, behavior analysts would readily agree: Behavior is complex and flexible. However, complexity and flexibility by themselves do not mean behavior shows free will. Rather, complex and flexible behavior could be the result of complex and flexible events, variables, and relations.

Suppose the notion of free will is taken to mean that a because a cause of behavior cannot be detected, behavior must be the product of free will. Here, behavior analysts suggest that we should keep looking, perhaps with a new investigative technique. Just because we have not yet detected a cause of behavior doesn't mean that one doesn't exist and we could not eventually find it.

Suppose the notion of free will is taken to mean that individuals have chosen some course of action, but could have done otherwise if they had wanted to. Here, behavior analysts suggest that we may usefully compare the outcome of the chosen course with outcomes of the courses not chosen. Perhaps the outcome of the chosen course in the past influences the behavior of choosing that course in the present. Perhaps individuals did not know about alternative courses of action that were available in the past, and if they had known about them, they would have chosen one of them, because they would be better off by doing so.

Suppose free will is taken to mean that individuals have chosen a course of action on the basis of their own beliefs, values, or intentions. Here, behavior analysts suggest we might usefully proceed by analyzing what such terms as beliefs, values, and intentions actually mean for the behaving individual. For example, they might they be related to past and present environmental circumstances for the individuals. If so, then a knowledge of those circumstances will allow us to better understand the individual's behavior.

Suppose free will is taken to mean that individuals have chosen a course of action based on a rational deliberative process. Here, behavior analysts suggest that the process itself, although not necessarily accessible to anyone else, may well be related to past and present environmental circumstances. Neither the process itself nor the act of choosing it is anything other than behavioral and related in an orderly way to environmental circumstances. In short, the terms deciding and choosing may be understood as referring to behavior that influences other behavior.

Summary and Conclusions

We began this chapter by tracing some historical influences in psychology. Originally, psychology was concerned with the structure and organization of mental life, as revealed through introspection. Introspective approaches were fraught with ambiguity. Psychologists then turned to an S – R formulation, where they emphasized only observable stimuli and responses. This approach also proved inadequate, as behavior was much more flexible than an S – R formulation allowed. Finally, psychologists turned to an S – O – R formulation, in which acts, states, mechanisms, processes, and the like inside the organism were inserted to mediate the relation between S and R and thereby provide what was thought to be lacking.

The acts, states, etc., were unobservable and were taken to be from a mental domain, instead of the behavioral domain. This move resulted in a position called mentalism. Mentalism involves explaining behavior by attributing its cause to phenomena from a domain that differs from the one in which behavior takes place. For behavior analysts, this mentalistic, mediational approach has persisted to the present. Much of contemporary psychology is one or another version of the S – O – R mediational approach, with different forms of psychology proposing different mentalistic mediators. The mentalistic mediators are often nothing more than explanatory fictions, postulated to possess exactly the causal properties that are necessary to explain some particular instance of behavior. Contemporary cognitive psychology is a conspicuous example.

Behavior analysts accept that some parts of the environment and some forms of behavior may not be observable to others. They are private, but their privacy does not mean they are part of another domain.

Finally, we have argued that behavior analysts assume that behavior is functionally related to environmental events, variables, and relations. From Chapter 1, we can say that the functional relations may be expressed in terms of contingencies, rather than fictitious inner entities.

Behavior analysts understand that no single experiment can conclusively prove or disprove that behavior is a subject matter in its own right, or the validity of various objections to a science of behavior. Rather, our point is that in the course of human history, comparable objections have been made about many different sorts of events in many different scientific disciplines. In the case of human behavior, the weight of the evidence shows that behavior can also be given an explanation in the terms of natural science. By arranging features of the environment, behavior can be predicted and controlled. This orientation to a science of behavior aligns behavior with other scientific subject matters. Behavior analysis is not simply a method to study behavior that occurs for some other reasons. Rather, it seeks to identify the causes of behavior wherever and whenever it occurs. Behavior analysts are just as much concerned with behavior outside the laboratory as it is with behavior inside the laboratory because the world outside the laboratory is continuous with the world inside. The laboratory provides the controlled conditions that help us to understand the more complex conditions of the world outside the laboratory. As we noted earlier, the orientation is entirely optimistic: By taking certain actions, we can make our lives more meaningful, and contribute to the welfare of all humans.

Reference

Watson, J. B. (1913). Psychology as the behaviorist views it. *Psychological Review, 20*, 158-177.

Key Terms and Concepts

René Descartes
Wilhelm Wundt
introspection
John B. Watson
classical S - R behaviorism
mediational S - O - R neobehaviorism
explanatory fictions
private, covert behavioral events
strong free will position
weak free will position

Study Questions

1. Briefly describe the mind-body interactionism of René Descartes.
2. Briefly describe what is meant by introspection.
3. Briefly describe the classical behaviorism of John B. Watson
4. Briefly describe what is meant by mentalism. Be sure to summarize the four points mentioned in the chapter.
5. Briefly describe how appeals to physiology in explanations of behavior can sometimes be mentalistic.
6. Briefly describe an example of an explanatory fiction.
7. Briefly describe what the chapter means by a private or covert behavioral event
8. What is the chapter's distinction between strong and weak versions of the free will argument as it applies to human behavior?
9. What is the behavior analytic answer to claim that human behavior shows free will?

Chapter 3

Genes, Selection, and Physiology

A behaving person is a biological entity. Indeed, in its early days, psychology was extensively influenced by biology, as early psychologists studied the physiological mechanisms that underlay behavior in attempts to link their field with the natural sciences. They found these mechanisms operated according to known physical and chemical principles. Knowledge of these mechanisms and their operating principles was important because it cast doubt on the kind of explanations offered by Descartes—that behavior should be explained by the action of animal spirits in our nervous stem and pineal gland. Of course, modern biology has advanced a great deal since these early days, and has contributed a great deal more to our understanding of the participation of physiological processes in behavior.

In this chapter we review some fundamental contributions that the study of physiology has made to behavioral science. We start with the role of genes, and in particular with the sense in which genes cause behavior. We then examine the important principle of selection, which is so prominent in modern biology. Our primary concern is not the selection of bodily features such as size and shape of bird's beaks, although we use such examples to illustrate how selection works. Rather, our primary concern is how the principles of selection might be applied to the selection of behavior. Selection may be seen as an important causal mode in the life sciences that replaces the traditional sense of cause as the push or pull of mechanical forces.

Chromosomes

The nuclei of human body cells typically have 46 chromosomes, arranged in 23 pairs. An exception is the nuclei of reproductive cells (sperm cells in males and egg cells in females), which have only 23 chromosomes, or one member of each pair. At conception, each parent or donor then ordinarily contributes one chromosome, resulting in 23 pairs in the body cells of offspring. Chromosomes can be ordered by size and are generally referred to by their rank in the size ordering: We designate the largest as chromosome 1 and the progressively smaller chromosomes with smaller numbers. The exception is the chromosomes of the reproductive cells, which are designated as the 23rd pair even though they might be as large as the fifth pair of chromosomes. Different species have different numbers of chromosomes. For example, a fruit fly has 8, a laboratory mouse has 40, a laboratory rat has 42, and a chimpanzee—our closest relative among the primates—has 48.

A chromosome is made up of a very large, complex organic molecule called deoxyribonucleic acid, abbreviated DNA. DNA is very important in the study of genetics, so we will spend some time on it. DNA consists of two long strands or sequences of chemical material, twisted around each other but joined at particular locations in the sequence. A common metaphor for the structure of the DNA molecule is a twisted ladder, with rungs joining the two side rails. A more technical name for shape of the DNA molecule is double helix. A common way of talking about the structure of the chromosome is by referring to the number of rungs in the DNA that makes up the chromosome. Some single chromosomes have around 50 million rungs. Others have as many as 250 million rungs. One estimate is that for humans, the total number of rungs in all 46 chromosomes is over 3 billion. For comparison, the loblolly pine has 23 billion, or around seven times as many.

Genes

A *gene* is a section of DNA that provides a recipe or set of instructions for making or regulating the biochemical material involved in our growth, development, and reproduction. We use the term recipe here to characterize a gene, rather than the term blueprint, because the term blueprint incorrectly suggests genes consist of little copies of the developed organism, and that growth and development conforms to those copies. The gene itself can be short or long, and is typically identified in terms of the sequence of rungs that make it up. Overall, genes constitute only a very small percentage, perhaps as low as 2 percent, of the total DNA in human chromosomes. At present, geneticists are still debating the exact number of human genes because they are still debating exactly how to define a gene. Besides, geneticists are still discovering that sequences of DNA first thought not to play a role in our growth, development, and reproduction do so after all. Recognizing such uncertainties, we can say that for humans, one current estimate is that the total number of genes in all chromosomes is between 23,000 and 25,000. For comparison, a representative single cell bacterium contains around 2,000 genes. To keep us humble, we need to recognize that this figure can vary widely in living organisms: A rice plant has around 36,000 genes.

Most genes provide a recipe for how developing cells arrange new chemical material as they divide and grow. The function of other genes is more subtle or indirect: They modify or regulate other sections of DNA, such as by activating or de-activating them in response to environmental stimulation or other factors. In this regard, we note that a caterpillar and a moth still have the same genes, even though the physical appearance of a caterpillar obviously differs from that of a moth. It is just a matter of which genes switch other genes on and off during the life cycle of the organism. Finally, some sections of DNA may once have had similar functions as outlined above, but over evolutionary time their functions have become unclear. Geneticists once referred to this material as *junk DNA*, suggesting that it had no function. However, as time has passed, scientists are finding out that in many cases, what was thought to be junk DNA actually has some very subtle functions after all, either singly or in combinations with other genes. For example, it may be involved in regulating growth and development in combination with other genes, or it may activate or deactivate other genes.

At present, some human traits are said to be *single gene traits*, in the sense that the traits are related to single genes on the chromosome. Some examples are attached vs detached earlobes, ability to roll one's tongue, the shape of the hairline—relatively flat or with a widow's peak in the center, and some health-related conditions like cystic fibrosis. More common are *multiple gene traits* that come about through a combination or blend of several genes. Some examples are eye color, skin color, and overall body size, again recognizing that a person's height or weight is obviously also influenced by environmental variables such as nutrition. In humans, the genetic information about the biological sex of the offspring is carried on the 23rd pair of chromosomes.

An exciting scientific project currently underway is *mapping the human genome.* The term genome refers to the full set of recipes and other informational material represente by the genes in the chromosomes. Of course, there isn't just one human genome, as there are over 6 billion living humans, with over 6 billion sets of genes and chromosomes. The genome that is being mapped actually consists of the genomes of several individuals, randomly selected from a pool of diverse individuals. To be sure, a large percentage of the genes is going to be the same for all humans, presumably greater than 99 percent, because we are of the same species. We all have cells and cell walls, and usually the other features that commonly identify us as humans. The point is that if scientists can compare the DNA of one person with a given trait to the DNA of a person without that trait, we may be able to identify the recipes for particular properties or other functions that are contained in the various sections. Then scientists can identify what variations in those sections produce variations in those properties or functions.

The task is daunting. Let us apply an extended metaphor. Mapping the human genome is a little like trying to understand the content of a book written in a language about which we know only a very few things. The book corresponds to the genome. The book has 23 chapters. A chapter corresponds to a pair of chromosomes. We know the alphabet of the language has only 4 letters—a, t, g, and c. [Those familiar with the molecular features of genetics recognize that these letters represent adenine, thymine, guanine, and cytosine, the chemical bases that constitute the rungs joining one rail of the spiraling DNA ladder to the other, but this information is not critical to the metaphor.] We know the letters always occur in pairs: a is always paired with t, and g is always paired with c. [Again, those familiar with the molecular features of genetics recognize that the chemical properties of these bases mean that adenine on one rail always bonds with thymine on the other, and guanine always bonds with cytosine, when the two DNA strands join together, but as before this information is not critical to the metaphor.] Altogether, the book has over 3 billion pairs of letters. Each chapter does have a special sequence of letters at its beginning and end. However, as species evolve and even individual organisms grow, the sequence gets closer together, meaning the length of the chapter becomes shorter and shorter. A chapter consists of a sequence of paragraphs. The paragraphs correspond to genes. Each paragraph has a special sequence of letters that identifies where it starts and ends. A paragraph consists of a sequence of words. Each word consists of a sequence of only three letters. [Again, those familiar with the molecular features of genetics recognize that the three letters constitute the recipe for an amino acid, again not critical to the metaphor.] As in any book, the paragraphs can consist of any number of words. In addition, seemingly random or repetitive sequences of these pairs of letters are interposed at various places in the text. These sequences can be of various lengths. They can also fall within and between paragraphs, which make it very difficult to identify where a given piece of legitimate and meaningful text starts and stops. To continue the metaphor, it is as if the author's word processing program has randomly left in passages during the editing and revising process, in something resembling a "track changes" command. [Remember we have so-called "junk DNA," some of which is not actually junk after all.] Moreover, in many instances the meaning of one sequence of letters depends on the meaning of a sequence in another place in the same or even a different book. On the basis of this kind of information, geneticists are trying to figure out the equivalent of who the central characters are in the book, what the plot is, in what town the action takes place, and how everything turns out in the end for the central characters.

In sum, we can note four ways that DNA is important in our growth, development, and reproduction. First, DNA carries information that guides physiological growth and development, through the particular sequence of chemical material that makes it up. One sequence means the physiology of the organism will develop in one way, whereas a different sequence means it will develop in a different way.

Second, DNA provides for replication. During growth, development, and reproduction, the two strands of DNA uncoil and divide. After a series of chemical processes each strand ends up responsible for the production of another strand. A common metaphor here (admittedly somewhat different from the twisted ladder) is that the two strands are like a zipper: They first unzip, a new strand is produced, and then the strands zip together again.

Third, the possibility exists that during growth and development, some features of the sequence will not be correctly replicated. We may have irregularities or errors in the process that are called *mutations*. The mutations may come about at various stages in the cascade of chemical processes supporting growth and development, or be attributable to toxins from the environment. During replication, some material may be left out, some extraneous material may be added, or some material may be inserted in the wrong place. Many mutations are incidental and largely neutral. Of course, some mutations are harmful, and the organism with them will probably not survive gestation. For example, the cells in our bodies need to have walls, and if the recipe for making cell walls is not accurate, we will not survive. Still other mutations may well be beneficial and serve the organism well in its struggle to survive. For example, we may be able to produce an enzyme throughout our lives that allows us to metabolize lactose in milk, permitting us to domesticate cows and live an agricultural lifestyle, rather than as hunter-gatherers. Mutations are one source of changes in lineages of organisms as they evolve over time.

Fourth, the DNA provides the means by which the characteristics of the recipe are replicated, meaning retained and expressed, in future generations of a population. How then do organisms change over time? Perhaps the simplest way to answer this question is to say that the recipe changes over time. As we have seen, one source of changes in the recipe over time is mutations. A second source is the DNA of parents or donors, who contribute a range of different characteristics through the DNA they contribute. A third source is called *epigenetics*. For this source, suppose experience with the environment switches on some gene, thereby producing a unique chemical. Now suppose that the chemical modifies the person's DNA. The result is that the person's biological make up changes. When the biological make up changes, so does the potentiality for its behavior to change.

Genes as Causes of Behavior

To better understand the causal role of genes, let's turn to the example of a potter who makes a vase out of clay. We can start with a simple question: What is the cause of the vase? To answer this question, we can usefully apply the thinking of the ancient Greek philosopher *Aristotle* (ca. 384 BCE–322 BCE), who suggested we use the word cause in several different senses. One sense of cause is what Aristotle called a *material cause*. For Aristotle, a material cause was the stuff out of which something was made. The material cause of the making of a clay vase was the clay, mixed with water to a certain consistency so that the clay would respond to the potter's hands and hold its shape. A second sense of the word cause is the action of potter's hands. Clearly, we can say that the potter's hands caused the clay to become a vase rather than, say, a bowl. A third sense is the ultimate use of the vase, perhaps to hold flowers. Here, we can say that what caused the potter to make the vase was the goal of having some container to hold flowers. A fourth sense is a smaller model of the vase, perhaps a picture or image that guided the potter in the process of crafting the vase; the picture caused the potter to put pressure at particular points on the vase during the process, so the vase would end up looking like the picture.

We focus below on the first two senses of cause. As a material cause, the clay of an appropriate consistency makes it possible for the potter's hands to have an influence, and for that influence to be retained. Behavior analysts ask analogous questions when it comes to behavior: What is the cause of the behavior of interest? For behavior analysts, genes and the physiology they yield are a material cause, corresponding roughly to the consistency of the clay. Nevertheless, a lump of clay will not assume the form of a vase without something from the environment affecting it—the potter's hands. So also will behavior not assume the form it does without something from the environment affecting it. In the case of operant behavior, the action of the environment is the contingency, as described in Chapter 1. Just as the clay needs to be of a certain consistency to retain the influence of the potter's hands, so in the case of operant behavior does an individual's physiology need to have certain properties to retain the influence of the contingency it has experienced.

Genes predispose an individual's susceptibility to influence from the environment. In the example above, the clay is predisposed to be susceptible to the influence of the potter's hands because the clay has a certain consistency. So also is an individual predisposed to be susceptible to certain influences of the environment because the individual has certain genes. Thus, we can see that understanding the influence from the environment is critical because an individual necessarily lives in an environment that can have differential effects. Nevertheless, the clay and the potter's hands are different types of causes—one cannot be reduced to the other. Similarly, the physiology of the living individual and the influence of the environment are different causes—one cannot be reduced to the other. Just because environmental events *can* influence substances or individuals doesn't mean that all substances or individuals *will* necessarily encounter those events, or that the events will necessarily influence all substances or individuals to the same degree.

In sum, genes don't cause behavior in the ordinary sense of the word cause. For example, they do not establish an unavoidable, inescapable destiny for an individual. Rather, genes provide the physical basis for the structures and processes that participate in behavior, as that behavior occurs in the context of environmental circumstances.

Selection

We turn next to the principle in biology called *selection*. Selection was emphasized by Charles Darwin (1859) in his famous book, *On the Origin of Species by Means of Natural Selection*. At the time of Darwin's book, a popular view was that species were organisms that possessed special sets of characteristics, each assigned in a way that differed from another. Darwin proposed an alternative view based on the principle of selection.

In abstract terms, selection consists of repetitive cycles of (a) variation, (b) interaction with the environment, and (c) differential replication as a function of the interaction. Selection starts with random variation of certain characteristics in a population of individuals. Suppose some of these characteristics mean individuals who have them will hear better, see better, run faster, jump higher, or have body parts that differ from others. Now suppose that some of the characteristics allow individuals to better access food or avoid predators. This is the stage of interaction with the environment. These individuals are more likely to survive and reproduce. We can say that these characteristics favor the individuals who possess them in their struggle for survival. Individuals who possess fewer of the favored characteristics are less likely to survive and to contribute fewer if any descendants to the next generation. Future generations then consist of a higher proportion of the descendants of individuals with the favored characteristics due to the differential effects on reproduction. This is the stage of differential replication. The process of selection leads to species as we know them, involving descent with modification from earlier forms of the individuals. In an important sense, the environment selects individuals by how well their characteristics meet the demands of the environment. The ability to meet the demands of the environment is called *fitness*. We will see shortly how the environment selects behavior as a characteristic of living individuals. For now, let's examine how it selects a specific bodily feature: the shape of birds' beaks.

In one part of his travels, Darwin found populations of finches that lived in the Galapagos Islands, off the northwest coast of South America. He observed that the shapes of their beaks varied from island to island. One explanation of this phenomenon was roughly as follows. At first, suppose the beaks of the birds in a given island varied randomly, ranging from thick and strong to pointed and thin. All birds, regardless of the shape of their beaks, had ready access to a wide variety of food that was available in the environment. Darwin wasn't sure of the underlying mechanism for the random variation—he speculated something internal was responsible, but he didn't know then what we now know about genes. We would now say that the random variation in the beaks was attributable to mutations in the genes of the birds in the population.

Now suppose the environment on the island changed in some fashion, such as more or less rain, or higher or lower temperature. The change in the environment meant a change in the particular type of seed that was available. The seed that was now available had a tough shell, and birds with thick and strong beaks were better able to crack open and eat the seeds than were birds with pointed and thin beaks. In other words, the shape of a bird's beak now had a consequence that it didn't have before: Birds with thick and strong beaks had better access to food. As a result, they were favored in the struggle for survival. As a result, these birds were the ones that differentially reproduced and whose characteristics were differentially replicated in the population. As a result, the population came to contain more birds with thick and strong beaks, and fewer with pointed and thin beaks. Different islands may well have had different climates or different processes, but the principle of selection applied in any case.

The examples above outline how the environment selected body characteristics such as the beaks of birds. What was important was how well a beak allowed a bird to adapt to the challenges of its environment. One kind of beak was not necessarily or inherently superior to the other across all situations. Rather, it was favored in particular environmental circumstances—fitness. It did not necessarily represent a progressive improvement by design.

Darwin argued that such events played out over tens or hundreds of millions of years of evolutionary time. Environmental changes can be caused by any of several events, ranging from natural disasters like earthquakes, volcanoes, or drought, to meteor strikes. The example of bird beaks above is not the only way the environment might select a body characteristic, but is useful to illustrate the principles involved in selection. We move now to another example of how the environment selects properties of living individuals: the selection of behavior.

The Selection of Behavior

An important point is that just as body characteristics are selected, so also are behavioral characteristics. For example, consider unconditioned respondent behavior. Let's suppose that in the ancestral past, the nervous systems of a population of individuals varied randomly. The random variation in the nervous systems was attributable to random variation in the genes of the individuals in the population (mutations), or to the mixture of genes provided by parents or donors. For simplicity, let's now suppose the random variation meant that when the individuals came in contact with a predator, the individual's autonomic nervous systems responded in varying degrees. Let's say that for some individuals, the heart rate increased only a little, for others an intermediate amount, while for still others a great deal. In this example, the predator may be considered an unconditioned stimulus, and the change in heart rate an unconditioned response.

Let's further suppose that the more the heart rate of a given individual increased when it encountered a predator, the more likely it was to escape from the predator, for example, by running faster and longer. More blood would be pumped to the muscles, meaning the muscles would have the benefit of increased oxygen, nourishment, and removal of waste products. These individuals would survive. By surviving, they would be the ones to reproduce and replicate themselves. They would pass on their nervous systems and other characteristics to the next generation, as would that generation to the next, and so on. Those individuals whose heart rates didn't increase might not be able to run as fast or as far, and their prospects for survival were thereby reduced. They would not be the ones that were reproducing, and future generations of the species would not have their characteristics.

In a general sense, then, we can say that in the case above, the individuals who responded greatly to events in their environment were the ones who survived, reproduced, and passed on their characteristics, especially their sensitivity to unconditioned stimuli, to their offspring. The individuals who are alive today are their descendants, having inherited this form of sensitivity. In addition, we can say that for many individuals, the sensitivity to unconditioned stimuli is one of the important characteristics of being alive.

A similar line of reasoning may be applied to conditioned respondent behavior. We will use parallel language as much as possible to describe this line of reasoning. As before, let's suppose that in the ancestral past, the nervous systems of individuals in a given population randomly varied. As before, the random variation in the nervous systems was attributable to random variation in the genes of the individuals in the population (mutations), or to the mixture of genes provided by parents or donors. The random variation meant that the nervous systems of the individuals changed to varying degrees when the individuals came in contact with a conditioned stimulus that was associated with an unconditioned stimulus in the environment. The nervous systems of some individuals changed only a little, those of others an intermediate amount, while those of others changed a lot. These changes in the nervous system meant that some individuals responded only a little, others responded an intermediate amount, while still others responded a lot to the conditioned stimulus.

Let's further suppose that the more a given individual responded to a conditioned stimulus in its environment, the better was its chance of survival as compared with an individual who responded in a lesser fashion. For example, suppose an individual came in contact with a conditioned stimulus, such as the noise of rustling leaves, that was correlated with the appearance of a threatening unconditioned stimulus, such as a predator. Individuals will presumably run away from the predator. Now they have had an experience in which the noise of rustling leaves is correlated with the predator. Individuals whose heart rates increased a great deal to the conditioned stimulus may have actually been able to run faster and longer and better evade a predator, thereby contributing to its survival. In contrast, individuals whose heart rates increased less to the conditioned stimulus may not have been able to run as fast or as far, meaning they could be caught by a predator. On the basis of current thinking, then, we can say that the individuals who responded greatly to conditioned stimuli that were correlated with unconditioned stimuli in their environment were the ones who survived, reproduced, and passed on their characteristics, especially their sensitivity to conditioned stimuli, to their offspring. As before, the individuals who are alive today are their descendants, possessing this form of sensitivity. In addition, we can say that for many individuals, the sensitivity to conditioned stimuli is one of the important characteristics of being alive.

The Selection of Operant Behavior

The situation is somewhat different for operant behavior, but we can nevertheless apply the principles of selection in a meaningful way. Recall that operant behavior is a function of contingencies—of actions yielding consequences. It is useful for us to recognize that an individual's operant behavior comes about because the individual experiences certain contingencies, and these contingencies change an individual's nervous system so that its behavior changes in the future. We will try to use language in the case of operant behavior that is parallel to the language we used in the cases of unconditioned and conditioned respondent behavior. This time, however, we will focus on the role of consequences, rather than antecedent eliciting circumstances.

As before, let's suppose that in the ancestral past, the nervous systems of individuals in a given population varied randomly. The random variation in the nervous systems was attributable to random variation in the genes of the individuals in the population (mutations), or the mixture of genes provided by parents and donors. The random variation meant that the nervous systems of the individuals changed to varying degrees when the individuals experienced operant contingencies. The nervous systems of some individuals changed only a little, those of others an intermediate amount, while those of still others changed a lot as a result of their experience with operant contingencies. These changes in the nervous systems meant that the behavior of some individuals changed only a little because of the experience with the contingency, the behavior of others changed an intermediate amount, while the behavior of still others changed a lot. To use a concrete example, an individual might do something that was associated with getting food, such as foraging in an apple orchard and picking red rather than green apples

Let's further suppose that the more a given individual's behavior changed as a result of its experience with a contingency in that environment, such as picking red rather than green apples in the orchard, the better was its chance of survival as compared with an individual who responded in a lesser fashion. In the case of responding that resulted in food, the advantage would be straightforward. The individuals with a nervous system that changed after experience with a contingency, with the result that their behavior changed, might have some advantage in securing food or avoiding predators. They would survive and reproduce, in contrast to the others who would perish. Here, we can say that in the case of individuals with particular nervous systems, and hence the case of individuals who engage in operant behavior, their operant behavior was selected by the contingencies that existed in the environment. On the basis of current thinking, then, we can say that the individuals who responded greatly to the contingencies they experienced were the ones who survived, reproduced, and passed on their characteristics, especially their capacity to respond to operant contingencies, to their offspring. Genes might also affect the range of conditions that serve as a reinforcing consequence for contingencies, as well as the amount of random behavior that is often the source of operants. Indeed, the probability that a food-deprived individual will survive is enhanced if access to food is an effective reinforcing consequence. As before, individuals who are alive today are their descendants, having inherited the characteristics related to operant contingencies. In addition, we can say that for many individuals, the sensitivity to operant contingencies is one of the important characteristics of being alive.

Over time, both the unconditioned and conditioned respondent behavior as well as the operant behavior might change still further. There was random variation in the nervous systems, and in light of the advantage conferred by being able to respond to events experienced in the environment, the dominant form of sensitivity in the population might continue to shift in a particular direction. As with body characteristics, we can meaningfully state that behavioral characteristics were selected by the environment. The unconditioned sensitivity to forms of environmental stimulation tends to be studied in ethology and zoology. The sensitivity to conditioned stimulus–unconditioned stimulus relations in the case of conditioned respondent behavior and to the contingencies of operant behavior tends to be studied in behavior analysis.

Summary and Conclusions

We have seen that an individual's physiology is relevant to an understanding of its behavior because its genes determine the features of the environment to which the individual can respond, and indeed the possible forms of that response. In short, the genes provide the physiological foundation of the sensory systems that are stimulated by the environment, the muscular systems that do the responding, and the neural systems that link the sensory and muscular systems.

The concept of selection applies just as much in the science of behavior as elsewhere in biology. An individual's behavior is selected, just as the features of its body as a member of a species are selected. In the case of operant behavior, the selection is by consequences, such as reinforcement. An individual's physiology is changed by exposure to operant contingencies, such that the individual responds differently in the future. The susceptibility to operant influences is an important characteristic of living individuals.

Importantly, we need not conceive of a behaving individual as literally empty or as a black box that produces the observed effect according to processes about which we need not concern ourselves. A behavioral account of an event has two gaps. One gap is during an event, when a given stimulus leads to a given response. A second gap is between events, when one event affects the probability of behavior in future, similar circumstances. Information about physiological events during these gaps is important because it can help to identify new possibilities for prediction and control of behavior through an intervention.

For example, suppose that we have independent knowledge of how an individual's body has already been changed through its interaction with the environment. Given this knowledge, we can predict and control what its behavior will be when it next encounters particular features of its environment. We wouldn't have to reconstruct its history.

Similarly, suppose that we have independent knowledge of how to change an individual's body directly. Having done so, we might well be able to control its behavior by presenting stimuli that will cause desired forms of behavior based on what its current body state is. For example, we might have independent knowledge of how to change an individual's body by surgery, a shot, or a pill, so that the individual will respond in desired ways when presented with a given stimulus.

Of course, at issue in a practical sense is whether we will actually have this kind of a priori knowledge at the time we wish to predict and control. After all, we may not have the technical apparatus to actually measure the existing state of an individual's body in the field, so that we can apply just the right stimulus at just the right time based on that state to produce a given form of behavior. Similarly, it is difficult to perform surgery in the field and modify an individual's body every time we want the individual to behave in a particular way. The ordinary way of predicting and controlling behavior is by arranging antecedents and consequences in the environment. Thus, a science of the relations between behavior and environment will always be able to make a contribution.

In closing, behavior analysts view the relation between behavior analysis and the science of physiology in practical terms. In principle, we can use either environmental or physiological means to predict and control behavior, depending on what our own circumstances are at the time. One form of knowledge is not necessarily superior to another, or necessary to validate another. Behavior analysis and physiology can work together in the cooperative venture of a science of behavior. In practice, however, we need to be aware of any practical circumstances that might limit our efforts.

Reference

Darwin, C. (1859). *On the origin of species by means of natural selection.* London: Murray.

Key Terms and Concepts

gene
DNA
junk DNA
single gene traits
multiple gene traits
mapping the human genome
mutations
Aristotle
material cause
fitness
selection of bodily characteristics
selection of behavior

Study Questions

1. Why does the chapter suggest the term recipe is more appropriate for a gene than blueprint?
2. Briefly describe the twisted ladder metaphor for the structure of DNA.
3. What are two functions of genes?
4. What is an example of a single gene trait?
5. What is an example of a multiple gene trait?
6. What are four ways that DNA is important in our growth, development, and reproduction?
7. Briefly describe the sense of cause as it relates to Aristotle's metaphor of the potter crafting a vase.
8. In what sense can we say that genes cause behavior?
9. What are the three stages in the repetitive cycle of selection?
10. Briefly describe how the principle of selection applies to the shape of birds' beaks.
11. Briefly describe how the principle of selection applies to the development of respondent behavior.
12. Briefly describe how the principle of selection applies to the development of operant behavior.

Chapter 4

The Nature of Verbal Behavior

Perhaps the single most important aspect of our being human is our ability to engage in verbal behavior. For behavior analysts, *verbal behavior* is operant behavior that develops through social interaction with others. A distinguishing feature of verbal behavior is that it is reinforced through its effects on the behavior of others, rather than through its direct or mechanical effects on the environment.

Let's consider an example. Suppose we are thirsty. If we are near a drinking fountain, we can push down a button on the drinking fountain ourselves and produce water. Our response of pushing down the button has a direct, mechanical effect on the environment—doing so produces water. This response is clearly an operant response. The reinforcer is the water we produce. However, the behavior is not verbal because it doesn't affect another person. Alternatively, if we are not near a water outlet, we can ask someone who is for a glass of water. Our response here affects another person—a listener. Our asking for a glass of water is an operant response. As before, the reinforcer is the water we receive. This response does constitute verbal behavior according to our definition because the water is provided only through the mediation of a listener (Skinner, 1957).

We speak of the social interaction between a speaker and a listener as a *verbal episode*. In verbal episodes, particular forms of a speaker's behavior, such as speaking, writing, or in some cases even gesturing affect a listener. The speaker's behavior is then followed by reinforcing consequences that the listener mediates. The consequences determine whether the speaker engages in the verbal behavior again. Verbal behavior consists of processes in which speakers learn to engage in the responses in question, and listeners learn to respond on the basis of that behavior (or perhaps more technically, any auditory or visual stimulation that the behavior produces). Together, speakers and listeners form a *verbal community*, which is the name for the group that interacts verbally.

Many different consequences can be involved in verbal episodes. Sometimes, the consequences are material and tangible, as in the example above when we receive a glass of water through the mediation of a listener. Material consequences are also conspicuous when shopkeepers guide cus-

33

tomers to the requested size and style of shirt. At other times, the consequences are more subtle and generalized, as when speaker A converses with listener B and B provides social attention or nods of approval during the conversation. In addition, once acquired, the verbal behavior of speakers can be extended so that it occurs in a variety of other circumstances, sometimes involving only the speakers who are also their own listeners. After all, sometimes people do enjoy singing in the shower. Worth noting for present purposes is that in all cases, the verbal behavior has developed during the lifetime of the speaker, and owes its current strength to its history of interaction with others.

The Evolution of Verbal Behavior

To be sure, nonhumans can vocalize in a number of different ways, and those vocalizations might well affect other nonhumans. An important question is whether these nonhuman interactions constitute verbal behavior as we have defined it here. A representative example is vervet monkeys in Africa (Cheney & Seyfarth, 1980). Suppose a troop of monkeys is foraging for food. Some monkeys are foraging on the ground, and others are foraging in the trees. Primatologists have observed that when a monkey sees a snake nearby in the grass, the monkey raises a particular alarm. Upon hearing this alarm, the monkeys that are foraging on the ground rear up. After they have done so, they are in a better position to see and thereby avoid the snake. When a monkey sees a predatory bird like an eagle flying above the troop, the monkey raises a different alarm. Upon hearing this alarm, the monkeys that are foraging in trees leave the trees and move to dense thickets. After they have done so, the eagle can no longer see them. The monkeys have avoided the eagle. In each case, we have monkeys that are responding differentially to vocalizations from other monkeys.

Although these instances do resemble verbal behavior, the resemblance is only superficial. The forms of responses for both the monkeys that raise the alarms ("speakers") and those that respond to them ("listeners") have likely evolved as innate behavior patterns, rather than as operant behavior. Suppose that in the ancestral past, some monkeys raised differential alarms when faced with different kinds of predators, and some didn't, either because their alarms were nondifferential or the monkeys didn't raise any alarms at all. When alarms were raised, the alarms were innate forms of behavior, evoked by the predators themselves. Now suppose other monkeys responded differentially on the basis of the alarms, and some didn't, either because their responses were nondifferential or the monkeys didn't respond at all. Among these possibilities, a survival advantage accrues to the monkeys that raised differential alarms in combination with those that responded differentially. For this process to be operant verbal behavior, the monkeys that raised differential alarms would have to be doing so because the monkeys that responded differentially provided reinforcement for the differential alarms, for instance, by giving food or positive social attention for the differential alarms. There is no evidence that such events took place.

To be sure, early in the evolutionary history of humans, vocalizations were likely evoked through processes of natural selection and survival, such as those described above for vervet monkeys. However, later in our evolutionary history, the nervous system that regulates our vocal apparatus changed. These changes meant that our verbal behavior came under the control of operant processes. As a result, operant vocalizations came to be involved in the lives of our ancestors, for example, through caregiving and delivering instructions to members of the social group. Whatever was the origin of the vocalizations, speakers learned to say things because doing so affects listeners, for example, by changing what listeners did or said with respect to speakers. Similarly, speakers changed what they did or said with respect to listeners. Thus, human verbal behavior may be understood as more complex than vocalizations innately evoked by environmental threats.

Verbal Behavior, Language, and Communication

Given the approach outlined above, the term *language* may be understood as a set of reinforcing practices conventionally adopted within a verbal community of speakers and listeners. By reinforcing practices here we mean, In what antecedent circumstances does a response in a particular class customarily meet with approval or other reinforcing consequences? Consider a light with a wavelength of about 700 nm. According to the conventional practices of English speakers, speakers meet with approval when they say the color of such a light is "red." According to the conventional practices of Spanish speakers, speakers meet with approval when they say the color of such a light is "rojo." On this view, language is not a thing or set of hypothetical "rules" that is possessed by speakers and listeners, such that vocalizations are then processed according to the rules in some hypothetical spot in our brains. These hypothetical rules do not cause speakers to speak in the way they do, nor do they cause listeners to understand what speakers are saying. Rather, the term language is simply a name for the interactions that take place between speakers and listeners. These interactions have been shaped and maintained by the conventional practices of the verbal community. The verbal responses themselves are emitted in characteristic circumstances, have a characteristic topography, have a characteristic organization (described as grammar and syntax), and have characteristic consequences. We have many different languages because we have many different verbal communities with many different verbal practices—red for some, rojo for others.

The term *communication* is sometimes used in conjunction with verbal behavior, for example, to imply the transmission of a common nonphysical or mental entity called a "meaning" from the mind of the speaker to the mind of the listener. Clearly, it is important to recognize that the behavior of a speaker affects the behavior of a listener. However, to hold that some nonphysical entity is transmitted from the mind of a speaker to the mind of a listener moves the analysis out of the realm of natural science, and invokes a variety of mentalistic considerations. For behavior analysts, communication may be understood as indicating that the operant behavior of a speaker is reinforced via the mediation of a listener. The term nonverbal communication is misleading. It may imply that the behavior of a speaker is not vocal or oral, but according to the definition of verbal behavior provided earlier in this chapter, it doesn't have to be. For instance, it can be gestural. As verbal behavior, the response of beckoning with one's finger can be equivalent to the vocalization of "Come here."

In our everyday discourse, words are said to have a *meaning*. It is not idle to ask, What does the term meaning actually mean? For behavior analysts, meaning is a matter of the circumstances in which the verbal behavior customarily takes place, and the subsequent responses it engenders. It is often useful to distinguish between meaning from the point of view of speakers and from the point of view of listeners. From the point of view of speakers, meaning is a matter of what causes speakers to say what they do. To ask speakers what they mean is to ask them to identify the contingencies that have caused their behavior. From the point of view of listeners, meaning is a matter of what an utterance causes listeners to do. To ask if listeners understand the meaning of a sentence is to ask what the sentence causes listeners to do: To what extent is the sentence a discriminative stimulus for some form of behavior? In this way we can see that meaning, speaking, and listening are always behavioral matters.

We can carry out a similar analysis for the term *reference*. According to a traditional view, the meaning of a word is often established by determining its referent. Unfortunately, the traditional view introduces many mischievous ideas about verbal behavior, not the least of which is that for every word there must be some entity or thing to which the word corresponds. This idea is another version of a mentalistic view of meaning. The mentalistic view conjures up minds and other domains in which the supposed activities take place—the meaning or referent is communicated from the mind of the speaker to the mind of the listener. For behavior analysts, if the term reference is relevant, it simply identifies the principle of stimulus control. To ask what a term refers to or what is its referent is simply to ask what events normally occasion the verbal response in question, as an instance of verbal behavior. For behavior analysts, it is just as mischievous to say a word refers to an object as it is to say stepping on the brake at a traffic intersection refers to a red light. To be sure, it is correct to say that stepping on the brake at an intersection is occasioned by a red light as a feature of the environment, just as it is correct to say that saying a word is occasioned by some property of the environment, but the behavior in each case does not occur as a matter of some mediating mental process called reference.

The Functional Analysis of Verbal Behavior: Contingencies and Units

As with other forms of operant behavior, the contingency is the fundamental unit of analysis for verbal behavior. Discriminative stimuli occasion the verbal behavior, and reinforcers maintain the verbal behavior. As we will see shortly, we can identify different categories or classes of verbal behavior on the basis of different categories or classes of discriminative stimuli and reinforcers in the contingencies that cause the verbal behavior in question. As we will see later in the chapter, verbal behavior is not generally considered to be produced like beads on a string, where saying one word stimulates saying the next in a sequence in something like a sequential S-R respondent process.

We can easily compare the behavioral view with a traditional view. In a traditional view, words are the fundamental units of verbal behavior. They are taken to be independent, autonomous things that symbolically represent or refer to other independent, autonomous things. If the represented things are not in some observable dimensions, the things are assumed to be in some other dimension, which is unobservable. The meaning of the word is determined by ascertaining what those other things are. One implication of this traditional view is that the meaning of a word is some sort of a mental thing that is possessed. The word can therefore be "used" in the same way that other possessed things are used. For example, speakers can use the word to express meanings or intentions. The meaning of a word is something that speakers first formulate in their minds, using processes that almost certainly include mental representations of events. Speakers then communicate that meaning to the mind of the listener. Speaking or writing therefore represents a sort of information processing activity of the human organism. This activity is carried out according to the rules of an innate, mental language acquisition device, which has evolved in the brains of humans alone to process the underlying structural, grammatical, and syntactical features of language in the same way that our stomachs have evolved to process the food we eat. In any case, because language is assumed to follow rules, the processing of language is assumed to be most appropriately analyzed in structural units applicable to logic. Words can therefore be construed as symbols for objects. Moreover, words are the principal components of sentences. A sentence is held to express a proposition, which has a logical content. An enduring concern is the logical status of the words as reflected in the structure of a sentence and as they contribute to the logical content of the proposition. And so it goes.

In contrast to the view above, behavior analysts adopt a functional approach to verbal behavior. This approach differs appreciably from the structural approach of a traditional view. A structural approach emphasizes the parts of speech in an utterance (noun, verb, adjective, adverb, preposition, subject, object, etc.). A functional approach recognizes that one can indeed classify the structural parts of speech in an utterance, but the question is what circumstances lead to the development and emission of those parts of speech. For behavior analysts, the instances of verbal behavior called parts of speech are themselves derived from social interaction with the verbal community. Thus, always at issue are the functional relations that underlie any form of behavior, respondent or operant, nonverbal or verbal. We do not ordinarily say a speaker "uses" a word any more than we say a person "uses" a push to ring a doorbell. Rather, we simply note that speakers are behaving verbally according to the conventional practices and prevailing contingencies of their verbal communities.

Traditionally, the sequence of words that is said to express a complete thought is called a sentence. For behavior analysts, a sentence is typically a series of words emitted sequentially, but occasioned, as a unit, by some further state of affairs. To talk of sentences as expressing "propositions" is often not helpful because such talk implies mysterious logical activities in a mental domains are causing the behavior. Traditionally, the activities are assumed to have some logical properties that dictate their behavioral significance. In contrast, according to behavior analysis, we need to recognize that speaking or writing in sentences occurs because listeners encourage speakers to do so. When speakers are young, listeners may well respond appropriately when vocalizations consist of a single element. However, as speakers mature, listeners encourage and then reinforce more complex utterances. As speakers learn what is acceptable according to the conventional practices called grammar and syntax, words in one location of the sentence influence others, to produce agreement in case, tense, and number. The influence can become very complex, as in recursive sentences: "The canary that the cat ate sang." The point is that the nature of the environment determines the nature of the resulting verbal behavior, rather than supposed innate rules of grammar encoded in hypothetical brain structures. If the concept of a rule is meaningful, it simply describes the conventional practices or contingencies of a given verbal community. Any functional link between words in a sentence is not a simple, mechanical association of S to R, as beads on a chain, but rather a relation of operant stimulus control.

To be sure, verbal behavior does commonly take the form of words or phrases, organized into sentences according to the conventional grammatical and syntactical practices of the verbal community. For behavior analysts, these structural units clearly do exist and are important units of analysis. Nevertheless, they exist and are important because listeners have shaped them. For example, listeners reinforce speaking in sentences because the sequential framework provided by a sentence benefits listeners: It provides an additional source of discriminative control for any subsequent behavior of listeners. We can cite two examples to illustrate how the sequence of verbal responses makes a difference. The first example is from the sport of tennis. In tennis, listeners know which player has how many points because the conventional practice is to announce the server's score first. The second example is Roman numerals. When we write the Roman numeral for the Arabic numeral 4, we write IV, not VI. Putting the I and V in a specific order is reinforced according to the conventional practices of the group—the I preceding the V indicates the sequence is occasioned by one less than V, whereas the I following the V indicates it is occasioned by one more. Speakers then adopt this practice for IX and XI, for the arabic numerals 9 and 11.

The Mand Relation

A great deal of verbal behavior develops as a result of elementary verbal relations. Suppose a speaker is deprived of something or under painful stimulation. A response is emitted, and is reinforced by a reduction in the deprivation or painful stimulation that is mediated by a listener. Behavior analysts call this form of verbal behavior a *mand*. Here, the term mand suggests a sense of the imperative, as in command or demand. For example, if a child cries when it is thirsty, the parents might provide some water. The child's crying affects the parent, who gives water to the child. The crying then develops as an operant response: The child might cry when it is only a little thirsty, and not so extremely thirsty that it is distressed and the crying is respondent. The vocalization can develop as full-fledged verbal behavior as the child matures, and the verbal community reinforces more appropriate forms of response, such as politely asking for water, instead of simply crying. In any case, receiving the water from an obliging listener represents the reinforcement. In this sense, mands are sometimes described as naming their own reinforcer.

A mand is an imposition on listeners, in that when speakers mand, listeners provide or do something that directly or immediately benefits only the speaker, not the listeners themselves. Nevertheless, listeners may supply the consequence because it may be of indirect benefit to them. For example, it may be important to the listener to take some action given the mand, as when a parent does something to relieve a child's demonstrated distress. In addition, providing or doing something establishes some basis for reciprocity in social interactions, as in "I'll scratch your back now and you can scratch mine later." As speakers' experiences with the verbal community increase, speakers learn to soften their mands. After all, listeners may find it tiresome when speakers continually demand that listeners stop what they are doing and attend to them. To increase the probability of reinforcement among listeners, speakers my then find it useful to be polite in tone, or add "Please" to their mands. Everyday discourse reflects many such instances.

The Tact Relation

Now suppose a speaker is in contact with some object, situation, or event in the environment, or some property of an object, situation, or event. A response is emitted under the discriminative stimulus control of this feature. A listener in the verbal community finds it useful to know about this feature, and might then indicate approval, recognition, or gratitude as social reinforcement when the speaker talks about it. Behavior analysts call this form of verbal behavior a *tact*. Here, the term tact suggests the sense of "is in contact with." For example, suppose A needs to keep an appointment at 1 pm. A is not in contact with a clock, but B is. A then asks B what time it is. A's behavior is a mand. B then states that the current time is a few minutes before 1 pm. B's behavior is a tact. A then provides a reinforcer for B's tact, in the form of saying thank you, and leaves in time to keep the appointment.

A tact is an imposition on the speaker, in that when speakers tact, speakers provide or do something that directly or immediately benefits only the listener, not the speakers themselves. There is no material benefit for B to go out of his or her way to tell A the time. Nevertheless, the social reinforcement of approval, recognition, or gratitude is strong enough to support the interactive verbal behavior that takes place, even though the exchange of a material consequence like food or water is not necessarily involved.

A special case of a tact is a *concept*. A concept may be defined in behavioral terms as generalization within a class of discriminative stimuli and discrimination between classes of discriminative stimuli. For example, consider the discriminative stimulus of a triangle. A triangle is defined as a bounded geometric figure with three sides. It doesn't matter whether the triangle is large or small, acute or oblique, a right triangle or an equilateral triangle. All triangles differ from circles, squares, and rectangles, among other geometric figures, by virtue of their respective properties. If we are asked to supply the name of a bounded geometric figure with three sides, and we say triangle, our verbal behavior reflects the concept. Concepts, then, are matters of stimulus control, rather than mental or cognitive entities that are possessed. Concepts developed as tacts constitute a great deal of scientific verbal behavior. Consider our definition of operant behavior as a form of behavior that is reinforced by its consequences. The functional relation matters in the definition of the class of discriminative stimulus called operant behavior, not the particular species emitting the response or the particular topography of the response or the particular reinforcer for the response.

A further special case, related to a concept, is an *abstraction.* An abstraction is a verbal response that is occasioned by some particular form of discriminative stimulation, even though other forms of discriminative stimulation are present. Color naming is a suitable example. We say a stop light, fire hydrant, or apple is red, even though the other features of those objects differ.

Sometimes statements take the form of tacts, but the contingencies that control those statements differ from those that control tacts. Suppose mischievous older brother A steals a cookie from the cookie jar. Now suppose a parent asks, Who took the cookie? and A answers that younger brother B did. A's statement has the form of a tact. However, what contingencies control A's statement? A is seeking to avoid punishment for stealing a cookie from the cookie jar. A's behavior is motivated by the possibility of aversive stimulation. Consequently, A says something that avoids the aversive stimulation. A's behavior has the form of a tact, but is actually a mand. Thus, lies, fibs, exaggerations, and misrepresentations may be understood as mands, in that they are functionally related to certain outcomes.

The Intraverbal Relation

As can be seen from the above examples, and as we mentioned earlier in this chapter, verbal behavior does not generally occur like beads on a string. Rather, it is operant behavior, emitted and reinforced under particular circumstances. However, in some cases, verbal behavior does take the form of a sequence or chain of words. Behavior analysts call this form of verbal behavior *intraverbal*, to indicate the word-to-word linkage that exists between words. For example, if a speaker is reciting the alphabet or even a memorized poem, often one letter or word becomes the stimulus for the next, and so on. Sometimes game shows on television are based on intraverbals, as when contestants try to guess a famous saying or quotation given just a few letters or words from the longer verbal expression. Crossword puzzles give clues to fill in the squares based on intraverbals. Often criticisms of a behavior analytic approach to verbal behavior assume behavior analysis generally regards words as emitted in a serial process like beads on a string. However, such an assumption is incorrect. Although this form of verbal behavior clearly exists and is relevant, all verbal behavior is not of this type.

Grammar and Syntax

Our review to this point has concerned a few elementary verbal relations. Verbal behavior has other features, notably grammar and syntax. How do behavior analysts accommodate these features?

For behavior analysts, grammar reflects operant processes. In many instances, if we want to talk about an event that happened in the past, we add the ending -ed to the verb. If we want to talk about more than one object, we add the ending -s to the noun. In these cases, we are engaging in a special kind of tacting. We indicate agreement in case, tense, and number between subject and verb of a sentence because the verbal community reinforces it. The behavioral nature of this process may be seen when we consider the case of the child who says "goed" instead of "went." The child has obviously not observed anyone saying goed or been taught to say goed. Rather, the behavior just generalizes from prior situations to new, as other forms of behavior generalize to new situations. The child tacted an action in the present by saying go. In previous instances the child learned to tact past events by adding -ed to the verb. The child simply combines the two tacts and says goed.

Similarly, syntax reflects operant processes. As we saw earlier, the verbal community teaches us to avoid confusion in tennis by reinforcing our saying the server's score first. The verbal community teaches us to avoid confusion in Roman numerals by reinforcing our putting the letters in a certain order. Similarly, the verbal community teaches us to provide supplemental information in a sentence by reinforcing our putting words of the sentence in a certain order, according to the conventional grammatical practices of the verbal community. Syntax doesn't mean we covertly emit and rearrange words, but rather that the ordering of words reflects a secondary source of control. Our having said one word exerts influence on our saying further words in the sentence, with various endings to the words that indicate the relations among the words so ordered.

Higher-order Verbal Relations: Equivalence Relations

The term *equivalence relations* refers to the development of a special kind of stimulus control in verbal behavior. To illustrate, let's consider the case of a young, typically developing child that is just learning to read. Suppose the child is presented with a picture of a dog. Then, the child learns to equate the picture with the spoken word "dog" rather than the spoken word "cat." Here we can say that the picture exerts stimulus control over the spoken word "dog" rather than the spoken word "cat." Now suppose that the child is presented with the spoken word "dog" and the child learns to equate the spoken word with the letters D-O-G on a card rather than the letters C-A-T on a card. A wide variety of recent research has shown that if the child is presented with the letters D-O-G on a card, the child will reliably pick a picture of a dog rather than a picture of a cat on the very first opportunity. Here, the letters D-O-G control the child's response of picking the picture of a dog, even though there has been no history of reinforcement for the child's doing so. Similarly, if the child is presented with the spoken word "dog", the child will reliably pick a picture of a dog rather than a picture of a cat. Here, the spoken word "dog" controls the child's response of picking the picture of a dog, again even though there is no history of reinforcement for the child's doing so. The responses in question show that the pictures, spoken words, and written words are related in a way we can call equivalent, even though these stimuli have not had any explicit, prior training that would directly produce the relations we have observed.

Why then does a child reliably pick a picture of a dog rather than a picture of a cat when presented with the letters D-O-G? Even though the child is very young, we can usefully turn to an analysis of the child's prior experiences. Presumably, the child has had a number of experiences in the past with being presented with a variety of other pictures, and then learning to equate particular spoken words with the pictures. Similarly the child has had a number of experiences in the past with being presented with a variety of other spoken words, then learning to equate particular written words with the spoken words. The child has also had a number of experiences in the past with being presented with a variety of other written words, then learning to equate particular pictures with those words. Given that speakers have had a number of these experiences in the past, we can say the speakers have learned the generalized tendency to regard a picture of a dog, the spoken word "dog," and the written letters "D-O-G" as equivalent, rather than as isolated and disconnected features of the verbal environment. In a similar fashion, we can say that speakers have learned the generalized tendency to regard a picture of a cat, the spoken word "cat," and the written word C-A-T as equivalent. Equivalence relations seem to be at the heart of the "understanding" of verbal behavior—we can be said to understand verbal behavior when we view spoken words, written words, and pictures of actual objects as equivalent, even when we have not had a direct history of reinforcement for doing so. At this writing, a great deal of research is going on with nonhumans to determine whether they form equivalence relations in the same way as humans.

Verbal Regulation

Verbal behavior is of tremendous importance when it comes to understanding the human condition. It is unquestionably the principal medium through which humans interact socially. As we mentioned earlier in this chapter, we cannot go back hundreds of thousands of years and determine precisely how the various forms of verbal behavior evolved. Perhaps the earliest form of verbal behavior emerged as some contribution to caregiving or instruction within the family or social group. The wonder of a Shakespearean sonnet or a Nobel Prize winning piece of literature stands at the other end of the evolutionary process.

If an early form of verbal behavior was in fact related to caregiving or instruction, then the groundwork was established for what would evolve as *verbally regulated behavior*. As the term suggests, in verbally regulated behavior, some instance of behavior is regulated by a verbal discriminative stimulus. A common name for a verbal stimulus of this sort is a "rule." Verbal stimuli can function as discriminative stimuli, just as nonverbal stimuli do. They can supplement nonverbal auditory and visual discriminative stimuli, or perhaps replace them entirely. However, the richness and complexity of the verbal discriminative stimuli makes them markedly superior to nonverbal stimuli.

For behavior analysts, rules can be understood from the point of view of either speakers or listeners. Suppose a speaker is said to be following the rules of grammar. In this case, the rule is a description of the conventional practices of the verbal community, for example, with regard to generating an utterance that has the conventionally approved structure. Suppose a listener is said to follow a rule, say by looking both ways before crossing the street. The rule specifies a form of behavior and suggests that adverse consequences will take place if the listener's behavior does not comply with the rule. In either case, there is nothing hypothetical or from a mental dimension.

The behavioral sense of rules here differs from the rules of the mentalistic tradition, mentioned earlier. In the mentalistic tradition, a speaker is said to be following a rule when speaking, and a listener is said to be following the same rule when parsing the sentence to understand what the speaker is saying. The rule is said to be a mediating phenomenon from another dimension, perhaps operating through hypothetical brain processes as a causal variable. Behavior analysts regard the whole enterprise as not a particularly useful way to conceive of what goes on when individuals behave as speakers, listeners, or both.

Let's consider the following example from the history of technology. The example concerns blacksmiths and how to best operate the bellows to produce a desired temperature in the blacksmith's forge. According to Salaman (1957, p. 112, as cited in Skinner, 1969), in the late middle ages blacksmiths developed a verse that guided the operation of the bellows:

Up high, down low,
Up quick, down slow—
and that's the way to blow.

By heeding the message and correlating the tempo of the verse with the tempo of the operation of the bellows, a blacksmith was able to produce the desired temperature in the forge. In addition, the blacksmith could teach the verse to an apprentice. The apprentice could then recite the verse and also produce the proper temperature, but without having to go through an extensive learning history involving direct effects on the forge of various patterns of operating the bellows. In addition, the verse freed up the blacksmith to concentrate on the work at hand, rather than diverting his attention to constantly supervise the apprentice. The verse was a useful discriminative stimulus for the apprentice, and a labor-saving device for the blacksmith.

One of the hallmarks of a culture is verbally regulated behavior, and the systematic behavior patterns thereby generated would not be as strong, if they would exist at all, without verbal behavior. Countless examples exist, from laws ("Drive on the right-hand side of the road" [in the US, but not in England or Japan, of course]) to aphorisms ("A stitch in time saves nine") to advice ("Do unto others ...").

Interpretation

In much of our everyday lives we seek to make sense out of events we have observed. For example, if some principle has been developed in the laboratory under controlled conditions, we may apply this knowledge in the world outside the laboratory, even though conditions aren't as well controlled as in the laboratory. Behavior analysts call this principle *interpretation*. Thus, we interpret the evolution of species through the mechanism of natural selection, or earthquakes and continental drift through the mechanism of plate tectonics, even though we haven't actually manipulated anything. Many scientific theories are interpretations in this sense.

In the case of behavior, we may know that laboratory analyses have shown subjects like rats or pigeons will learn more quickly when a reinforcer is delivered immediately after a response. In fact, learning may be slowed if a reinforcer is delayed, even though the magnitude of the reinforcer is large. We may then look at an instance where we are having some difficulty teaching our dog to sit on command. In practical terms, we might interpret the problem as having to do with how quickly a reinforcer is delivered after the to-be-learned response. It may be more reasonable to see if the reinforcer can be delivered more quickly after the response, rather than, say, increase the magnitude of the reinforcer. Our conclusions come from applying what we know from elsewhere to good benefit, rather than from carrying out an analysis under controlled conditions, which may not be practical.

Verbal Behavior, Folk Psychology, and Mentalism

Our everyday language can also set traps for us. Suppose that we are presented with an apple. When asked to name it, we learn to say "Apple." In other circumstances, if we hear the word "Apple," we might then start looking around for the apple. We often approach situations by assuming that if we hear or read a word, then there must be an object to which the word corresponds. In other words, we come to view a word as a thing that refers to another thing. Much of our Western culture is based on such assumptions.

Now suppose we hear the word "belief." We might then assume that there must be an object or entity to which the word corresponds. We can't observe such an entity, so we further assume it must be unobservable and mental. The same goes for such words as "desire" and "intention."

The term *reification* is sometimes used in connection with our mischievous tendency to assume that if we use a word as a noun, there must then be some independent thing or object that actually exists to which the noun refers. Many problems can arise from reification, but the problems are particularly acute when we use terms that suggest psychological processes. Suppose we say an individual does something intelligently. The term is actually an adverb that describes doing something efficiently, wisely, with a minimum of errors, and so on. It is only a small linguistic step to reification and saying that the individual behaves in the way observed because the individual has intelligence. What started out as a descriptive term is linguistically converted to a noun. The noun is assumed to refer to an entity that actually exists in another dimension. The entity is assumed to cause behavior. Some individuals are assumed to posses a great deal of it, others less. The problem is that this entire approach is not particularly helpful if we want to understand why the individual does something intelligently. To understand why we must examine the contingencies that promote the behavior that is called intelligent.

Folk psychology is the name given to culturally based explanations that appeal to reified causal entities from another domain. These explanations sound convincing because we have learned to talk this way in our culture. However, closer reflection suggests the explanations that result are not particularly helpful. Some words illustrating folk psychology relate to mental states, beliefs, intentions, ideas, perceptions, intelligence, and so on. As suggested in Chapter 2, the supposed causal entities of folk psychology are the stuff of mentalistic explanations. The objection is not so much that the entities of folk psychology are unobservable. Rather, the objection is that they owe their strength to spurious social and cultural factors, rather than any contribution to understanding, prediction, and control. They then interfere with our ability to identify variables and relations in the behavioral dimension that actually do cause our behavior, nonverbal as well as verbal.

Summary and Conclusions

We have seen that verbal behavior is operant behavior, reinforced through the mediation of other persons who have learned to respond to the verbal behavior according to the conventional practices of the verbal community. Such matters as meaning, reference, and communication are indeed important in an understanding of verbal behavior. From a behavioral point of view, meaning is not a matter of transmitting something mental from the mind of a speaker to the mind of a listener. Rather, meaning from the standpoint of speakers is a matter of what causes speakers to speak as they do. Meaning from the standpoint of listeners is a matter of what the verbal behavior causes the listeners to do. Reference is a matter of what events occasion the verbal behavior. Communication is simply another way of saying that verbal behavior influences the behavior of listeners, regardless of its topography. On this view, language is the name of the set of conventional practices that prevail in a particular verbal community, rather than an internalized set of hypothetical rules for generating utterances.

We can classify verbal responses based on the contingencies that promote them. By so doing, we can identify the elementary verbal relations associated with mands, tacts, and intraverbals. Grammar and syntax reflect operant processes where the verbal community teaches us to respond in ways that take into account additional features of what we are speaking about. In more complex cases we learn relations during our development among various forms of stimulation, such as among written words, pictures, and spoken words, in the phenomenon called equivalence. Equivalence relations allow us to move beyond isolated, restricted usages in a way that is said to show true understanding. Verbal behavior can exert a very strong effect on our behavior as listeners, as when we follow the advice offered in some verbal statement. Scientific verbal behavior often shows abstraction and higher order concepts, where these phenomena suggest control by very subtle aspects of what we are speaking about. In addition, much scientific verbal behavior is interpretive, and consists of statements in which known principles are applied to explain events that have not been directly subjected to controlled experimental analyses.

Finally, behavior analysts are very concerned about verbal behavior in psychology that is mentalistic and that shows the influence of folk psychology. Folk psychology arises for several reasons, but perhaps the most prominent is the tendency toward reification. Reification comes about when we assume that if a word is used, there must be something that actually exists to which the word refers. Our generally mentalistic culture freely invokes entities from folk psychology in causal explanations of behavior. Behavior analysts argue that doing so interferes with an effective understanding of the contingencies that actually cause our behavior, both verbal and nonverbal.

References

Cheney, D. L., & Seyfarth, R. M. (1980). Vocal recognition in free-ranging vervet monkeys. *Animal Behavior, 28,* 362-367.

Salaman, R. A. (1957). Tradesmen's tools. In C. Singer, E. Holmyard, A. Hall, & T. Williams (Eds.), *A history of technology* (vol. 3) (pp. 110-123). London: Oxford University Press.

Skinner, B. F. (1957). *Verbal behavior.* New York: Appleton-Century-Crofts.

Skinner, B. F. (1969). *Contingencies of reinforcement.* New York: Appleton-Century-Crofts.

Key Terms and Concepts

verbal behavior
verbal episode
verbal community
communication
meaning
reference
mand
tact
intraverbal
equivalence relations
verbally regulated behavior
interpretation
reification
folk psychology
language
grammar
syntax
concept
abstraction

Study Questions

1. How can animal cries be sometimes mistaken for operant verbal behavior?
2. Why is communication a troublesome word to use in explanations of verbal behavior?
3. Why is reference a troublesome word to use in explanations of verbal behavior?
4. For behavior analysts, what is the meaning of verbal behavior from the point of view of speakers? Of listeners?

5. Distinguish between a traditional account of meaning and a behavior analytic account.
6. Why do behavior analysts not consider verbal behavior to be generally like beads on a chain?
7. How do behavior analysts account for grammar and syntax?
8. What is the definition of language in behavior analysis?
9. How is folk psychology related to mentalism?
10. What does it mean to say that behavior is verbally regulated?
11. What is an example of a concept?
12. What do behavior analysts mean by interpretation?
13. Give an example of the following classes of verbal behavior: mand, tact, intraverbal.
14. What do behavior analysts mean by equivalence relation?

Chapter 5

Self

The term "self" is central to much of psychology. For instance, we often speak of the importance of a sense of self, as it relates to self-confidence, self-control, self-esteem, or self-satisfaction. We often speak of being self-conscious, self-reliant, or self-righteous. We might reflect on our current situation and say such things as "I was not acting like myself" or "I wanted to do it by myself."

Clearly, each of us is an individual. Unless we have an identical twin, each of us has a unique genetic endowment. However, the fingerprints of identical twins are not identical, and different environmental conditions may cause the genes of one twin but not the other to switch on or off, resulting in the expression of differences between the two. Moreover, the experiences we have during our lifetimes are unquestionably unique, regardless of whether we have an identical twin. Our goal in this chapter is to develop an account of these undeniably important personal aspects of our lives that is consistent with the scientific approach to behavior we find in behavior analysis.

Individuality

Sometimes a sense of self is said to be related to our *individuality*. What, then, does individuality mean? As noted above, each of us is unique. If we have a core at the center of our being, it starts with our genetic endowment. Our interaction with the environment during our lifetime then cements our uniqueness. We can be said to know ourselves when we know what we are doing and why. If we can be said to know ourselves better than anyone else knows us, it is because we have learned to observe our own behavior and identify the causes of that behavior better than anyone else has. We are constantly able to observe ourselves and assess those causes. We know things about ourselves that no one else knows because no one else has the same extensive history of observing what we do and why. We may have private thoughts, wishes, desires, fears, and so on that no one else is aware of at the time they are occurring.

For behavior analysts, self-knowledge is the result of interactions with our social environment. As we grow up, we are routinely asked what we have done in the past, what we are currently doing, and what we are likely to do in the future. These questions largely concern our observable behavior, although they may also concern our emotional responses, sensations, feelings, and thoughts. We are also asked *why* we have done, are currently doing, and will probably do certain things. These questions concern the contingencies that cause our behavior. Our social environment then reinforces correct responses. Given this approach, we can see that self-knowledge consists in self-tacting.

As a hypothetical example, let's suppose that there is an omniscient person who knows everything about our genetic endowment, and had observed us at every instant throughout our lives as we interacted with the environment. Presumably, such an omniscient person would be able to accurately predict our behavior. The private thoughts, wishes, desires, fears, and so on mentioned above were caused by something, so presumably the omniscient individual would know about these internal phenomena. Where is our individuality then? It has not gone anywhere. We are the same unique individuals we always were. We are unique at home, work, or school, on Mondays, Wednesdays, or Fridays. Events that were reinforcing in the past will likely continue to be.

This hypothetical example raises the question of what we mean by individuality. Perhaps a traditional understanding of individuality is that it implies qualities of which no one else is aware. But we have seen that this omniscient person is aware of these qualities. If not, how could the person have accurately predicted our behavior? Of course, no such other person exists, nor could one. The point is that individuality simply means the unique constellation of events, variables, and relations that have come together at a unique locus to constitute the unique behaving person we call ourselves. The confluence takes place in the one domain, not in two or more, as much of traditional Western culture would argue. Self-knowledge is a matter of understanding what these variables and relations are, how they have come together, and how they contribute to our lives.

Self as Agent

In many instances, language of the self is concerned with the self as an *agent*. As traditionally conceived, the sense of self as an agent implies humans are wholly autonomous beings who have conceptions of themselves as they exist in the world, and how they voluntarily interact with the world. They are not lashed and prodded through life by mechanical forces beyond their control. They have free will and freedom of choice. They can therefore initiate behavior, based on their individual purposes, intentions, goals, beliefs, values, wishes, wants, and desires. Their behavior shows particular patterns over time that cannot be explained by any relation to physical forces in the environment. As traditionally conceived, such terms as agency and freedom are assumed to reflect inner, mental causes of behavior, if the notion of cause is even appropriate in those cases. An explanation of behavior would have to reflect features of a mental domain, rather than an analysis of functional relations between environmental circumstances and performance in the behavioral domain. Nearly all of this approach is orthodox mentalism. As we have seen, behavior analysts argue that the question of how purely mental events can produce physical events like behavior remains intractable.

Traditional psychology might argue that mental terms and concepts are necessary to account for particular patterns of behavior that are organized over time, as implied by such terms as intention or purpose. Behavior analysts ask, Who says behavior analysts can't account for particular patterns of behavior over time? On what basis is it necessary to embrace agency or free will to account for some particular pattern of behavior organized over time? One reason for the embrace of agency and free will is an assumption that a cause must be contiguous with behavior. If we have difficulty finding a contiguous cause in the environment, then we must invent one, put it inside a person in a mental domain, and use mental terms to describe how it mediates the relation between environment and behavior. Behavior analysts do not find it necessary to assume a contiguous, mediating cause from a mental domain to explain behavior. Rather, the sense of cause as the fact of a functional relation is sufficient, without regard to its temporal parameters. The first step is to recognize what can be a cause in the behavioral domain. The second step is to identify what the cause actually is.

What Does Agency or Freedom Mean?

So, for behavior analysts, the important questions concern the meaning of such terms from our ordinary language as agency and *freedom*.

For behavior analysts, talk of agency and freedom may be compared to talk of sunrises and sunsets. Talk of sunrises and sunsets is not literally about an ethereal chariot that pulls the sun from beyond the eastern horizon in the morning and deposits the sun beyond the western horizon in the evening. Rather, talk of sunrises and sunsets is one way of talking about the beginning of light and dark periods of the day. An important consideration is that we can talk about those periods in terms of the facts of astronomy when necessity demands.

Now let's consider talk of agency and free will. For behavior analysts, such talk is not literally about some autonomous entity inside us that causes our behavior, any more than talk of sunrises is about an ethereal chariot. To be sure, for centuries people have assumed that individuals do have some autonomous entity inside us that causes our behavior. As we have seen, such assumptions are at the heart of folk psychology. Behavior analysts take the position that we have more effective ways of addressing our concerns about the causes of behavior, particularly when we use such terms as agency or freedom.

Behavior analysts suggest that when we speak of agency, we are actually talking about the characteristics of acts in context, rather than supposed features of mental entities like minds. As anticipated earlier in this chapter, the meaning of agency or freedom is related to our capacity for self-analytical repertoires. These repertoires generally involve our tacting past behavior and the conditions that affected it, present behavior and the conditions affecting it, and probable future behavior and the conditions likely to affect it. These tacts then exert discriminative control over subsequent behavior in what we call self-management. We then obtain more reinforcement than we could in the absence of such tacts. The process is not mysterious: The analytical tacts we have learned to generate about ourselves exert the same discriminative control as analytical tacts others may make about us. What is important is to understand the experiences necessary for the self-analytical tacts to develop, and once developed, for them to exert discriminative control. Under the influence of social contingencies that are cherished for extraneous reasons, people may mistakenly attribute this process to something from another domain called agency, but closer analysis suggests the concern is actually with something from the one, behavioral domain. Again, our self-analytical repertoires develop during our lifetimes, when we are asked to identify what we are doing and why. The repertoires then expand under correlated experiences with ourselves as both speakers and listeners. The repertoire presumably has both overt and covert components.

Some of the covert components are concerned with the *feeling of freedom*. Clearly, individuals do have feelings associated with being a so-called agent. We feel free when we experience respondents related to the opportunity to pursue reinforcers. We feel the loss of freedom when we experience respondents related to the prevention or loss of opportunity to pursue reinforcers, or perhaps even experience respondents related to impending aversive stimuli. The reinforcers in question are not necessarily food or water, although sometimes they can be. Sometimes they are related to more generalized social and personal circumstances of living, like opportunities for interaction with others or the ability to pursue individual interests that are reinforcing. In an important way behavior analysts want people to feel freer than they ever have. We can engender these feelings by enhancing the effectiveness of our behavior in pursuit of reinforcers. After all, this state of affairs causes our feelings of freedom. We probably don't feel free to enjoy a refreshing swim in a lake on a hot summer day if we don't know how to swim. We don't feel free to enjoy the benefits of a library if we don't know how to read. No doubt feelings and a traditional conception of agency outlined earlier in this chapter contribute to the popular appeal of traditional psychology. Some traditional psychologists talk of self-efficacy (Bandura, 1997), internal versus external locus of control (Rotter, 1954), and self-actualization (Maslow, 1954; Rogers, 1961), often in efforts to dispel mechanical conceptions of behavior. After all, no one appreciates being called a mechanical robot, which is how many people view the alternative. Behavior analysts argue that to equate behavior analysis with a mechanical viewpoint is a mistake. The very conception of operant behavior means that individuals are interacting with their environments, not just lashed and prodded in a mechanical way through life. Indeed, the notion of being lashed and prodded through life is a legacy of classical S - R behaviorism, which behavior analysis replaced with its concepts of operant processes and selection by consequences.

In contrast with traditional mentalism, the feelings of freedom and agency may be understood as respondents brought about by stimuli correlated with impending changes in reinforcement. After all, a stimulus correlated with an impending increase in reinforcement leads us to feel good, and one correlated with an impending decrease in reinforcement leads us to feel bad. The stimuli are often verbal, or at least the result of verbal processes, as implied by the treatment of self-analytical tacts above. When we can accurately state what we are doing and why, we are likely to achieve more reinforcement in our lives than when we can't. We then experience the respondent condition we call "feeling good about ourselves." When we can't state what we are doing and why, we are likely to achieve less in our lives than when we can. We then experience the respondent condition we call "feeling bad about ourselves."

Often a claim is made that belief in agency or freedom is useful and adaptive, if not necessary to understand and explain behavior. This claim is based on the utilitarian value of the belief: If we believe we are free, the probability is decreased that we will be coerced or manipulated into some particular form of action by others. Although there may well be some value in such a position, we need to recognize that our behavior is inevitably a function of the environmental circumstances in which we live. If we don't recognize this fundamental fact, then we run the risk that in the long term, certain of our behavior patterns may well prove troublesome. For example, suppose we believe we should be free to buy a ticket in a state-run lottery. After all, buying the ticket is customarily regarded as a voluntary action, not compelled by any other person or entity. We may further believe no one should be able to impose restrictions on our voluntary behavior. However, lotteries are gambling systems. They are not philanthropic systems. They pay us for giving them our money. Many pay us only 90 cents for every dollar we give them. If an individual has a particular kind of history related to intermittent reinforcement, the particular way the individual has won prizes in the past may produce a behavior pattern where the individual continually buys tickets to play the lottery, even at the expense of necessities. In extreme cases the individual may resort to embezzlement or theft to support gambling losses. We can see then that the behavior pattern that developed under the belief that it was voluntary has a troublesome outcome. To be sure, not every instance of gambling leads to such an unfortunate outcome. Nevertheless, what is most useful is to recognize that agency entails developing self-analytical repertoires that tact past and present behavior, as well as the circumstances of which that behavior is a function, and circumstances that are likely to influence us in the future. Those repertoires promote self-management skills that will be of inestimable value to us. The result will be even stronger feelings of the sort we currently identify as freedom, and even greater improvements in human welfare.

The Self in Behavior Analysis

As suggested previously in this book, behavior analysts accept that humans may have experiences that no one else can see. In some cases these experiences involve our innermost sensations and feelings. In other cases, these experiences involve engaging in activity that is not observable to anyone else. Behavior analysts accept that we can usefully take these experiences into account to understand human behavior. However, behavior analysts do not view these experiences as qualitatively different from experiences that others can see, just because no one else has access to it. Thus, behavior analysts do not distinguish between (a) the mind, as an entity from an unobservable, mental domain; and (b) the body, as an entity from an observable, physical domain. Rather, behavior analysts integrate the various elements of the human experience into a functional whole. For behavior analysts, then, the sense of self does not mean that inside us we have some unobservable inner being that differs from the being that others see.

For behavior analysts, we are always single, integrated individuals living our lives, adapting (or in unfortunate cases, not adapting) to the circumstances in which we find ourselves. We have sensory systems, which enable us to come into contact with events and relations in the environment. We have motor systems, which enable us to operate on the environment. We have nervous systems, which link sensory and motor systems. Our nervous systems change as we experience events and relations in the environment, leading us to behave differently when we encounter certain events and relations in the future. We can respond to features of the external environment, such as lights, odors, tones, and flavors. We can respond to features of the internal environment, such as aches, pains, sensations, and feelings. In addition, when we think, reflect, fantasize, or contemplate, we are behaving in ways that have stimulus properties. In some cases, we are behaving verbally. The stimulus properties of these forms of behavior are as much part of the environment as are external features like sights and sounds, even though they are not accessible to others. They can then guide subsequent forms of behavior, just as can external features of the environment.

Given this alternative point of view, behavior analysts regard an important sense of the term *self* as identifying an individual who behaves in organized and consistent ways as a result of its unique experiences, particularly as those experiences are related to reinforcers (Skinner, 1953). As an illustration, we can consider what is called *self-management*. In the case of self-management, we must identify who is doing the managing, and who is being managed. Traditional approaches invoke the mind in the mental domain as doing the managing, and the body in the physical domain as being managed. Behavior analysts talk instead of the single individual who is interacting with various features of the environment. The single individual then plays two different roles: the *managing self*, who engages in *managing responses*, and the *managed self*, who engages in *managed responses*.

For instance, suppose we set an alarm clock before we go to bed, to be sure we get up from our warm, cozy bed in time to keep an appointment in the morning. It is the same individual who sets the alarm clock and gets up in the morning. Suppose we write out a grocery list to be sure we purchase only needed items at the market. It is the same individual who writes out the list and purchases the items. Of interest in such cases are the circumstances that get us to set the alarm or write out the list, on the one hand, and then to actually get up or to actually purchase the listed items, on the other hand. A ringing alarm doesn't inevitably cause us to get up nor does the list inevitably cause us to purchase the items. The point is that there is no entity from another domain called the self that is inside us and causes our behavior of setting alarms, arising, writing out lists, or purchasing items. Rather, a ringing alarm may well make it more probable that we will arise at a specified time or a list may well increase the probability we will buy the needed items. Setting alarms and writing lists are instances of operant behavior, and may be understood in terms of the contingencies we have experienced. We are the *managing self* when we engage in the *managing response* of setting the alarm clock or writing a list. Such responses influence the response that comes next. We are the *managed self* when we engage in the *managed response* of getting up on time or buying listed items.

Often self-management competes with more immediate contingencies. For example, we engage in the managing response on Sunday night of setting the alarm clock, to be sure we engage in the managed response of getting up on time on Monday morning. However, as we noted above, when Monday morning actually comes, we turn off the ringing alarm clock, roll over, and go comfortably back to sleep. Such conflicts are ordinarily overcome by a supplemental managing response, such as putting the alarm clock across the room. The alarm clock is then so loud that we cannot go back to sleep. We get up to turn off the alarm clock, and as long as we have arisen, we might as well stay up and get going with our day, as we intended the night before. Similarly, when we are actually at the market, we might spend our money on various "impulse" items the store owner has cleverly placed near the check out counter, and not have enough money left to purchase what we really need. To overcome these competing responses, we might engage in a managing response by writing out a list. We might then subtract the cost of each item we purchase to ensure we remain within our overall budget, as the managed response. In more general terms, a managing response creates additional circumstances that make the managed response more probable. An appeal to an internal entity from another domain is neither necessary nor helpful. Indeed, to invoke an internal entity from another domain is actually to reduce, rather than promote the likelihood of adaptative behavior. We fail to pay attention to the circumstances in our environment that do cause our behavior.

Summary and Conclusions

The self is an important concept in traditional psychology. Traditional psychology operates from the perspective of two domains: the mental and the physical. Given this distinction, the mental domain is traditionally taken as more important. It supposedly contains the unobservable mental causes of behavior, one of which is the sense of self. In contrast, the physical domain is less important. It supposedly contains only behavior.

Behavior analysts approach the self quite differently. The self implies an individual with a functionally organized repertoire. Self-management means arranging the environment to promote desirable behavior. The response of arranging the environment to promote desirable behavior is called the managing response. The desirable behavior itself, which is said to show self-management and is typically delayed from the behavior of arranging the environment, is called the managed response. Individuality means the unique collection of experiences that makes each one of us who we are. The terms agency or freedom simply mean that as living organisms we have the capacity to act in various complex ways. Often our behavior is guided by our self-analytical statements of what we are doing and why. Feelings of freedom are brought about by repertoires that are effective in deriving reinforcement from the environment. Behavior analysts want to make people feel freer than ever before, by promoting more effective self-knowledge of the contingencies that cause their behavior.

References

Bandura, A. (1997). *Self-efficacy: The exercise of control.* New York: Freeman.
Maslow, A. (1954). *Motivation and personality.* New York: Harper and Row.
Rogers, C. (1961). *On becoming a person: A therapist's view of psychotherapy.* London: Constable.
Rotter, J.B. (1954). *Social learning and clinical psychology.* New York: Prentice-Hall.
Skinner, B. F. (1953). *Science and human behavior.* New York: Macmillan.

Key Terms and Concepts

self
individuality
agent, agency
freedom
feeling of freedom
self-management
managing response
managed response
managing self
managed self

Study Questions

1. How do behavior analysts define the term self?
2. What does individuality mean in behavior analysis?
3. Distinguish between traditional and behavior analytic accounts of agency.
4. Distinguish between traditional and behavior analytic accounts of freedom.
5. What does the feeling of freedom mean in behavior analysis?
6. Distinguish between the managing response and the managed response in matters of self-management.

Chapter 6

Consciousness and Awareness

As mentioned throughout this book, behavior analysts approach the subject matter and methods of psychology quite differently than do traditional psychologists. Traditional psychologists typically claim the business of psychology is to account for the nature and functioning of various inferred mental phenomena in our lives. One of the most prominent of these mental phenomena in traditional psychology is consciousness. In contrast, behavior analysts emphasize behavior in relation to environmental circumstances. One might wonder, then, whether behavior analysts have anything meaningful to say about consciousness. This matter is particularly important because behaviorism is commonly thought to deny or ignore the relevance of any talk of mental phenomena. To be sure, much of the force behind the historical and conceptual development of behaviorism in the first quarter of the 20th century was its concern about what the mentalistic psychology of the time had to say about consciousness. However, for behavior analysts, the term consciousness concerns aspects of human functioning, rather than some causal or mediating state or process in a mental domain. In this view, behavior analysts ask what is at issue when such terms as consciousness are used.

What Does Consciousness Mean?

For behavior analysts, an examination of the ways we use the term *consciousness* indicates that we are said to be conscious or have consciousness when we are able to sense and respond to the environment in particular ways, where we are included in the environment just as much as are nominally external objects, events, and relations. We may not be sensing and responding at exactly the moment in question. However, if we are not, we have the potential to do so at some other time. In ordinary circumstances, we are said to be not conscious when we are not responding to the environment, as when we are sleeping. We say in ordinary circumstances because after all, we do roll over in our sleep. Further, we might scratch our nose when we are asleep and some prankster tickles it with a feather. Readers may also be aware of what reflexes are often elicited when we are asleep and a prankster dips our fingers into a cup of warm water.

Of special interest is self-consciousness: our responding to our behavior and the circumstances that cause it. Behavior analysts are vitally interested in understanding how individuals come to respond to their own behavior. As mentioned in Chapter 5, responding to oneself is of central importance in self-management. According to a behavior analytic view, consciousness is not a mental state or process that causes us to respond to our own behavior, or mediates such responding. Rather, it is the fact of such responding. As we will see shortly, the important question is how responding to our own behavior and the circumstances that cause it comes about.

For behavior analysts, individuals may often behave in certain ways, given certain environmental circumstances. The important sense of a causal analysis of behavior lies in determining functional relations among (a) antecedent circumstances in the environment, (b) behavior, and (c) the consequences of the behavior. These relations exist whether individuals are able to describe them or not. It is one question to ask what specific features of the environment influence that behavior. It is a second and different question to ask whether individuals can describe what they are doing and why. A great deal of the traditional talk about consciousness assumes that what is introspectively "observed," such as feelings (e.g., of anxiety), sensations, images, and the like, reflects causes of behavior from a mental domain that differs from than the one in which behavior takes place. According to a traditional view, these mental causes mediate the causal relation between the environment and behavior. Behavior analysts disagree with this traditional assumption. To the extent that talk of feelings, sensations, images, and the like is meaningful, behavior analysts suggest that such talk is ordinarily about behavioral phenomena. The talk is about effects, rather than causes. Some prior events caused the feelings, sensations, or images that are reported. Behavior analysts suggest it is useful to trace these earlier events back as far as practical in order to understand where the feelings, sensations, or images come from, and how they then might be related to subsequent behavior. Thus, behavior analysts are very much interested in consciousness and introspection, not as aspects of mental life that explain behavior but rather as aspects of the behavioral functioning of humans that need to be explained.

Clearly, people do make introspective statements about their sensations and feelings. They can imagine what it would be like to be in situation X, Y, or Z. They can make statements about what caused them to engage in some form of behavior in the past, what is causing them to engage in some form of behavior currently, and what is likely to cause them to engage in some form of behavior in the future. Of course, some individuals are more skilled than others at introspective describing their feelings, sensations, or behavior and the conditions that cause them. Given that introspective statements are a form of behavior that can and does occur, the origins of that skill need to be understood. Thus, introspective statements are just as appropriate for a science of behavior to consider as any other form of behavior.

Behavior analysts ask such questions as the following about the nature and causal status of the introspective statements: How did these statements come about in the first place? What do such statements in fact describe? Do these statements influence subsequent behavior, and if so, according to what processes? To answer these questions, we now need to expand on an important concept, that of private or covert behavioral events, which was introduced in Chapter 2.

As we have seen, behavior analysts acknowledge that many important events take place within the skin, and that many of these events are unobservable and inaccessible to others. Behavior analysts further acknowledge that an understanding of events within the skin can contribute to an understanding of overt behavior. However, behavior analysts do not assume that talk of these events implies that a mental domain actually exists that differs from a behavioral domain. In addition, behavior analysts do not assume that these events have any special properties, structure, or nature simply because they are within the skin. Finally, behavior analysts also do not assume that they need to be analyzed differently than does observable behavior.

We have suggested that self-consciousness is concerned with our responding to our own behavior. That we can respond to our own behavior is not as curious as it sounds. Suppose we make a fist, and then raise our index finger. Presumably, we can state in a reasonably accurate way that we are indeed raising our finger. Now suppose we again make a fist, and rise our index finger, but this time with our eyes closed. Again, we can presumably state we are doing so. The point is that we are responding, in this case verbally, on the basis of discriminative stimulation from our own behavior of raising our index finger. If our eyes are open, our verbal response might be based on visual stimulation, but if our eyes are closed it presumably is not. If our eyes are closed, the statement is presumably based on the proprioceptive and interoceptive sense of our behavior of rasing our index finger. In either case, the stimulation from the finger raising is the stimulus condition that occasions our verbal statement. As described, both the finger raising and our verbal statement are public.

Now suppose that instead of visibly moving our index finger, we just tighten the muscle in the finger, but not enough to see it move. In this case we might say we are on the verge of raising our index finger. The tightening of the muscle is a private behavioral event, in the sense that no one else has access to it. If we say out loud what our finger is doing, even though our finger is not visibly moving, our statement is public. However, suppose we whisper to ourselves what our finger is doing, where no one else could hear what we whisper. Here, our statement is private. The possibilities outlined above are admittedly simplified instances of responding to our own behavior, but they serve to illustrate the point. In summary, the behavior with respect to which we are responding can public or private, nonverbal or verbal, and our responding can be public or private, nonverbal or verbal.

In some cases, when traditional psychologists talk about mental events, behavior analysts say the talk is actually about a *private, covert behavioral event*, rather than about some causal or mediating mental state or process from another domain. The private behavior is related to public circumstances just as much as public or overt behavior is. The talk is not literally about brain states because the brain does not have the kind of sensory receptors that permit speakers to come into contact with brain states and speak about them in the observed way.

Of course, not all of the so-called mental phenomena identified in traditional psychology can be construed as private behavior. Behavior analysts suggest some talk is simply metaphorical or even about *explanatory fictions*. Considerable inspection of this talk and the circumstances that give rise to it are necessary to determine whether the talk is actually about some natural event, or whether it is simply some metaphorical talk about fictitious entities. We make use of these several categories of behavior in what follows.

Private Behavioral Events

Let us now continue to elaborate on the concept of private behavioral events. Two cases are of importance. The first is when we learn to describe our internal sensations and feelings. The second is when our own covert operant behavior influences us. Let's look first at how we learn to describe our internal sensations and feelings.

Verbal Reports About Our Internal Sensations and Feelings. In the case of sensations and feelings, the object of the talk is certain changes or new conditions that develop in our bodies when we come in contact with significant stimuli in our environment. These new conditions are then sensed by our interoceptive and sometimes proprioceptive nervous systems, in ways that are analogous to the ways in which our eyes and ears in our exteroceptive nervous system sense common public stimuli such as lights and tones.

Important questions now are, How are we able to talk about our feelings, sensations, and behavior? For example, what experiences lead us to describe one pain as sharp, and another as dull? These questions are not idle ones, as they have far-reaching implications for our world view. A traditional position, such as one derived from the position of Descartes, might hold that we are just able to describe our feelings and sensations because we are human. The self (or for Descartes, the religious Soul) can just observe the internal panorama of events and apply a private language to describe those sensations. This whole story, of course, subscribes to the traditions of a dualistic metaphysics, with assumptions of both physical and nonphysical domains of existence.

A thoroughgoing behavioral psychology like behavior analysis views these matters very differently. We ordinarily experience the pain as it occurs, although there are exceptions: Athletes might not feel pain at the time they are injured because of the intensity of the competition, and soldiers might not feel time at the time they are injured because of the intensity of the battle. Our ability to function in challenging circumstances may also benefit from specialized physiological mechanisms that inhibit or block pain. In any event, the main problem that needs to be resolved is in the field of verbal behavior: How is a vocabulary descriptive of our internal sensations and feelings like pains acquired and maintained?

We begin our answer by repeating that verbal behavior of any sort develops through the interaction with others. To illustrate, we can consider a simple case involving exteroceptive stimulation: How do we learn to say a red light is red, rather than some other color? Well, in the presence of the red light, when we respond by saying "Red" a listener reinforces our response by saying "Correct, it's red all right." If we say "Green," a listener does not say we are correct. An important feature of this case is that the listener must be in contact with the red light, as the occasion on which to administer the reinforcement necessary for the verbal behavior to develop. In simple terms, the listener needs to knows when to provide the reinforcement necessary for the verbal response. A public stimulus like a red light satisfies this requirement. Now we can consider the case of verbal behavior that is occasioned by internal sensations or feelings. If we say we are in pain, the listener is not in contact with that pain. Hence, the listener operates at a handicap because our pain is not a basis that the listener can use for providing the differential reinforcement necessary for a response occasioned by the pain to develop, in the same way that the listener can use the publicly available red light as a basis for providing the differential reinforcement necessary for a response occasioned by the red light to develop. The pain is private. We are the only ones who are in contact with it. The situation is much the same if the listener was trying to teach us to label a light as red or green, but the listener was blindfolded and does not know what color the light actually is. In neither situation is the listener is in direct contact with the relevant stimulus. As a result, the listener cannot use it as a basis for providing the differential reinforcement necessary for our verbal behavior to develop.

The fact remains, however, that we do learn to describe our innermost feelings and sensations. Therefore, it follows that there must be one or more ways for listeners to work around the limitation described above. In other words, there must be some public antecedent condition that is common to both ourselves as speakers and others as listeners that listeners can use as a basis for administering the differential reinforcement necessary for the verbal behavior to develop. What are the ways then that a listener can work around the limitation and promote verbal behavior under the control of private forms of stimulation, such as pain? This question is important for parents who want their children to tell them where it hurts.

One way is when we engage in some *collateral behavior*. Here, listeners reinforce our talk of being in pain when we hold some afflicted area, perhaps also moaning and groaning as forms of unconditioned responding. The pain develops some measure of stimulus control, such that the next time the pain is present, we can talk about it.

Another way is when there are *public accompaniments*. Here, listeners reinforce our talk of being in pain when they see that we have been struck by some object or that we have fallen down and suffered tissue damage. For example, we may be bleeding or some area might be inflamed. Indeed, listeners may even mistrust verbal reports of pain if those reporting the pain do not engage in some collateral response like holding an afflicted area and moaning, or if listeners have not observed some public accompaniment that might have caused the pain. We might regard the speaker as a malingerer or hypochondriac. In those cases, the reinforcers for pretending to be in pain are gratuitous attention, or escape from unpleasant work.

In future cases, there might be generalization based on the properties of the private experience. Suppose we experience pain caused by a sharp object. Others see that we have had the public accompaniment of contact with the sharp object. Others then approve and interact meaningfully with us when we talk of experiencing a sharp pain. The internal sensation of pain acquires some measure of discriminative control over our verbal behavior. Later, we describe pains resembling the original pain as sharp, even if they weren't caused by a sharp object. Similarly, suppose we experience pain caused by a dull object. Others see that we have had the public accompaniment of contact with the dull object. Others then approve and interact meaningfully with us when we talk of experiencing a dull pain. Later, we describe pains resembling the original pain as dull, even if they weren't caused by a dull object. Again, given this sort of approval and meaningful interaction from listeners, the internal sensation of pain initially acquires stimulus control. Later on, similar pains occasion a similar verbal response, according to the process of stimulus generalization.

In sum, verbal behavior about internal sensations and feelings is acquired on the basis of public features of some situation, and then transfers to those sensations and feelings. In future situations, control can be exerted by the sensations and feelings alone, resulting in speakers' being able to talk about their own internal world.

The Influence of Covert Operant Behavior. Now let's look at how we are influenced by our own covert operant behavior. Here, we are concerned with the traditional topic of *thinking*. We have more to say about thinking in Chapter 7 that follows. For now, let us say that in many cases, what we mean by thinking is engaging in some form of behavior that exerts stimulus control over our subsequent behavior. Often thinking takes the form of covert operant behavior. However, strictly speaking, we can think publicly. Indeed, we do so when we write notes to ourselves as reminders.

One common case of the term thinking targets our own behavior. We learn to speak about our behavior and the conditions that cause that behavior when those with whom we live ask us what we have done in the past, what we are doing currently, what we are likely to do in the future, and what circumstances are related to those forms of behavior. It is useful for others to find out. Consequently, they socially shape and differentially reinforce appropriate answers.

Once others teach us to describe our own behavior and the conditions to which it is related, we can generate verbal descriptions in other circumstances, as we try to adapt to the whole range of circumstances in which we live. In an athletic competition, we may tell ourselves to "Pay attention!" or "Watch the ball!" or "Bend your knees!" The resulting responding constitutes a form of discriminative stimulation that is just as useful to us as stimulation that comes from others. Sometimes our talk may be out loud. However, in many cases, the responding that influences us is private, or covert.

Covert behavior means we are engaging in the same type of responding as when we respond publicly, with the same organ systems, but our responding is at a reduced magnitude. Our everyday words like thinking or imagining typically apply in this case, when we are influenced by our responding to ourselves and our life circumstances. As is probably evident to many readers, this sense of thinking is very close to the way behavior analysts treat the phenomenon of self-consciousness.

To be sure, the extent to which we respond to ourselves, and the extent to which we are then influenced by such responding, differs widely across individuals, based on how well we have learned via our interactions with others. Nevertheless, the interesting point is that such descriptions come about because of social interactions. When consciousness is viewed as largely self-descriptive verbal behavior, the important implication is that consciousness is socially induced.

The famous French philosopher René Descartes is credited with the saying "Cogito, ergo sum"—"I think, therefore I am." From the point of view of behavior analysts, Descartes had it somewhat backwards. It would have been more accurate to say, "I am, therefore I can think."

Consciousness From a Traditional Point of View

Early versions of psychology assumed mental life in the form of consciousness was the appropriate subject matter of psychology, and introspection as a form of "inner observation" was the appropriate method to investigate consciousness. A particular problem in the early study of consciousness was the lack of agreement regarding the findings. For example, often the supposed research results in one laboratory could not be replicated elsewhere. In a famous article, Watson (1913) questioned the whole introspective project. Watson did not deny that some important events take place inside the skin, and that psychology needed to provide an account of these events. What Watson disputed was the mentalism associated with the way traditional psychology sought to do so. As an alternative, Watson proposed a natural science approach to the study of behavior, in which events taking place inside the skin were conceived as natural events to be accommodated in the same way as events outside the skin, as stimuli, responses, and so on.

Despite arguments by Watson and others, a conception of consciousness as some underlying phenomenon from a mental or cognitive domain that differs from behavior in a behavioral domain has flourished in traditional psychology. Indeed, many contemporary researchers have applied new technology, such as brain imaging, to support inferences about longstanding mental concepts as well as develop new ones. They have argued that improved mathematical techniques allow us support inferences about mental life that could not have been supported earlier. Let us now further examine some representative statements about how traditional positions have tended to view consciousness.

Consciousness is commonly viewed as a mental entity or mental state that possesses some "content." The mental state has something to do with receiving sensory input from the environment and then being able to reflect on the sensations resulting from that input and how we are responding to it. It is linked to memory processes, except that it is more like a temporary buffer on a computer than a longer-term location in which data are stored and from which retrieved. Its content is a copy or representation of a sensation, feeling, image, or even the characteristics of an event in the near past. However, the content is held to be part of our immediate experience—a "raw feel," and different from the content associated with such other mental processes such as memory. It is based on a subjective conception from individuals who report they are having these experiences, and that they are aware of who they are and that they are having them. In certain cases we are able to do things automatically, without benefit of consciousness. The exact proportion of things that are said to require and not require consciousness so conceived is a matter of empirical investigation.

We might contrast consciousness with the term unconscious. One sense of unconscious is that individuals are sleeping or even "knocked out": They are relatively inert and don't respond to much of anything for some period of time, perhaps from a blow to the head. They then regain the ability to respond as they recover. While knocked out, individuals are obviously not conscious of anything, including their own behavior.

Another sense of the term unconscious was discussed extensively by Sigmund Freud. At the end of the nineteenth and early in the twentieth centuries, Sigmund Freud theorized about "the unconscious mind." With frequent usage over time, this phrase became shortened to "the unconscious." Among other attributes, the Freudian unconscious was a repository of various biological urges, such as sexual motivation and aggression. Individuals were not aware of these urges, but the urges were powerful determinants of behavior nonetheless. The maladaptive behavior of a client in Freudian psychoanalysis, said to be unconsciously motivated, is an instance.

Freud believed an individual's personality was composed of three components: id, super-ego, and ego. The individual had a certain biological character ("id"), but typically lived in a social setting with prescribed rules of conduct ("super-ego"). Often an individual's biological character came into conflict with social rules, which for Freud meant that the components of an individual's personality typically came into unconscious, but nevertheless real, conflict with each other. When the components were in conflict, the individual experienced anxiety. Freud further believed that another component of the personality ("ego") might use various unconscious strategies or defense mechanisms to protect itself against the anxiety created by the conflicts. Individuals were not able to verbally report that they were engaging in these strategies. The defense mechanisms might appear to work in the short term, but they only caused problems in the long term. Freudian psychoanalysis sought to identify the source of the conflict, then strengthen the personality components so that the unconscious conflicts could then be brought up to the conscious level, dealt with more constructively, and ultimately resolved.

Of course, a great deal more could be said about traditional ideas and research into the area of consciousness. The review above is intended to be only brief and illustrative. Clearly, consciousness and introspection, taken for granted as mental phenomena that underlie behavior, have continued to be of prime importance in traditional psychology. The alternative view of behavior analysis, based on the principles of natural science, has much to offer.

Awareness

In traditional psychology, one very common example of a conscious mental state or process that supposedly mediates responding to a stimulus is *awareness*. Framed as an experimental question, at issue is whether a participant's behavior in an experiment will change only if the participant is aware of the experimental manipulations, where by aware we mean that the participant can describe those manipulations.

Actually, there is a great deal of research on this experimental question, some of which has been carried out by behavior analysts. One well known experiment is Hefferline and Keenan (1963). In this experiment, participants received monetary reinforcement when muscle tension in their thumb was about half that required to produce a visible contraction. Thus, the response was private. Interestingly, the participants showed the reinforced increase in muscle tension, even though it was not visible. In addition, the participants were unable to describe the reinforcement contingencies, even though their responding had clearly been under the control of the contingencies.

In another experiment, Thaver and Oakes (1967) presented participants with pairs of verbs. One verb was previously identified as a hostile verb, while the other was previously identified as neutral. The researchers then had participants compose sentences using the verbs. For half the participants, the researchers said "Good," a social reinforcer, when the participants used the hostile verb in their sentences. For the other half of the participants, the researchers said "Good" when the participants used the neutral verb in their sentences. The participants were then presented with two ambiguous pictures and asked to write a story at least one page long about each picture. Participants wrote more hostile stories when the researchers had previously said good after the sentences that used a hostile verb, and participants wrote more neutral stories when the researchers had previously said good after the sentences that used a neutral verb. To be sure, some participants were aware that their behavior had changed, where awareness was assessed by a series of questions at the end of the experiment. The important feature was that other participants were not aware in this way. Thus, the behavior of participants who were unaware reflected generalization without awareness from the previous manipulation.

The literature contains many investigations of the relation between conditioning and awareness. The two examples cited above are not intended to give an exhaustive review of this literature. Rather, they simply make the point that human operant behavior can and does change in response to reinforcement contingencies, even though participants are not aware of the contingencies. This finding confirms that it is neither correct nor even useful to view awareness as a conscious mental state that necessarily mediates changes in behavior.

Again, some research has shown that the behavior of participants changes in conditioning experiments only when they are aware (Spielberger & DeNike, 1966). In keeping with the present behavioral analysis, these cases may mean that the implicit self-descriptive verbal behavior called awareness contributes some uniquely necessary form of discriminative stimulation to the conditioning process. Further research will help us understand why awareness, understood as the stimulation of self-descriptive verbal behavior, provides necessary discriminative stimulation in some, but not all cases.

Some Contemporary Issues

We may now consider some contemporary issues in the study of consciousness. These issues are often thought to be critical to the study of consciousness as a mental state, but our purpose in considering them here is to show how they may be understood from the perspective of behavioral processes.

Blindsight. The first phenomenon we consider is *blindsight* (Weiskrantz, 1986). Blindsight refers to the rare but documented cases in which individuals profess to be blind, or at best not to be able to see very well or clearly, but then nevertheless respond quite accurately in visual discrimination tasks. The standard laboratory demonstration is when individuals are presented with a light in some portion of the visual field on a trial but then report they do not see the light. If the individuals are subsequently asked to indicate by pointing to a location in their visual field where the light was located on the trial, they say they are just guessing and point to some location. In fact, their responses are often more accurate than is expected on the basis of chance alone. At issue is how individuals can specify the location of the light when they report they haven't seen the light and are just guessing about its location. If consciousness as traditionally conceived is some mental or cognitive process that supposedly mediates the relation between environment and behavior, such that behavior cannot be properly understood without knowing the details of the mediating process, how is it that orderly behavior can take place without the apparent benefit of such a mediating process?

In these rare cases, the pupils, retinas, optic tracts, and optic pathways of the individuals are undamaged. Where the individuals have sustained damage is in the occipital cortex of their brains, for instance, through injury or stroke. Although the underlying physiological processes aren't thoroughly understood, one reasonable possibility is that branches of the optic tracts and pathways project to both (a) the occipital cortex, which makes possible verbalizations about the light; and (b) other areas of the brain, which make possible at least somewhat accurate responding with respect to location. Given the damage in the occipital cortex, the individual cannot verbalize about the light, but can respond somewhat accurately to its location. That the brain has multiple layers of systems, including some that are linked hierarchically, is well known. Consequently, in exceptional cases of physiological trauma it is possible for neural communication to take place in or to one system without communication in or to another.

Phantom Limb Pain. Another phenomenon is *phantom limb pain*. Suppose an individual has had a limb amputated. In a high percentage of cases, these individuals report pain or some other sensation such as itching in the absent limb. Of present interest is how individuals can be said to be responding to something that in one sense isn't there. How can individuals report pain in their leg when they have no leg? This state of affairs contrasts with blindsight, in which individuals do not verbally report the presence of a stimulus that is there and to which they are nonetheless responding otherwise.

Again, although the underlying physiological processes aren't clearly understood, one reasonable possibility is that as the brain adapts to the loss of the limb, neural stimulation from the nerve fibers that were previously connected to the now absent limb become rerouted in the brain, such that they end up projecting to pain or other sensory centers instead of to less distressing sensations. In other words, the condition felt as pain involves central structures as it receives projections from peripheral structures, and stimulation along the pathway from peripheral to central structures may be sufficient to produce the sensation. One promising therapy for phantom limb pain is to provide a visual simulation of the missing limb, such as through a mirror or computer generated virtual reality, so that visual input can override and correct the body sense input (Ramachandran & Blakeslee, 1998). Worth noting is that this therapy is based on behavior–environment relations.

Consciousness in the Laboratory. Other effects pertaining to the concept of consciousness have been noted in the literature over the years. In one kind of verbal learning experiment, participants are presented with a series of sentences. Then, in probe or test trials, sentences are presented again, and participants are asked to rate how familiar the sentences are to them. Interestingly, participants may report they are more familiar with a sentence they have actually never seen before than one they had seen previously. The sentence they had never seen before may actually be a composite of two sentences that they had seen previously. In this case, participants report something about their experiences, which on a traditional view is taken as an indication of consciousness or awareness, but the experience about which they are presumably reporting—hearing a specific sentence—never happened (Bransford & Franks, 1971).

In another kind of experiment, participants wear headphones in what is called a dichotic listening task (Hugdahl, 1988). In a representative case, one message is played in one ear and another message in the other ear, and the participant is then instructed to "pay attention" only to the first message and ignore the second. The participant may not be able to report anything about the second message except for superficial properties, such as whether the voice was male or female. Nevertheless, the participant's behavior may reflect a systematic influence of the second message, such as the extent to which it clarifies ambiguities associated with the first message. In this case, participants can report very little about their experiences, which on a traditional view is taken as an indication of the lack of consciousness or awareness. However, their behavior nevertheless reveals an important effect of the experience about which they cannot report. It follows that we need not view consciousness in traditional terms, as a necessary mediating state or process, but rather as a behavioral process related to the fact of whether or how individuals are influenced by stimulation in the environment, and the extent to which they can report that stimulation.

Summary and Conclusions

The conclusion that follows from the review above is that consciousness is a behavioral matter. For behavior analysts, we know ourselves when our verbal community encourages us to identify what we are doing and why. The "why" concerns identifying the antecedent and consequent conditions that provide the context for our behavior. In other words, the "why" concerns contingencies. If we focus on the role of verbal behavior, our ability to provide verbal reports about our own behavior and the circumstances that cause that behavior is itself a function of environmental relations. These verbal reports can then enter into contingencies that control subsequent behavior. However, any influence is again a function of environmental relations. As such, the influence is neither necessary nor automatic. To be sure, the actual neurological organization that allows an individual to come into contact with the behavior or experience that is the target of that report is an independent matter, clearly worthy of investigation in its own right. However, this neurological functioning is the subject matter of neuroscience, not behavior analysis. What is clear is that it is not useful to view consciousness in traditional terms as a matter of some single, overriding agent in a mental domain that has executive oversight and authority to mediate an individual's behavior.

References

Bransford, J. D., & Franks, J. J. (1971). The abstraction of linguistic ideas. *Cognitive Psychology, 2,* 331-350.
Hefferline, R., & Keenan, B. (1963). Amplitude-induction of a small-scale (covert) operant. *Journal of the Experimental Analysis of Behavior, 6,* 307-315.
Hugdahl, K. (1988). *Handbook of dichotic listening: Theory, methods, and research.* Hoboken, NJ: Wiley.
Ramachandran, V. S., & Blakeslee, S. (1998). *Phantoms in the brain: Probing the mysteries of the human mind.* New York: William Morrow & Company.
Spielberger, C. D., & DeNike, L. D. (1966). Descriptive behaviorism versus cognitive theory in verbal operant conditioning. *Psychological Review, 73,* 306-326.
Thaver, F., & Oakes, W. (1967). Generalization and awareness in verbal operant conditioning. *Journal of Personality and Social Psychology, 6,* 391-399.
Watson, J. B. (1913). Psychology as the behaviorist views it. *Psychological Review, 20,* 158-177.
Weiskrantz, L. (1986). *Blindsight: A Case Study and Implications.* Oxford: Oxford University Press.

Key Terms and Concepts

consciousness
unconscious
private behavioral events
explanatory fictions

collateral behavior
public accompaniments
stimulus generalization of pain
covert operant behavior
thinking
awareness
blindsight

phantom limb pain

Study Questions

1. What does consciousness mean in behavior analysis?
2. What does unconscious mean in behavior analysis?
3. How does our verbal community use collateral behavior to teach us to describe our internal feelings and sensations?
4. How does our verbal community use public accompaniments to teach us to describe our internal feelings and sensations?
5. How would we learn to describe a pain as a "burning pain"?
6. How does stimulus generalization allow us to describe pains we haven't felt before?
7. How does covert operant behavior come to influence subsequent behavior?
8. Briefly describe a research example showing that participants can come under the control of operant contingencies without being aware of those contingencies.
9. How does behavior analysis interpret the phenomenon of blindsight?
10. How does behavior analysis interpret the phenomenon of phantom limb pain?

Chapter 7

Thinking, Cognition, and Memory

As we saw in Chapter 6, behavior analysts emphasize that many important activities in our lives are unobserved by others, and that these activities are legitimately part of psychology. However, in contrast to traditional psychology, behavior analysts view these activities as similar in kind though not necessarily in degree to other behavioral phenomena. In particular, behavior analysts do not view these activities as caused by mental or cognitive phenomena with special causal status. Understanding these activities as behavioral and functionally related to the environment means that steps can be taken to promote and strengthen these activities to the benefit of the persons involved.

This chapter reviews the behavior analytic approach to thinking, cognition, and memory. We start with thinking. Clearly, humans do think. Just as clearly, thinking is a suitable subject matter for a science of behavior. As with other topics of this book, we need to specify what we mean by thinking: What activity is being described? What are its properties?

What is the Behavior of Thinking?

For behavior analysts, when we speak of *thinking*, we are speaking of a form of behavior in which people engage, not different in kind from other forms of behavior. This form of behavior is then either reinforcing in its own right, or else it contributes to discriminative control over other forms of behavior that follow. Let us illustrate with a few representative cases.

We begin by considering behavior that is reinforcing in its own right. Consider the behavior called *daydreaming*. Suppose we are in the grip of a cold, snowy winter. We might then think about having a picnic in the park on a warm, sunny, midsummer day. We might imagine what we have previously done in such circumstances—preparing a picnic basket, going to the park, watching the sights and listening to birds singing, leaves rustling, and children playing. Suppose we haven't seen loved ones for a long time. We might then think about reuniting with them. In these cases, we are presumably doing fragments of the same things we do in the actual case, but just at a reduced magnitude. If we are meeting loved ones at an airport, we might imagine what we would see while driving to the airport, and what we would see once inside the terminal. Even though our behavior is covert, the behavior is automatically reinforcing because it is related to reinforcement derived from engaging in the public form of the behavior. This notion of something being private and automatically reinforcing is not the same thing as being an autonomous, initiating, mental cause because there is always the link to some frame of reference that is external to the organism. The external, public event is reinforcing, and covert events associated with the public have similarly become reinforcing.

Now we can consider engaging in a form of behavior that contributes to discriminative control over a form of behavior that follows. Consider the behavior called *problem solving* or *making a decision*. Suppose we face a situation that calls for some action on our part. We might not initially know what to do, so we think. The function of thinking is to clarify the situation by providing new discriminative stimuli or supplementing existing discriminative stimuli, so that we can act effectively. The occurrence of a given form of behavior, whether overt or covert, sometimes sets the occasion for other forms of behavior. Here we are not talking about chains of S - R reflex units, but rather functionally organized sequences of operant behavior. Some early portions of this sequence may be functionally related to later ones. These portions may be covert until the final action, or they may alternate between covert and overt. If the behavior is verbal, they may take the form of mands or tacts relating to our own behavior, where we are our own listeners.

Suppose we are leaving from work for home. We need to stop at the market to buy groceries and at the dry cleaners to pick up some clothes. In order to not drive around unnecessarily, it is useful for us to identify the place at which to stop first, so that we can follow the most efficient route. To do so, we can engage in covert behavior that produces discriminative stimuli that will guide us. We can covertly leave work and covertly begin to drive, first imagining we turn left at this corner and then right on the next, to see whether the contemplated route is efficient. If it is not, then we might covertly try another route. When we identify a suitable route, we can then overtly drive that route. We might even talk to ourselves, overtly or covertly, as we remind ourselves to turn left or right at a particular intersection in the process of driving the route. The behavior of thinking has produced discriminative stimulation that guides us.

Much of the behavior called thinking involves covert, private activity. However, there is no requirement that our thinking be covert. We can engage in overt, public thinking as well as covert, private thinking. In the example above, we need to stop at the market to buy groceries. Which groceries will we buy? We have engaged in public thinking when we have written down the desired items on a list. However, suppose no paper and pencil are available. Then we would need to engage in private thinking: We note for ourselves which items we must buy and repeat them to ourselves several times, in an effort to be sure we do indeed buy them. To ensure we are really systematic, we might contrive a sentence in which the first letter of each word is also the first letter of the name of an item we need. Alternatively, we may imagine ourselves walking into the store, then down the aisles where the desired items are located. In any case, the effect is the same: We end up purchasing the correct items.

In other instances, the behavior that occasions the term thinking is close to that suggested by the related term *reasoning*. Here again the covert behavior is likely to be entirely verbal in character, and the covert verbal behavior in question occasions other verbal behavior. Reasoning then is the activity in which we produce discriminative stimuli, often verbal, that occasion other behavior that achieves some consequence. In this sense, the reasons given for a given form of behavior are statements about the causes of the behavior. The causes are the discriminative stimuli and consequences in the contingencies that engender the behavior in question. For behavior analysts, reasons are not something mental or cognitive that influences us through different, nonbehavioral processes.

Why does the behavior called thinking take the form that it does? Again, we are talking either about behavior that is automatically reinforcing, as in daydreaming or fantasizing, or else behavior that creates discriminative stimuli that contribute subsequently to reinforcement. The overt forms are defined by their relation to reinforcement, as is operant behavior generally. We may even respond on the basis of stimuli associated with incipient or inchoate forms of the behavior. The covert forms may well have been acquired in overt form, but then reverted to covert. Why did they revert to covert? There are several possibilities. One is the lack of material support. We can't engage in the overt form of thinking and write down a grocery list if we don't have a paper and pencil. Consequently, we behave covertly. Covert behavior is also faster, as well as more expedient or convenient, particularly when we learn to respond on the basis of inchoate or incipient forms. Finally, behavior might become covert because the overt form is punished. We learn to talk out loud. However, others may rebuke our being bothersome when we talk out loud to ourselves as we plan our days. If no one else is around, we may well revert to talking out loud to ourselves. A different sort of punishment—that of a competitive disadvantage—is likely if we publicly contemplate our strategy when playing chess or a card game. We can avoid aversive consequences if we covertly rather than overtly weigh the possibilities.

In summary, behavior analysts readily accept that people think. Behavior analysts are interested in accounting for why and how people do so. Behavior analysts even want to help people think better. However, behavior analysts do not accept traditional assumptions that thinking is a nonbehavioral activity or process from another domain, like a mental or cognitive domain. Rather, behavior analysts view thinking as a behavioral process, like any other form of operant behavior. Ordinarily we conceive of thinking as covert behavior. Some prior events are responsible for the behavior called thinking to be covert, as opposed to overt. In addition, some prior events are responsible for the behavior called thinking to influence subsequent behavior. When the covert behavior called thinking occurs, it can but doesn't have to influence subsequent behavior. By viewing thinking as operant behavior, behavior analysts argue that thinking can be made even more effective by the events individuals experience during their lifetimes. It follows then that with suitably favorable experiences, individuals can become even better thinkers than they already are. That outcome seems useful indeed.

Memory

According to a traditional view, the study of behavior is often reduced to the study of learning and memory. Indeed, the field of psychology often has textbooks and university courses bearing those specific titles. If the study of learning is held to involve respondent and operant conditioning processes, what then does a thoroughgoing behaviorism say about memory, and how does it differ from the traditional view?

For behavior analysts, *memory* is a generic term that identifies the reinstatement of a response after the passage of time. Two related terms are *remembering* and *recall*. Let us now look in turn at these terms.

An informal but representative analysis of remembering suggests three elements are involved: (a) a preceding event, such as contact with a stimulus that has occasioned an individual's response; (b) some time period or delay during which the stimulus from the original event is absent; and (c) another opportunity to engage in a response that is based on presence of the stimulus from the original event. We say an individual has remembered when the response in (c) reflects the influence of the event in (a) followed by (b).

As with any form of behavior, our physiology obviously participates in this process. Our physiology is changed by the events we experience, and we often use the word "stored" to reflect what we call the memory of the events. However, our language is misleading. What is "stored" is the changed physiology of the organism, not copies or representations of the events we experience. The changes mean that the next time we encounter the original or a similar situation, our behavior will reflect those prior experiences. An understanding of how these experiences change our physiology, as well as the various levels and systems of organization of our physiology within our nervous system, is clearly relevant to an understanding of how we will or will not respond in particular situations after the passage of time. This understanding will ultimately be achieved by the techniques appropriate to neuroscience as a discipline. Further, this understanding will constitute one kind of answer to questions about the nature of remembering.

Behavior analysts ask such questions as, What was the setting in which the to-be-remembered response was originally made? What is the to-be-remembered response? How similar is (a) the original setting, to (b) the test setting? What other events with what other stimuli and responses did the subject experience during the interval between the original and test settings? What other events with what other stimuli and responses did the subject experience prior to the original setting and response? The ecology of the to-be-remembered response is also relevant, for we wouldn't want to assume that the process of the reinstatement of a response after some period of time reflects some sort of general purpose mental mechanism that receives inputs and generates outputs, regardless of the ecology of those inputs and outputs. Thus, questions about remembering are viewed as questions about behavioral events. Such questions concern what is remembered, as well as how remembering works.

Earlier we mentioned that traditional views often emphasize a structural account of remembering. By a structural account we mean roughly that a subject is assumed to partition a to-be-remembered stimulus or response into different parts, and each part is assumed to be stored and retrieved by a different structure or system in the body. Such contrasting terms as short vs. long term memory, declarative vs. procedural memory, implicit vs. explicit memory, or episodic vs. semantic memory all seem to suggest that different structures operate in different situations. We review some traditional distinctions in what follows to establish some familiarity with how the reinstatement of a response can often differ across situations.

For example, we might be said to have *sensory memory* in tasks involving (usually briefly presented) stimuli. We might be said to have *iconic memory* when visual stimuli are presented for short periods, say of up to 1 s. We might be said to have *echoic memory* when auditory stimuli are presented for short periods, say of up to 4 s.

We might be said to have *declarative memory* in other cases. Declarative memory is made up of *semantic memory* and *episodic memory*. We speak of semantic memory when we remember the impersonal meaning of words. We speak of episodic memory when we remember personal or autobiographical life events, such as who, what, when, and where. Further, these episodic memories are said to be explicit—we remember specific events or information from the past, as evidenced by our ability to correctly state the information.

We might be said to have *procedural memory* in other cases. For example, we remember how to perform certain motor responses, like riding a bicycle or tying one's shoes. These responses are automatic, routine, and implicit. In contrast to declarative memory, procedural memory means we typically do not remember how specific events or information from the past have influenced these responses.

We might be said to have *short-term memory* and *working memory*. Short-term memory might be concerned with retention and maintenance of a limited set of items over a relatively short period of time, hence the name. An example would be reciting a telephone number that had just been given to you. Working memory is similar, in that it involves a short period of time, but it also involves manipulation of the contents. To use a standard example, suppose we want to calculate a 15 percent tip to a server at a restaurant. We might first calculate 10 percent, then add half to what we remember the first 10 percent to be.

We might also recall some events better than others. For example, upon smelling a fragrance, such as after shave or perfume, we might readily remember an episode with a loved one who wore that fragrance, as opposed to the color of the clothes the loved one was wearing at the time.

For behavior analysts, the important questions are, What is said to be remembered by whom, and for what purpose? That these are questions about behavior is precisely the point. Questions about remembering are questions about the context of behavior, where an important aspect of the context is temporal.

This approach also allows us to make sense out of a number of cases to which the term recall applies. Recall here implies how we might produce discriminative stimuli that facilitate the reinstatement of a response after the passage of time. For example, consider the case in which you can't remember where you left your car keys. For any number of reasons, the stimuli from where you actually did leave your car keys are weak or deficient. So, what do you do? A useful strategy is to try to provide stronger stimuli to reinstate prior responses. A common tactic is to remember the last time you drove the car. Where did you go? What time did you return home? Day or night? What did you do when you returned home? Where did you walk when you entered the house? What were you thinking at the time? And so on.

Consider the case in which you can't remember the name of a song you hear on the radio. In this case, the auditory stimuli of the musical notes are insufficient to occasion the verbal response of the name of the song. A common tactic is to start singing the lyrics to the song. Depending on your verbal history, just beginning to sing the lyrics may be sufficient. Alternatively, the title of the song may be embedded in the lyrics you sing.

Consider the case in which you remember an individual's face, but you can't remember the individual's name. When and where did you last see the individual? Was the individual alone or in the company of another? If with another, what was that person's name?

Can't remember the score in your tennis match? What was the last point you played? Which court was it in? Walk to that court, simulate hitting a forehand or backhand or serve, and see if the supplemental proprioceptive stimulation helps.

Consider the case in which you can't remember the year Christopher Columbus was said to have "discovered" America. Make a mnemonic: "In 1492 Columbus sailed the ocean blue." The mnemonic provides the intraverbal stimuli to occasion stating the correct year.

Want to recall a list of items for a test in a class? Make a mnemonic word based on the first letter of each item. Want to remember the seven colors of the visible spectrum? Try ROY-G-BIV, for red-orange-yellow-green-blue-indigo-violet.

Want to recall a list of items to purchase at the grocery store? Enter the items on a hand-held digital device, like your smartphone. If your smartphone is not convenient, make a mnemonic word based on the first letter of each item. Of course, if all else fails, you could always write down the items on a piece of paper.

Want to train yourself as a server in a restaurant to recall what each customer orders without having to write the order down? Look at each customer's face or clothing, and link the order to that clothing, and further to the location of each customer at the table you are serving. You can also hope they don't change their clothes or positions at the table until after you have delivered their food.

Many memory experts routinely make use of mnemonics and memory tricks, such as linking spatial locations (e.g., corners of the room) with each of a series of things they want to say. The familiar locution of "In the first place, ..." is literally an outgrowth of this tactic. With practice, many individuals can even respond on the basis of incipient or inchoate forms of the verbal stimuli they have developed, often quite rapidly.

That you can recall some features of an event but not others occurs often enough and needs to be accounted for. What if you were never in contact with the feature you can't recall? Other features present at the same time may interfere with your recall of the feature in question. What if you experienced some intervening events that are similar to the feature you can't recall? Those events may interfere with your recall of the feature in question. For instance, individuals of one generation who lived in the US may remember where they were early on the afternoon of Nov 22, 1963. Others may remember where they were on the morning of Sep 11, 2001. Probably not many will recall what clothes they were wearing on those momentous dates. The point is that such terms as memory, recall, and the like all pertain to behavioral processes. The behavior of remembering and recall is a function of prevailing stimuli and the consequences of the behavior.

Traditional Views of Thinking, Cognition, and Memory

The approach that behavior analysts take to thinking, cognition, and memory differs markedly from that of traditional psychology. In most of our Western intellectual tradition, including traditional psychology, a phenomenon must be publicly observable to count as behavior. In contrast, thinking, or perhaps *cognition* more generally, is not publicly observable. Accordingly, thinking or cognition is held to refer to the unobservable, inferred acts, states, mechanisms, processes, structures, or entities from another domain (e.g., mental, cognitive, "the mind") that accomplish the active reception, transformation, reduction, elaboration, organization, manipulation, selection, storage, and retrieval of information. These underlying, inferred states and processes then constitute the appropriate causally effective antecedents to be cited in the explanation of behavior. Thinking or cognition is presumably accomplished by elements of the CNS (central nervous system), but is not merely the operation of processes associated with perceptual input or motor output. Rather, it is the collection of processes between perceptual input and motor output. Individuals are said to be consciously aware of some, but not necessarily all of these processes. As mental or cognitive activity, as opposed to behavioral activity, thinking and cognition therefore need to be talked about in different terms and explained with different concepts than is publicly observable behavior.

In some accounts, thinking and cognition are compared to the processing routines and operating system activities in a computer. A computer has input devices, as in a keyboard, internet connection, or USB port. It has output devices, as in a video screen or printer. According to a computer metaphor, thinking and cognition involve what happens when information is moved from buffers or registers to memory locations and back again. At issue are the capacities and operating characteristics of each element in the system as well as the functional architecture of the system as a whole. In such accounts, the processing in the person's mind is held to be "innate," in the sense of being relatively fixed by the genetics of the person, and is therefore relatively independent of experience. After all, the capabilities of a computer are ordinarily determined by the innate capabilities of the operating system, rather than by what word processing documents or spreadsheets have been composed on it.

The traditional view argues that behavior is not causally related in any obvious one-to-one way to environmental stimuli in the observable domain. Therefore, behavioral output must be causally related to something other than the direct input from environmental stimuli. This other "something" to which behavioral output is causally related, and in terms of which a causal explanation of behavior is appropriately sought, is the mind and its unobservable cognitive structures that are said to underlie behavior. Thus, traditional psychology is talking about cognitive activities and the like whose origin and status are supposed to be independent of our life experiences, although the "content" may come from our experiences. Even so, the principal assumption is that specification of the cognitive structures and their operating characteristics is what is explanatory, not mental content per se. In some cases, traditional psychology assumes that the cognitive activities are genetically based faculties that have arisen through evolution to deal with specific problems of living (e.g., Pinker, 1994), rather than general purpose processes and faculties.

If one adheres to all of these hypothesized underlying structures and events, an explanation of behavior is neither complete nor satisfactory until the presumed unobservable, underlying structures and cognitive mechanisms have been identified. The study of observable behavior is just something to do until a really good theoretical, cognitive science comes along, which will ultimately supply the appropriate answers to questions about the causes of behavior. By that view, the chief value of the study of observable behavior is that it provides evidence of thinking and cognition. In other words, the study of observable behavior is useful to provide data that can be used as a basis for making inferences about unobservable, underlying processes.

The traditional view of memory is largely based on the metaphor of storage and retrieval. According to traditional accounts, incoming information is processed (or "encoded") and then retained in some location, where it is stored. The locations may have a fixed capacity for how much they can retain. There may be different time frames for the storage locations, as in short- versus long-term memory. There may be memory for experienced, nonverbal events as opposed to memory for verbal facts and figures. There may be memory for skills such as riding a bicycle that differs from memory for skills like remembering names, dates, telephone numbers, or the meaning of words. Various other complex routines may be called upon to retrieve the stored information. Like many other terms from the cognitive vocabulary, memory is presumed to refer to nonbehavioral activities or functions, but which nevertheless are causally responsible for behavior. Virtually any standard textbook can provide further details about the various models that have been proposed to account for memory. As before, what is of concern to behavior analysts is that such a view invokes mysterious mental powers and forces, beyond the behavioral domain. The implication is that little can be done about an important aspect of human behavior, which seems a troublesome implication indeed.

For behavior analysts, the trouble with traditional concepts is that they almost always conform to the categories of folk psychology or a dualistic metaphysics, rather than natural science. Descartes spoke of voluntary behavior as coming about when the Soul activated the brain and rest of the body through the pineal gland. How different is that from speaking of voluntary behavior as coming about when an Executive Function in the prefrontal cortex activates the brain and rest of the body? We can make a one-to-one correspondence between archaic dualistic concepts and modern cognitive science in many such cases.

By not treating covert activities as behavioral, traditional psychology limits the extent to which we can do things like improve our memories. To improve our memories, or improve our problem solving skills, or improve any of the other activities called cognitions, we need to understand that we are dealing with behavioral processes. The way to improve behavioral processes is to manipulate behavioral features of our lives: discriminative stimuli, responses, and reinforcers.

Summary and Conclusions

In conclusion, behavior analysts regard talk about thinking, cognition, or memory as reflecting any of three possibilities. First, the talk could be occasioned by private or covert behavioral events. Second, it could be occasioned by physiology. Third, it could simply be about explanatory fictions. We need to examine such talk to determine what occasions the talk. In the first case, verbal behavior about many phenomena traditionally assumed to be mental or cognitive could actually be occasioned by private or covert behavior taking place "inside the skin." Private or covert behavior resembles public or overt behavior except that it is reduced in magnitude and scope, perhaps to incipient or even inchoate form. In addition, private or covert behavior is functionally related to the environment, just as is public or overt behavior. Covert behavior is causal in the sense that it is an intermediate link in a chain of behavior. Its origin and subsequent influence (e.g., discriminative, eliciting, evocative) are a function of its relation to the environment. Thus, a thoroughgoing behaviorism does not ignore facts upon which a mentalistic statement is based. Rather, it seeks to formulate and study those facts in effective ways, for example, in terms of private or covert behavior.

In a second case, the talk assumed to be about cognitive phenomena could actually be occasioned by physiological factors. Physiological events that can be known about participate in every behavioral event. If they can be known about, they can be used as a source of information to predict and control behavior, if sufficient information about actually encountered features of the environment is lacking. They may also suggest additional possibilities for manipulation and intervention. Thus, they clearly have a pragmatic relevance for behavior analysts.

Finally, in a third case, some talk about phenomena traditionally assumed to be cognitive, if not most talk, is merely a function of fanciful explanatory fictions. Closer examination reveals that fictitious mental phenomena are the product of the various social-cultural contingencies of folk psychology. These phenomena are cherished for incidental and irrelevant reasons. As we have previously noted, they typically reflect cultural assumptions derived from metaphors or language use of converting adjectives or adverbs into nouns, rather than rather than any significant observational process.

In sum, behavior analysts suggest that for the traditional psychology, talk of mental phenomena as causes is one or more of these three kinds. The traditional position implicitly endows what it assumes to be mental phenomena with initiating, autonomous, or spontaneous causal properties, and ultimately interferes with the assessment of contingencies controlling the behavior in question, or in some cases with identifying the functioning of the relevant physiology. Traditional talk in folk psychology represents a surrender to mentalism, even though proponents claim it is just common sense.

Reference

Pinker, S. (1994). *The language instinct*. New York: Harper Collins.

Key Terms and Concepts

thinking
daydreaming
problem solving, making a decision
reasoning
sensory memory
iconic memory
declarative memory
semantic memory
episodic memory
procedural memory
short-term memory
working memory
remembering
recall
cognition

Study questions

1. What are two forms of behavior that occasion our saying someone is thinking?
2. Briefly describe how punishment induces the behavior of thinking to take a covert form.
3. What is the behavioral definition of memory?
4. Paraphrase the role of physiology in memory, according to behavior analysts.
5. If you can't remember where you left your keys, what do behavior analysts suggest you do to find them?
6. If you want to recall a list of items for a test in a class, what do behavior analysts suggest you do?
7. Paraphrase how the chapter suggests traditional psychology takes cognition to resemble the actions of a computer.
8. Paraphrase how the chapter suggests traditional psychology uses the metaphor of storage and retrieval to account for remembering.

Chapter 8

Knowledge and Truth

In much of our contemporary culture, knowledge is taken to provide the foundation for our behavior. For example, we often explain why an individual is able to do X by saying the individual "knows how to do X" or "has the knowledge to do X." As with other topics, behavior analysts agree that an understanding of knowledge is very important to an understanding of human behavior. We begin our review of the topic of knowledge by asking, What does knowledge mean?

Knowledge as Behavior

For behavior analysts, questions about knowledge are best viewed as questions about the behavior said to show knowledge, rather than as questions about mental states and processes. Suppose we ask what it means to say a person "knows how to use the word processing program." For behavior analysts, such a question concerns the effectiveness of the person's operant repertoire with respect to the word processing program, perhaps as compared to say, a spreadsheet program. To say a person "knows only slightly how to use the program" means that the person has a somewhat limited operant repertoire with respect to the program: The person can do some things like enter and edit text but can't take advantage of advanced formatting features or styles. To say a person "knows thoroughly how to use the program" means that the person has a comprehensive operant repertoire with respect to the program: As before, the person can enter and edit text, and in addition can take advantage of advanced formatting features and can even do desktop publishing. Again, knowledge is not understood as being a causal mental state of which behavior is a mere index. Indeed, framing the answer that way has all the deficiencies of mentalism, as we have discussed earlier. Rather, *knowledge* boils down simply to what a person can do.

The behavior said to show knowledge can be nonverbal, verbal, or even some combination of the two. In addition, the behavior can be either public or private. In some instances, verbal behavior constitutes a source of discriminative stimulation for the behavior that follows. Regardless, analyzing the behavior said to show knowledge is carried out by analyzing the contingencies responsible for the origin, nature, and limits of the behavior in question: What antecedents have occasioned the behavior, what behavior has actually taken place, and what consequences maintain the behavior?

Knowing How and Knowing That

In our everyday language, we sometimes we use the term knowledge in the sense of *knowing how*, and at other times we use it in the sense of *knowing that*. An example of *knowing how* is when we say we know how to ride a bicycle. Ordinarily, we say we know how to ride a bicycle when we are able to maintain our balance, pedal correctly, and so forth. Thus, the analysis of knowing how to ride a bicycle concerns the nonverbal contingencies responsible for bicycle riding—what kind of bicycle it is, whether we have ridden similar bicycles in the past, whether we have learned to maintain our balance and avoid skinning our knees and elbows, in addition to identifying the reinforcing benefits of moving easily from one place to another.

An example of *knowing that* is when we say we know that Washington, DC is the capital of the US. However, it is now useful to distinguish between two further senses of knowing that. The first sense of knowing that concerns a first order behavioral relation. In this sense, we say we know that Washington, DC is the capital of the US when we are asked what is the capital of the US and we then answer correctly. The analysis of this sense of knowing that concerns contingencies involving such things as a history of gold stars from teachers, approval from parents, and other recognition for correct answers to this question in the past.

A second but somewhat different sense of knowing that concerns a higher order behavioral relation. In this second sense, we say we know that we know how to ride a bicycle, or we know that we know that Washington, DC, is the capital of the US. Here, we are saying that we can engage in the behavior in question when circumstances warrant, rather than that we are currently engaging in that behavior. In this second sense, one set of contingencies has already produced a given form of behavior, such as when we ride a bicycle or answer a question about the capital of the US. A further set of contingencies produces further behavior, typically verbal, with respect to that already existing behavior. This kind of second order relation may seem superfluous until we encounter such everyday questions as, "Do you know whether you have studied enough for the exam?"

In sum, the term knowledge typically means that a person can effectively engage in one or more skilled forms of operant behavior when the occasion arises. If the question is, "What causes this knowledge?", the answer is, "The contingencies to which the individual has been exposed." If the question is, "Why is the knowledge limited?", the answer is, "Because those contingencies were limited." If the question is, "Why is the knowledge thorough?", the answer is, "Because those contingencies were thorough."

Knowledge From a Traditional Point of View

In contrast to behavior analysis, much of traditional psychology assumes that knowledge is some sort of internal possession or state that is produced by various mental processes. A common statement is that knowledge consists in *justified true belief*. The justification is the logical basis, the true is a correspondence with reality, and the belief is the content of the mental state. Knowledge is sometimes said to differ from opinion because the former is universal, necessary, and certain, whereas the latter is at best particular, contingent, and probabilistic. For example, following from its commitment to a symbolic-referential view of verbal behavior, much of traditional psychology assumes that first, individuals have the capacity to create mental symbols or entities to represent the world at large, with various meanings attached to them. Second, much of traditional psychology assumes that individuals have the capacity to manipulate these symbols internally in various ways, for example, by deductive logic. These manipulations ultimately result in one or another form of behavior, either verbal or nonverbal. The creation and manipulation take place in a mental, subjective, or cognitive domain (e.g., in the mind). Knowledge is the mental term that supposedly captures the totality of these assumed, underlying processes, as justified true belief.

Two features of a traditional position on knowledge are especially troublesome to behavior analysts. The first is that the mental states and entities are asserted to be responsible for behavior, but the processes according to which the presumed mental states are translated into overt behavior are only vaguely specified, if ever. Common statements are that the mental states and entities initiate behavior, they mediate relations between environment and behavior, or they afford *competence*, where competence means a supposed underlying mental phenomenon enables an organism to behave in a particular way. Just how a cause in a mental domain can cross a boundary and yield an effect in a behavioral domain is not clear.

The second feature is that the creation, manipulation, and subsequent causal influence of these mental states and processes are taken to reflect an independent contribution of the organism. Thus, the presumed mental states and processes by definition are not related to environmental variables or events. Indeed, the traditional position typically argues that an appeal to these mental phenomena rather than to environmental variables and events is *required* to adequately explain at least some, and perhaps all instances of behavior. The traditional position considers behavior analysis to be deficient precisely because it explains behavior by relating it to environmental variables or events and doesn't appeal to these sorts of causal, mental phenomena. Again, this view moves the traditional position beyond the sphere of scientific analysis.

As mentioned many times in this book, behavior analysts view the traditional position as seriously flawed. Much if not most of the traditional position is based on the mentalistic assumptions of folk psychology, rather than a modern, naturalistic view of the behaving individual. These assumptions (or perhaps more accurately, series of assumptions) lead us to look in the wrong places, such as a nonphysical or at least metaphorical domain, for the causes of behavior. Thus, the traditional position misrepresents the variables that are actually responsible for behavior. Further, the traditional position ultimately misrepresents the origin, nature, and maintenance of any private behavioral events that actually take place when individuals think or engage in other forms of covert behavior that are often involved in analyses of knowledge.

Truth

It is tempting to define Truth as an eternal, metaphysical reality that could not possibly be wrong. As with other matters, behavior analysts view truth in behavioral terms. To ask whether what a speaker says is true is to ask about the origin of the statement—why does the speaker make the statement in the first place? Then, we can ask what practical, effective action is occasioned by the statement. Suppose someone states that B. F. Skinner distinguished between respondent and operant behavior. In order to know the truth value of the statement, it is useful to know whether the statement is in fact a tact of the historical development of behavioral psychology (it is). We can then understand Skinner's contributions as compared with those of some other important figure, such as Ivan Pavlov's. Suppose someone states that given the lengths of two sides of a right triangle, we can find the length of the third side from the familiar Pythagorean theorem of $a^2 + b^2 = c^2$. In order to evaluate the truth value of the statement, it is useful to know how the equation was derived. We can clearly use the equation to promote effective action in Euclidean geometry, such as computing the length of the third side of any right triangle when we know the length of the other two sides. However, the equation does not hold for non-Euclidean geometry. Truth is often held to be independent of personal opinion. It has a certain generality that others can agree upon. How then do behavior analysts stand with respect to the thesis of "truth by agreement"? Consider a famous psychological arrangement known as the "Ames Room." Viewed from a particular location, the room appears to have a conventional rectangular configuration, with vertical walls and a horizontal floor and ceiling at right angles to the walls. A curious effect is found if someone is observed moving around in the room: The person appears to change drastically in size while moving. Nevertheless, the room still seems to be comprised of the same walls, floor, and ceiling. However, if viewed from any other vantage point, the rooms may be seen to be actually trapezoidal in shape, rather than rectangular. As a result of the consistent agreement among observations from a multitude of vantage points, we say the room is not truly rectangular. The room can be viewed by many observers from the multitude of vantage points, or by a single observer from the multitude of vantage points. The behavior analytic emphasis on effective action or the production of practical consequences handles this very nicely. Truth pertains to the degree that reinforcing consequences follow from the verbal behavior in question. A statement from one vantage point that the room is rectangular, whether by one observer or a multitude of observers, is not going to lead to effective action. Skinner (1957) summarized the behavior analytic position by saying "The extent to which the listener judges [a verbal response] as true, valid, or correct is governed by the extent to which comparable responses have proved useful in the past" (p. 427). In another, Skinner (1974) stated that "[A] proposition is 'true' to the extent that with its help the listener responds effectively to the situation it describes" (p. 242).

Verbal Processes, Truth, and Scientific Knowledge

Underlying traditional orientations to verbal processes, truth, and knowledge is a symbolic, referential approach to verbal behavior, as opposed to a functional approach based on the analysis of verbal contingencies. As described in Chapter 4, the traditional view suggests that words are the fundamental units of verbal behavior. They are independent, autonomous things that symbolically represent or refer to other independent, autonomous things, often in some other domain. Ascertaining what those other things are constitutes determining the meaning of the word. The meaning of a statement as a whole is a matter of its logical content. Worth noting is that the symbolic, referential approach to verbal behavior promotes a mentalistic approach to knowledge known as *epistemological dualism*. Readers may recognize that epistemology is a more formal, philosophical name for a concern with the origin, nature, and limits of knowledge. Analyses that involve epistemological dualism appeal to states and processes in the two domains of mental and physical. However, the two domains of mental and physical are limited to only the knower, rather than to both the knower and the known, as in other forms of dualism.

An important arena of debate here concerns scientific verbal behavior and knowledge claims. Scientific verbal behavior is often thought to lead to an especially valid form of knowledge because it rigorously observes the principles of logic. Traditional approaches argue that scientific knowledge comes about when scientists use observable data to test hypotheses derived from theories. An important consideration here is what experiences did scientists have that led them to formulate their theories and hypotheses in the first place? On the one hand, did they begin with careful observations, perhaps even comparing measurements across observations? Or did they simply accept popular ideas of dubious origin, and proceed to make observations or conduct experiments, believing that their ideas for their observations and experiments were the result of some special "insight" or other mental process, and their method would validate the merit of their ideas? The second possibility leads to epistemological dualism.

To illustrate what we mean, let's turn to astronomy. For the sake of argument, let's propose some things that we know are obviously questionable. Let's propose that the Earth is flat, stationary, and certainly at the center of the solar system, if not the whole universe. Let's further propose that the moon, sun, planets, and stars are arranged in a series of concentric spheres, which rotate around the flat and stationary Earth. We can predict the movements of the bodies in those spheres and test the predictions. If a given planet does not make continuous movement across the sky, for example, because it stops, reverses direction for some time, then reverses again to resume its original course, we can say that the sphere that contains the planet has stopped, reversed direction, then reversed again to resume its original direction of rotation. We can then allocate resources to conduct various other observations and measurements that would validate the theory, leading us to say we know the Earth is flat and stationary, with a collection of heavenly bodies that revolve around it.

We might further argue that the Earth couldn't possibly be rotating around a stationary Sun because if that were the case, an object dropped from the balcony of a tall building would land away from the base of the building, not next to it. In addition, there would have to be a 1,000 mph wind at the equator, because the Earth is roughly 24,000 miles in circumference and the Earth is supposed to rotate on its axis each 24 hours. We could allocate resources to conduct a variety of experiments that we might cite as further validating the theory. We could drop objects from the balconies of many tall buildings, and we could measure the velocity of wind at many points on the equator. Presumably, the results of these experiments would show that objects dropped from balconies land next the building, not away from it, and wind velocity at the equator is not 1,000 mph. The results would lead us to say we know the Earth is stationary and the moon, sun, planets, and stars revolve around it. We might then assume that the geocentric theory has been supported. Do we want to assume that the theory is true?

Now let's turn to psychology. Again, for the sake of argument, let's propose some things that we know are obviously questionable. Let's propose the theory of folk psychology that humans have little entities inside them in another domain that regulate behavior. The entities can then be investigated by making observations and conducting experiments. We can accept the theory that we have explained behavior when we have explained how these entities work. We might observe reaction times in an experiment and infer the structure, operating characteristics, and functional architecture of the entities, perhaps based on the metaphor of a computer. We might then assume that the theory about causal entities in another domain has been supported. Do we want to assume that the theory is true?

For behavior analysts, much of traditional psychology operates in just this fashion. An important question concerns the origin of the theory in the first place. In the cases reviewed previously, theories about a flat, stationary Earth or little entities inside humans are derived from social and cultural preconceptions, rather than from natural science considerations. Behavior analysts argue that the resources devoted to conducting observations and experiments based on traditional considerations could have clearly been put to better use. Regrettably, scientists often have distorted opinions of how and why they have been scientifically successful, based on appeals to their supposedly superior mental processes and insight. This is epistemological dualism.

As suggested above, then, epistemological dualism assumes that such terms as scientific insight, judgment, and ingenuity refer to actually existing mental acts, states, mechanisms, processes, or faculties that scientists have. Epistemological dualism further assumes that scientists are successful because these internal phenomena cause the scientists to do scientifically correct things, like correctly explain an event. An implication of these assumptions is that some scientists are more successful than others because they have better mental phenomena. Thus, we can see that researchers and theorists embrace epistemological dualism when they explain their own behavior of explaining in mentalistic terms, even though they may not seem to be appealing to metaphysical, transcendental properties of the object that is known, as in classical psychophysical dualism. Common examples are explanations that involve postulating constructs, testing hypotheses deduced from theories, building and testing models, and so on. These various entities and activities are viewed as mental creations in a domain beyond behavior. In short, scientific knowledge is held to come uniquely from mental or cognitive manipulations or processes involving the entities.

Behavior analysts view the process of science very differently. For behavior analysts, science consists of the operant behavior of scientists or the artifacts of such behavior—working at the bench, inventing and refining investigatory methods, writing books and articles to inform others, and so on. Scientists often begin by asking questions of nature, then trying to find answers. Some research might well consist of testing hypotheses, but not all does. Some research can be carried out just to see what happens, or to determine the conditions under which a given outcome will occur. An important feature of science is prediction and control—What can we do that will make things turn out in some reinforcing way? How can we "shape Nature as on an anvil," as Francis Bacon (1561-1626) once put it. Our laws and theories represent verbal discriminative stimuli of varying degrees of generality that guide us in our interactions with the world. Even when we cannot directly manipulate events, as in manipulating the motion of the Sun and planets, by studying them we can still create verbal discriminative stimuli that will guide us, for example, as to when to plant crops to gain a bountiful harvest or how to navigate the surface of the Earth.

Summary and Conclusions

For behavior analysts, questions about knowledge are always questions about behavior. Questions about the extent of knowledge are questions about the extent of the operant repertoire. Questions about the origin of knowledge are questions about the contingencies that have produced the operant repertoire. Knowledge does not imply mental states and processes that mediate an effective operant repertoire. Rather, the existence of an effective operant repertoire is what knowledge means.

A great deal of knowledge is verbal. Thus, a knowledge of the contingencies that generate verbal behavior is of utmost importance in understanding knowledge claims. Behavior analysts argue that the mentalistic contingencies of folk psychology do not lead to effective knowledge because they mask the influence of naturalistic contingencies that prevail in observation, description, and explanation.

The traditional view of the scientific method is that it involves postulating constructs, testing hypotheses deduced from theories, building and testing models, and so on. Unfortunately, in many cases these entities have been postulated without adequate recognition of their origin. Often theories in traditional psychology are derived from the nonbehavioral domain of folk psychology rather than observation and description of the behavioral domain. Regrettably, the result in traditional psychology has been a more or less continual lurching from one theory or model to another over the years, depending on the latest data set and the academic credentials of the psychologist offering the theory or model. Our point here is that even if cases can be identified where the testing of theories and hypotheses has been successful, this approach has been successful because at some level the verbal processes of psychologists take into account the important variables and relations in the behavioral domain. The testing of theories and hypotheses has not been successful because supposedly superior mental powers and faculties have caused the scientists who supposedly possess them to do good science. Indeed, behavior analysts argue that psychologists would be even further ahead if they directly and more explicitly analyzed how variables and relations from a behavioral domain influenced their verbal processes, instead of believing that they possessed supposedly superior mental powers and faculties, which in turn caused them to do good science.

References

Skinner, B. F. (1957). *Verbal behavior*. New York: Appleton-Century-Crofts.
Skinner, B. F. (1974). *About behaviorism*. New York: Knopf.

Key Terms and Concepts

knowledge
justified true belief
knowing how
knowing that
competence
epistemological dualism

Study Questions

1. Briefly summarize the chapter's argument that knowledge is a behavioral matter.
2. What is the origin of knowledge, according to behavior analysts?
3. Briefly describe what "knowing how" means.
4. Briefly describe what the first sense of "knowing that" means.
5. Briefly describe what the second sense of "knowing that" means.
6. According to behavior analysts, what does it mean to ask whether a statement is true?
7. Briefly describe how the traditional point of view conceives of knowledge. Be sure to include the two features of the traditional position on knowledge that the chapter says are especially troublesome to behavior analysts.
8. What does it mean to say that the aim of science is to predict and control?
9. What are some reasons for doing science, according to behavior analysts?

Chapter 9

Perceiving

In its most general sense, the process of perceiving involves a complex relation between stimulating features of the environment and our subsequent behavior. In this relation, our sensory end-organs are basically *transducers* that register input from the environment in one or another form of stimulus energy. The end organs then convert that input into a form that is involved in our body's response. The operating characteristics of our end-organs are a function of their physiology. These characteristics determine the nature of our contact with the stimulating features of the environment. Our experiences then largely determine the behavioral results of that contact.

For behavior analysts, perceiving may be understood as an important part of a behavioral event, rather than some process in a mental domain that mediates the relation between environment and behavior. Perceiving can be influenced by environmental circumstances, just as can overt, motor behavior. To be sure, sometimes individuals report stimuli that are not present. At other times, they do not or cannot report stimuli that are present. As implied above, the differences can come about as a result of either the way our sensory end-organs respond to the stimuli in question, or our experiences. In any case, what we do or do not perceive is not necessarily correlated in a one-for-one way with stimuli in the environment. Rather, when we do or do not respond to stimuli in our environment, we do well to remember we are always responding in orderly ways, on the basis of our physiology and past history.

We may now look more closely at what behavior analysts have to say about the ways we perceive our world.

Behavior Analysis and Perceiving

Ordinarily, we perceive a light as having some particular color or a tone as having some particular pitch because we are in contact with a stimulus in the environment that is the source of a particular form of energy. For example, to say we perceive a green light at a traffic intersection ordinarily means that we are in contact with electromagnetic stimulation with a wavelength of, say, 520 nm (nanometers). We step on the accelerators of our cars on this occasion because of certain consequences in the past for doing so—we proceeded safely through the intersection and to our destination then, and we can do so now. Similarly, to say we perceive a red light at a traffic intersection ordinarily means that we are in contact with electromagnetic stimulation with a wavelength of, say, 700 nm. We step on the brakes of our cars on this occasion because of certain consequences in the past for doing so—we may have avoided an accident then, and we can do so now.

To be sure, there are physically defined boundary conditions for our sensory processes. The typical range for human color vision is from around 400 nm, at the violet end of the visual spectrum, to perhaps slightly beyond 700 nm, at the red end. The typical range for human pitch perception is from around 20 Hz (Hertz), at the deep bass end of the auditory spectrum, to around 20,000 Hz, at the high frequency end. Perception of auditory intensity is measured in units of db (decibels). The typical range is from 0 db up to, say,120 dB. A quiet room with the sound of ventilation or an air conditioner is around 45 dB. We typically converse with each other around 60 dB. Loud noises such as heavy equipment, gunshots, amplified music, and the exhaust of jet engines measure from over 80 to over 100 dB. Sounds can have enough energy to be over 120 dB, but if we are near them we wouldn't hear them for very long because they would damage our ears.

However, there are exceptions to the general principle that what we see or hear corresponds in a one-to-one way with a stimulus in the environment. An exception in the area of vision is called a *Benham disk*. Suppose we are presented with a uniquely shaded disk. Half of the disk is solid black and the other half has arcs of black on a white background. When the disk is spun rapidly, many observers see a color, even though no colors (i.e., chromatic wavelengths) are actually present in the visual display to be seen.

Another exception in the area of vision is called *Mach bands*. Suppose we are presented with a visual display consisting of contiguous light and dark vertical bars. At the boundary between the bars, most observers see a contrasting narrow band where the edge of the lighter bar looks darker than the rest of the lighter bar, and a contrasting narrow band where the edge darker bar looks lighter than the rest of the darker bar, even though no contrasting lighter and darker bands are actually present.

An exception in the area of audition is called the *missing fundamental effect*. In audition, the sounds we hear often result from the blends of many frequencies. The lowest frequency of a musical tone is called its fundamental frequency, and we describe its pitch as being high or low. Typically, multiples of the fundamental frequency, called harmonics, are also present. Harmonics contribute to the pleasing qualities of tones, and our recognizing whether a flute or violin is playing the same musical note. We ordinarily identify a pitch based on its fundamental frequency. However, if the acoustic pattern is artificially altered so that the fundamental frequency and perhaps even the first one or two harmonics are removed, but other harmonics are still present, we still hear the pitch corresponding to the fundamental frequency, even though that frequency is not actually present. Clearly, then, we do sometimes see or hear things that aren't present.

In a related phenomenon, we respond only selectively to stimuli that actually are present. Suppose we are presented with two sequences of three sounds each, say a tone, a buzz, and white noise (a hiss, like static on a radio; just as white light is a mixture of many visual frequencies, so is white noise a mixture of many auditory frequencies). When the duration of each sound is very short, say around one-tenth of a second, we can report whether the order of the stimuli in the second sequence is the same as or different from the order in first sequence with a reasonably high degree of accuracy. Interestingly, however, we cannot report what the specific order of the three sounds was. That is, we cannot report whether the tone, buzz, or noise was first, second, or third. We say this phenomenon is interesting because we can understand speech signals that occur many times faster than such arbitrary sounds as tones, buzzes, or white noise (Warren & Ackroff, 1976).

There are, of course, many other such sensory phenomena. For example, an artificial sweetener like saccharin tastes sweet, even though it has no sugar or even calories. We see some colors like magenta through the combined stimulation of red and blue, rather than as a pure spectral color itself. Again, these phenomena come about because the physiological operating characteristics of the end organs and associated brain structures determine the very nature of our contact with environmental stimulation. Understanding the physiological operating characteristics of the end organs that function as transducers is clearly relevant to understanding how we perceive the world.

However, sometimes sensory phenomena come about for a different reason, related to the influence of environmental circumstances. Let us now look at two such examples. One is conditioned respondent seeing. Another is operant seeing. Here is where behavior analysis helps us to understand our perceptual processes.

Seeing as a Function of Environmental Circumstances

Conditioned respondent seeing is perceiving that comes about when we have customarily experienced two visual stimuli together. If only one of those stimuli is then present, we have a tendency to see the other. This phenomenon is modeled on standard forms of conditioned respondent behavior. For example, suppose Pavlov's dogs experienced two stimuli together, say the illumination of a light followed by food. If the light is illuminated, the dog will have a tendency to respond by salivating, the same way as it does when food is presented. Suppose we experienced two visual stimuli together. If one stimulus is presented, we will have a tendency to respond in the same way as when we see the other.

An example of conditioned respondent seeing in the life of humans outside the laboratory would be a modified deck of playing cards. During our lifetimes, we have customarily seen hearts and diamonds that are colored red, and spades and clubs that are colored black. If we see a red suit, we are disposed to see a heart or diamond. If we see a black suit, we are disposed to see a spade or club. Now suppose we show an individual a card from a modified deck, say a red spade. When the card is presented for a very brief period of time, the individual might see the card as a heart. Here the visual response comes about because two stimuli have customarily been experienced together—red and a heart. If the stimulus has one customary feature—the color red, the individual has a tendency to see the other customary feature—the heart shape, even though the heart shape is not actually present.

The *Stroop effect* is somewhat related but not identical. This effect occurs when a participant is presented with word, such as "blue," that is written in red ink. The participant is then asked to name the color of the ink. Under these conflicting circumstances, the participant takes longer to do so than when the word "blue" is written in blue ink. The Stroop effect is ordinarily understood as a conflict created by semantics (word meaning) and perception (color). The subject takes longer to resolve the conflict when the color named is incompatible with the color of the ink.

Operant seeing is based on the operant model of behavior involving consequences. We see things when the things to be seen are important to us. For example, if we are waiting for a friend to pick us up in a car, we look in the direction from which we are told the car will be coming. We may perceive cars with a color and style similar to our friend's as the car coming to pick us up.

Another important case is seeing in the absence of the thing seen. In everyday language, we are talking about images or visualization. In one standard example (Skinner, 1953), suppose we are told to imagine a cube that is 3 inches on a side. One face of the cube is painted red, and two other faces, opposite to each other but adjacent to the red face, are painted blue. Now the lager cube is sliced into smaller, 1-inch cubes. How many smaller cubes have a side that is red and a side that is blue? The answer is 6, where the 6 cubes are at the intersections of the red side with each of the two blue sides. We answer this problem by doing much the same thing as we do in the presence of the thing seen.

Some standard "optical illusions" offer additional examples. The familiar *Müller-Lyer illusion* concerns judgments of "arrows" (i.e., lines) with arrowheads at each end that point inward (>—<) or outward (<—>). The arrows are actually of equal length. Typically sighted individuals report that arrows are longer with inward rather than outward pointing arrowheads, even when they are instructed that the lines are the same length. This familiar effect is no doubt attributable to a history of judging lengths based on the overall length of the visual display, rather than just elements of the display. Pigeons show the same effect.

A more complex problem in visual imagery involves *mental rotation*. In a common form of this problem, a participant is shown a line drawing of a three dimensional object. Then the participant is shown a second line drawing of the same three dimensional object, perhaps rotated on one or more of its axes. The participant is asked whether the second object is the same as the first, and the latency to do so is recorded. On average, the results indicate that the more the second object is rotated from the first, the longer is the latency to judge it as same or different. A traditional account might state that it is as if the participant "mentally rotates" the visual image of the second line drawing, compares it with the first, and judges it as the same or different. The time that the participant takes to "mentally rotate" the image and make the comparison is reflected in the latency. Behavior analysts recognize that an important process is transpiring in this problem, and that it is important for an adequate science of behavior to account for it. Behavior analysts do so in terms of operant seeing, rather than events in a supposed mental domain.

More specifically, the analysis of so-called mental rotation is that participants are doing much the same thing as when an object is actually present and they are watching it as it is actually rotated to a given orientation. Participants have learned to do "much the same thing" at some prior point in their lives. A common example is rotating a map so that it corresponds to our surroundings. In other cases, objects are often encountered under less than perfect conditions of illumination or perspective, and participants have some experience evaluating what these objects are. Such fundamental processes such as generalization and discrimination are involved, as when a child is playing and looks at a toy building block from different angles, or hidden behind other blocks with only a small portion showing. What is involved is a behavioral process involving precurrent responses, rather than a mental process.

Some Representative Studies of Perceiving

We may now examine some representative studies of perceiving. We review them here to illustrate general principles consistent with a behavior analytic view of perceiving, even though the authors are not behavior analysts.

A classic study in the analysis of perceiving is Held and Hein (1963). In their study, pairs of new-born kittens were put in a circular experimental apparatus for three hours a day over several weeks. The apparatus had a pattern of vertical bars on the wall created by black and white strips of masking tape, separated by a strip of bare metal. Extending diametrically across the apparatus was a rotating arm, fixed at the center. One kitten, designated the active kitten, was harnessed at one end of the rotating arm. The active kitten could move the arm either clockwise or counterclockwise, up or down, or toward or away from the center of the apparatus. The other kitten, designated the passive kitten, was suspended in a small gondola at the other end. The gondola in which passive kitten was suspended was linked to the movement of the active kitten. Consequently, the passive kitten saw the same things the active kitten did, but not as a consequence of its own movement. When the passive kitten was not in the apparatus, it was housed in darkness with its mother and littermates.

Each day after the kittens had been exposed to the apparatus, the researchers tested both visually guided behavior and perceptual responsiveness of the kittens. The tests of visually guided behavior involved paw movement, avoidance of a visual cliff, and blinking at an approaching object. The tests of perceptual responsiveness involved eye tracking of a moving object, pupillary reflex to a light source, and adjustment of paw placement.

In the tests of visually guided behavior, the paw movement task involved slowly lowering the kitten toward the surface of the table. The researchers measured how many hours of exposure to the apparatus were required before a kitten would extend its paws to meet the table. The visual cliff task involved placing a kitten on a bridge with a deep side to the left and a shallow side to the right. The researchers measured how many hours of exposure to the apparatus were required before the kitten would perceive depth and avoid the deep side. The final test involved moving an experimenter's hand toward a kitten's face. The researchers measured how many hours of exposure to the apparatus were required before the kitten would blink. In all three tests, the active kittens engaged in the response of interest before the paired passive kittens did.

In the tests of perceptual responsiveness, the eye tracking task involved moving an experimenter's hand across a kitten's visual field. The researchers observed whether the kitten would move its eyes to track the hand. The test of the pupillary reflex involved shining a light in a kitten's eyes. The researchers observed whether the kitten's pupil would contract. The test examining adjustment of paw placement involved placing a kitten's paw on a vertical surface. The researchers observed whether the kitten would adjust its paw to an intersecting horizontal surface. In all three tests, the active and passive kittens performed equivalently. These results indicated that the differences between performances on the behavioral tasks were not due to simply physiological deficits between the perceptual systems of active and passive kittens.

The implication of this research is that perceptual responses are actively shaped by an organism's behavioral interaction with its environment. Both active and passive kittens saw the same things, but the perceptual responses of the active kittens, which experienced consequences of their behavior when they moved toward or away from stimulus features of their environment, developed much sooner than those of the passive kittens.

For humans, an important study of perceiving is Stratton (1897). Stratton fit himself with a set of glasses that had an inverting lens on the right eye. This lens inverted the visual image, such that up was down and vice versa. At first, Stratton was disoriented and confused. However, after eight days, he reported he was functioning normally, walking around his house and even outside. He would experience occasional discomfort when attempting some new task and his kinesthetic sense did not match his visual input, or when concentrating on some task. Overall, however, he adapted well. Subsequent research with modern technology has confirmed the adaptiveness of the visual system in such cases (Dolezal, 1982).

Another important study of perceiving in humans is Gregory and Wallace (1974). This study concerns recovery from blindness. The individual in this study was a man, designated by his initials as S. B., who had substantially lost his vision at the age of 10 months. His retina and central pathways and structures functioned satisfactorily. The cause of his vision loss was related to opacity in his corneas. His sight was restored through surgery when he was 52. Here, we are interested in what he could and could not do after his surgery.

Gregory and Wallace (1974) report that when the bandages were removed after S. B.'s surgery, he saw faces as only a blur. He understood what a face was, and that voices came from faces. He further recognized voices, so he came to recognize who the face was based on the voice, but initially he was unable to do so, nor could he recognize facial expressions. About two months later, he had learned to navigate around hallways and through doors without touching them. His locomotion and navigation were facilitated when he was familiar with the layout of a room, and had judged distance when blind by the number of steps it took him to cross a room. He could tell the time by looking at a clock on the wall. His ability to tell time was apparently related to a watch he had when he was blind, according to which he could determine the time by touching the hands. He could visually recognize upper-case but not lower-case letters of the alphabet. While blind, he had learned to identify raised upper case letters by touch when they appeared on blocks, but his training had involved only upper case letters.

His performance on a number of perceptual problems was similarly interesting. A Necker cube is a two dimensional line drawing of a three dimensional object. Typically sighted individuals recognize it readily and report that its perspective reverses. S. B. was unable to identify what it was or that it reversed. He was also tested on some optical illusions. When tested on the Müller-Lyer illusion, S. B. reported the illusion in the same direction as sighted individuals though of somewhat less magnitude. He was unable to formulate coherent responses to Rorschach inkblots, suggesting he didn't see any figures or outlines. When shown slides of common scenes like a bridge over a river, he was unable to identify the water or the bridge.

S. B. did learn to adjust in many ways. He was able to work and did rely on his restored vision to perform many tasks. However, he learned to read only a few simple words. In addition, he became afraid when crossing a street, which was something he had done readily when blind. Ultimately, he became depressed when he was unable to recover completely from the effects of his blindness, which disappointed him greatly. Tragically, he took his own life two years after recovering his sight.

Again, our point in reviewing these cases is that the process of perceiving involves the active relation between behavior and its consequences. It is not something that causes behavior. Rather, it is part of the behavior itself. If we want to understand perceiving, we have to understand who is doing the perceiving, what is being perceived, and what is the consequence of the perceiving.

Attention

Another perceptual phenomenon is *attention*. For behavior analysts, attention describes the fact of stimulus control, namely, that responding varies when properties of the discriminative stimulus vary. Put simply, we are said to be paying attention to a traffic light at an intersection if we step on the brake when the light is red and step on the accelerator when the light is green.

In contrast, a traditional position might characterize attention as some sort of unobserved but nonetheless inferred mediating process or filtering mechanism. The process might further be characterized as a mental or cognitive activity, and inferred to cause observed behavior in some way. The argument might be that there are a multitude of stimuli that are available in the environment at any given time. Consequently, it is necessary to identify which stimuli are relevant, and how they enter into causal relations with behavior, either in part or in total.

Again, behavior analysts agree that there are many stimuli in the environment, and that understanding which stimuli do come to influence behavior is an important matter. For behavior analysts, the antecedent stimuli that come to influence behavior are those that participate in the relevant contingencies. In other words, the stimuli that come to influence behavior are those correlated with a state of affairs wherein a specified response produces a specified consequence. Stimuli outside the boundaries of one's sensory processes do not influence behavior because one is not in contact with those stimuli. Some variations in stimulus control across species may be understood as genetic predispositions. For example, pigeons pay attention to, meaning they come more readily under the stimulus control of, lights rather than tones if these stimuli signal when their responses can produce food, but tones rather than lights if these stimuli signal when their responses can avoid shocks (Foree & LoLordo, 1973). Other variations within individuals may be understood as related to the history of the individual in the environment in question. One individual may pay attention to one stimulus, and another may pay attention to a different stimulus.

A more complex case may now be considered. Suppose we go to the symphony, and we are said to pay attention to the strings. What state of affairs does such a statement describe? Perhaps we are describing that we are overtly turning our heads to better focus our contact with the contribution of the string section of the orchestra. This sort of precurrent behavior is obviously consistent with one sense of paying attention. The consequence is that we can more meaningfully discuss the beauty of the music with our friends after the concert.

Another sense of paying attention is possible, however. In this sense, we covertly listen to the strings, to the exclusion of, say, brass, woodwinds, and percussion. This sense lacks overt characteristics. For behavior analysts, we are simply doing the same thing that we do when we engage in overt behavior, but at a covert level. Based on our history, we may have been presented with situations in which we learned to engage in covert action that would sharpen our contact with a given stimulus, say, by changing our orientation to it. If one or more other stimuli are present, we might maintain our orientation to the first stimulus and not orient toward the others. As a result, the first stimulus exerts control, and the others do not. According to this model, we might come to pay attention to many features of the environment and not others, and the relations might then generalize to other, novel circumstances. We might more usefully talk of attending, as an activity, rather than attention, as the existence of a controlling relation.

Isn't this analysis simply saying that attention is the same as a mediating process? Well, perhaps in some respects, but not exactly all respects. Recall that the term mediation in traditional mediational accounts means that we respond on the basis of some unobserved, underlying, and mediating process or mechanism in a mental domain, not on the basis of how the environment is influencing us. Moreover, the origin of this mediating process or mechanism is innate. In contrast, behavior analysts are talking about processes in the behavioral domain, not a mental domain. In some sense the process might not be observable to another person, but the lack of observability does not mean that the process takes place in another domain. In addition, behavior analysts argue that the effects come about because of behavioral relations we have experienced in our lifetimes, not because of an inferred mental process that is hypothesized to be innate. To be sure, the nature of our contact with environmental stimulation is determined by the operating characteristics of our sensory end organs, but this recognition differs from an inference that we must have some innate causal process or mechanism in another domain.

Dreaming

A final perceptual phenomenon that we may address is *dreaming*. Obviously, in dreaming we often do not literally come in contact with the dreamed about events. How then might dreaming be understood?

Dreaming is an extreme case of covert seeing in the absence of the thing seen, or covert hearing in the absence of the thing heard. As in other cases, we are doing what we might do in the presence of the actual objects dreamt about. Our contact with what we are doing comes about through our interoceptive and proprioceptive systems. After all, we are able to describe the positions of our hands, arms, and legs if blindfolded and deprived of visual stimulation, and dreaming is a related case. Just as a novice typist might get confused when trying to type while blindfolded, because stimulus control through interoceptive and proprioceptive stimulation has not developed to the point that accurate typing is possible, so also do we get confused when dreaming. (We should add that the actions of skilled typists are not ultimately influenced by proprioceptive stimulation arising from successively struck keys. The feedback from proprioceptive stimulation is too slow. Rather, for skilled typists the actions of striking several keys in rapid succession are integrated into a single functional unit.) The point is that in dreaming, we don't have adequate interoceptive and proprioceptive stimulation to make the production of a given sequence of events meaningful. The result is that actual events may get modified or left out, or implausible or perhaps even impossible events may get interjected. To dream is to behave. When we dream, we do not create a copy or an image that is then perceived according to a mediating process from a mental domain. Just as with other topics, we can give a thoroughgoing behavioral account.

A Traditional View of Perceiving

According to traditional positions, the study of perceiving is important because it represents a window through which we can observe how the mind works. Perceiving is assumed to involve several stages of pre- and nonbehavioral mental activity. The first is taking in a stimulus—receiving it. Further steps involve processing it, perhaps in several ways including encoding it, transforming it, reducing it, and elaborating it. Actual behavior follows in due course, after the prior steps. One never actually sees the environment, but rather only some copy or representation of it. To understand behavior a researcher or theorist must be able to specify the process or mechanism according to which the copy or representation is created. Some researchers and theorists in the area of *psychophysics*, one of the classic areas of experimental psychology, sought to mathematically describe the relation between the subjective, psychological properties of the copy or representation, as reflected during a discrimination procedure, and the actual, physical properties of the stimulus, as measured using the instruments of physics. Sensation was ordinarily said to refer to the early, peripheral stages of registering a stimulus at the end organ. Perceiving was then said to refer to the later, central stages of "making sense" of the stimulus.

The principal reason for the traditional position is that behavior typically does not correspond in a one-for-one fashion with the environment. Individuals may see things that aren't literally there, or fail to see things that are. Moreover, different individuals may see entirely different things, even when looking at the same object. Necker cubes reverse when we stare at them, and Müller-Lyer arrows appear to be of different lengths when they actually aren't. In classic research involving ambiguous figures, some see a duck, while others see a rabbit. Some see an old lady, some see a young lady. Therefore, the argument goes, there must be something else going on, beyond just responding to the external world. The "something else" was assumed to be the creation of an internal representation or copy of the external world, such that responses occur to the internal representation, rather than to the external world itself.

The traditional position is generally referred to as involving a *copy theory*. With respect to the traditional position, behavior analysts ask, "If all this is actually going on, who makes the copy, and who sees it?" Thus, behavior analysts point out that this whole story simply defers the question and begins a regress. If individuals don't see the external world but only a copy, then wouldn't another individual be needed to create and see the copy, and so on? To solve the problem of who sees the copy, many positions end up appealing to mentalism. As we have argued elsewhere in this boo, mentalism offers no real explanation. We can stay within the behavioral domain and understand perceiving as a matter of stimulus control, related to the contingencies we experience in our lives.

Summary and Conclusions

Traditional positions in psychology often assume that there is perceiving, as mental activity, and behavior, as motor activity. The mental activity of perceiving is then taken to cause the motor activity of behavior. The mental activity is correlated with the central nervous system, whereas the motor activity is correlated with the peripheral nervous system. As we have seen, behavior analysts do not grant the traditional distinction between mental and behavioral domains that is such a vital part of traditional position in psychology. Behavior analysts regard the process of perceiving as part of a behavioral event, rather than some underlying or mediating mental activity. As a result, behavior analysts question the value of much of the traditional approach to perceiving.

Studies of perceiving have shown that in many instances we respond in a one-to-one fashion with environmental stimulation. However, we do not always do so. In some instances we report stimuli that aren't present. In others we do not or cannot report stimuli that are present. To understand perceiving it is helpful to know the operating characteristics of the sensory end-organs as well as our experiences with the stimuli in question. To assume perceptual processes are mental and differ from behavioral processes, as does traditional psychology, means that the causal contributions of environmental circumstances to perceiving are not appropriately recognized.

The operating characteristics of our end organs may lead us to report a stimulus that isn't actually present, as in a color on a Benham disk or an auditory frequency in the missing fundamental effect. Our experiences can lead us to report the lengths of visual stimuli as different when they actually are the same, as in Müller-Lyer arrows. Subjects benefit from experiences during their early lifetimes in which they actively make responses and directly engage the sensory consequences of those responses, as in Held and Hein's (1963) kittens or the case of S. B.'s recovery from blindness.

According to a traditional view, attention is a mental act that filters the processing of stimuli. In contrast, for behavior analysts attention is simply the name for the effective stimulus control relation, although the stimulus that influences the response is not necessarily the one an observer thinks it is or wants it to be. In cases of conditioned or respondent seeing, we report seeing a stimulus that is not actually there to be seen. Behavior analysts explain these phenomena by suggesting that when a stimulus is actually present, we respond to it in many different ways. We then report a stimulus as present when it actually isn't because we are responding in many of the same ways as when the stimulus is actually present.

Traditional accounts of perceiving rely heavily on a copy theory, according to which our end organs contribute to the construction of a copy of a stimulus in the mind. Behavior analysts do not find this account helpful. On the one hand, the account involves dubious appeals to other domains. On the other hand, it seems to disregard the contingencies in the one, behavioral domain that do influence our perceptual processes.

References

Foree, D. D., & LoLordo, V. M. (1973). Attention in the pigeon: The differential effects of food-getting vs. shock-avoidance procedures. *Journal of Comparative and Physiological Psychology, 85*, 551-558.

Dolezal, H. (1982). *Living in a world transformed*. Chicago: Academic Press.

Gregory, R. L., & Wallace, J. G. (1974). Recovery from early blindness: a case study. In R. L. Gregory (Ed.), *Concepts and mechanisms of perception* (pp. 65-129). London: Duckworth.

Held, R., & Hein, A. (1963). Movement-produced stimulation in the development of visually guided behavior. *Journal of Comparative and Physiological Psychology, 56*, 872-876.

Skinner, B. F. (1953). *Science and human behavior*. New York: Macmillan.

Stratton, G. (1897). Upright vision and the retinal image. *Psychological Review, 4*, 182-187.

Warren, R. M., & Ackroff, J. M. (1976). Dichotic verbal transformations and evidence of separate processors for identical stimuli. *Nature, 259*, 475-477.

Key Terms and Concepts

transducers
Benham disk
Mach bands
missing fundamental effect
conditioned respondent seeing
Stroop effect
operant seeing
Müller-Lyer illusion
mental rotation
attention
dreaming
psychophysics
copy theory

Study Questions

1. Fill in the blanks: According to the traditional position, the _____ activity of perceiving causes the _____ activity of behavior.
2. What is the range in nm for human perception of color?
3. What is the range in Hz for human perception of pitch?
4. What is the range in dB for human perception of auditory intensity?
5. How does conditioned respondent seeing come about?
6. Give an example of conditioned respondent seeing from outside the laboratory.
7. How does operant seeing come about?
8. Give an example of operant seeing from outside the laboratory.
9. Explain mental rotation in behavioral terms.
10. Briefly describe the procedure, results, and implication of Held and Hein (1959).
11. Briefly describe how Gregory and Wallace (1974) studied S. B.'s recovery from blindness, and the results of their study.
12. Compare what behavior analysts mean by attention with the traditional position.
13. Briefly describe the behavior analytic account of dreaming as covert visual or auditory behavior.
14. According to traditional positions, why is the study of perception important?

Chapter 10

Purpose, Intention, and Belief

In our everyday lives, we often explain our behavior in terms of our purposes. After all, we commonly view ourselves as rational human beings who have conceptions of who we are and what our behavior will do for us. We do not think of ourselves as reacting in a blind, stereotyped, and mechanical way to physical forces in the environment.

Behavior analysts agree that it is not useful to explain our behavior as stereotyped and mechanical reactions to physical forces in the environment. However, behavior analysts are also careful not to appeal to mentalism in their explanations of behavior. In this regard, when explanations of behavior appeal to purposes, behavior analysts ask, What does it mean to say our behavior shows *purpose*? The ordinary sense of the term purpose seems to imply that future states and processes, perhaps even in a mental domain, cause present behavior. However, it doesn't appear reasonable that a cause from the future can produce an effect in the present, especially when cause and effect lie in different domains. Indeed, this sense of purpose seems to imply mentalism. As we have seen, behavior analysts reject mentalism. Let's now look at the alternative way that behavior analysts understand explanations that invoke purpose and related words from our everyday vocabulary.

Behavior Analysis and Purpose

As we have seen throughout this book, behavior analysts explain behavior by looking to past consequences of our behavior in a particular situation, and to how closely the current situation resembles the past situation in which that behavior produced the specified consequence. According to this view, our behavior is adaptive and flexible, rather than stereotyped and rigid. Even when different instances of our behavior achieve the same kind of outcome, we do not always engage in that behavior in exactly the same way, or with exactly the same topography. An old folk saying is that "You cannot step into the same river twice." In a similar way, behavior analysts say that no response is identical in all respects to a previous one—even one of closely related form—if only because the history of the current response includes one or more of the previous responses. For behavior analysts, successive responses may be understood as forming a functional group, or class, on the basis of their resulting in a common class (again a functional grouping) of environmental consequences. This co-variation imparts order to the inherent variability in behavior and enables us to describe behavior in generic terms—in terms of classes. For example, when we print a letter of the alphabet with paper and pencil, we do not always make the letter in exactly the same way. Rather, our behavior is organized into different classes, where the class boundaries are distinguished by what does and does not achieve a given outcome. As reviewed extensively in chapter 1, we say that behavior has a "generic" property, based on the contingencies that cause it. We write an "A" and not a "B" when doing so is effective in achieving a given outcome, such as being understood by a prospective reader. Although there are many different ways to write an A, ordinarily none are so different that a prospective reader can't discern that we are writing an A. The behavior of writing a B has its own class membership, as does the behavior of writing other letters. The notion of a class of behavior is partly what gives rise to our intuitive conception that behavior is "organized." More specifically, behavior is organized with respect to the contingencies that cause it.

What then about sequences of behavior that extend over time? We are talking here about engaging in sequentially organized movements, extended over time, that culminate in a single outcome. Let's consider the example of typing the word "the." When we first learned to type, we probably did so by typing one letter at a time. Perhaps if we are anything less than a professional typist, we might still type some unfamiliar words one letter at a time. However, as our experience increases, the series of responses involved in typing the word "the" becomes unified or integrated. The responses are a functional whole—something we as actors accomplish, even if our responses happen to involve what formerly were independent movements.

We can next examine a more complex case of a sequence of behavior extended over time. Suppose we want to brew a cup of coffee. We proceed through several stages:

1. We get the coffee container, then
2. grind the coffee if it is in whole bean form, then
3. put the ground coffee in the coffee maker, then
4. fill the coffee maker with water, then
5. turn on the coffee maker to heat the water, then
6. wait for the heated water to drip through the ground coffee, then
7. pour the freshly brewed coffee into a cup.

We have engaged in a *chain of responses*. Fulfilling the requirements of one portion (or "link") of the chain leads to the next link, where each link is defined by its own set of circumstances and consequences. The responses of each link are class-based, just as any response is. The behavior in each link is organized with respect to its ultimate consequence, namely, how it contributes to securing a cup of coffee. We learn to make the sequence of necessary responses, and to engage in the behavior called "making coffee" and to which we might informally apply the term "purposive," on the basis of our past experiences.

Critics often claim that according to behavior analysts, the behavior in one link causes the behavior in the next in a rigid, mechanical way. Behavior analysts argue not so. Everyone agrees, behavior analysts included, that an important issue is how to account for the sequential organization of behavior seen in a chain. For behavior analysts, the sequential organization of behavior originates in the environmental contingencies, rather than in any intrinsic connections between the responses in the links. Worth noting is that putting the whole beans in the filter before grinding them just doesn't result in the reinforcing consequence of a good cup of coffee. Having the whole beans at hand is the occasion for putting them in the grinder, leading in turn to later stages and the cup of coffee. In a like manner, attempting to walk through a doorway without first opening the door is also not likely to be reinforced.

The term purpose is meaningful because behavior is related to environmental circumstances in two important ways. First, the term purpose correctly suggests behavior is functionally related to its consequences. Second, the term purpose correctly implies that (a) a consequence can affect an extended sequence of behavior, and (b) the sequence of behavior doesn't consist of a series of independent elements linked together mechanically. If the above treatment of the term purpose sounds familiar, it is. Operant behavior as described in chapter 1 is the very field of purpose, analyzable in terms of operant contingencies. What behavior analysts reject is the notion of purpose as some future cause of behavior from a mental domain, rather than as a characteristic of contingencies in the one, behavioral domain.

Behavior Analysis and Intention

The term *intention* often arises along with purpose. Just as it was useful to clarify the meaning of purpose, so also is it useful to clarify the meaning of intention.

In a broad sense, the term intention means engaging in operant behavior. We say we have an intention when we are disposed to behave in a way that achieves some consequence we have achieved in the past. In a more precise sense, we might say we have an intention when we can state just what the consequence is and how the behavior is expected to achieve it before we engage in the behavior. Furthermore, we can state what other related forms of behavior will achieve the same consequence.

As we have seen in earlier chapters, we learn to describe our behavior and the conditions of which it is a function because the verbal community has taught us to do so, by approving our descriptions when they are accurate. Such descriptions are typically about the important features of the environment, such as the contingencies that engender some form of our own operant behavior. In more technical language, these verbalizations may be called *self-tacts*. As we saw in Chapter 6, a history is responsible for the development of descriptive verbalizations about our behavior and its causes. The verbalizations don't emerge spontaneously as the product of an autonomous, all-controlling mind. The history may not be equivalent for all individuals, with the result that the descriptions individuals generate may differ considerably. Moreover, just because we say something that appears to be about our behavior and its causes doesn't mean that the statements accurately reflect that behavior and its causes. We often say we intend to do one thing but actually end up doing something else. We may say we intend to stop at the market on the way home from work and buy just a gallon of milk—nothing more, but we end up buying much more. We may even forget to buy the milk. For behavior analysts, we say that we have intentions when we are engaging in operant behavior, and an important part of the discriminative stimuli that guide our operant behavior is self-generated verbalizations, or self-tacts. These verbalizations may well be just as influential as verbalizations arising from others. Importantly, they are features of the behavioral rather than mental domain.

Behavior Analysis and Belief

A final term that we may address is *belief*. When we speak of belief in behavior analysis, as well as purpose and intention, we are typically speaking in dispositional terms. More specifically, dispositional terms like belief describe the tendency to engage in one form of behavior or several related forms of behavior in some specified situation. To say a person believes that a given team will win an athletic contest is to say that the person has a tendency to say so, wear team colors, promote the team's good fortunes, extol the team's virtues, and so on. Importantly, such instances of behavior are not evidence of belief as a mental state. In behavior analysis appeals to mental states are mischievous. Rather, such instances of behavior are what belief means.

Many common mental terms are dispositional, and we can make two further points about them. The first is that their usage as descriptive terms does not imply that they are literally entities from a mental domain that cause behavior. Rather, dispositional terms may be understood as effects. The specific causes of the behavior in question would have to be identified in an independent analysis of the contingencies associated with the behavior. If we want to informally use such dispositional terms as beliefs in a causal explanation of behavior, then we presumably need to identify what caused the beliefs or other dispositions in the first place, and what caused them are contingencies.

As we suggest above, dispositional terms can be useful in informal settings. For example, suppose we identify a person as a liar. We can then behave cautiously with respect to what the person says, for example, when the person gives us a tip on which stock to buy. Behaving cautiously in such situations is quite an adaptive thing to do. However, it is not particularly useful to explain the behavior of such persons by saying that they told an untruth *because* they were liars. Rather, the telling of an untruth is an instance of being a liar, not a cause. Being a liar is being a person who displays an extended pattern of telling untruths. It is in this sense that recognizing the person as a liar is meaningful in a correlational rather than causal way. The causal implications of dispositional terms are further illustrated by considering what to do if a child is lying. Identifying the child as a liar does not inform us what we should do about it. Instead, we need to examine the circumstances in which the lying occurs, and teach alternative repertoires that replace lying.

The second point is that dispositional analyses do not apply to all mental terms. For example, we previously considered thinking. In its ordinary usage, thinking is an actual, ongoing activity in the behavioral domain. It is not a disposition in the same sense as intention or belief. If we take a dispositional approach to all mental terms, we risk treating a disposition as a mental cause, and doing so is problematic.

Of course, we can say we believe that something is the case, when it actually is not the case. Suppose we state we believe that we can name in correct order the first six presidents of the United States. If we think about this statement, we either can or can't name the presidents in correct order. If we can name the presidents, the statement asserting our belief correctly reflects our behavior. But suppose that when we are asked to name the presidents, we mistakenly name the seventh president as the sixth. Our belief seems to have been false. How can we believe something that is false?

It is useful to start our discussion by examining what occasions our saying we believe we can name in correct order the first six presidents of the United States. The presidents we have named are in fact six of the early presidents, although perhaps not the first six. Next we need to examine why we say we believe the six we can name are in fact the first six. One possibility is that we are *lying*. Lying is a function of its own set of environmental relations. For example, we might be seeking undeserved credit or avoiding deserved blame for some aspect of our behavior, based on our assessment of what the audience knows. Lies typically change when the audience changes. False beliefs do not. For the sake of continuing our analysis, let's assume we are not lying. Were we once told that the six we named were actually the first six? Was there a misprint in a book we once read? Were we once presented with the actual names of the first six presidents, as well as the seventh, but then in reciting the names skipped the name of the sixth and jumped to the seventh, as some sort of generalization? In point of fact, the second president was John Adams, and the sixth was his son, John Quincy Adams. Maybe we skipped the name of the son, because we had already mentioned one president whose last name was Adams, and went on to the seventh, Andrew Jackson, whose last name is very different. Any of these possibilities might be the case. A functional approach to verbal behavior allows us to untangle problems nominally associated with "false beliefs." In contrast, a traditional approach based on mental states does not.

Traditional Views of Purpose, Intention, and Belief

The preceding treatment of purpose, intention, and belief contrasts with that of traditional psychology. To understand the contrast, we may turn to a review of the historical record. During the last quarter of the 19th century, when structuralism and functionalism prevailed, psychology was assumed to be a science concerned with the structure of mental life, particularly as revealed in introspective accounts of conscious content. As we have seen, legitimate questions were then raised about this approach to psychology. In distinct contrast to this approach, early behaviorists came along in the first quarter of the 20th century and sought to make behavior, rather than mental life, the principal subject matter of psychological science. In so doing early behaviorists advocated the use of objective observational methods, rather than introspection.

Some early behaviorists talked in mechanical terms about behavior, and promoted mechanical models of behavior that, at least in principle, could do the same things that behaving organisms did. The aim was to get by without appealing to the former mental terms, which were regarded as not scientifically respectable. A common example was a thermostat. The function of a thermostat is to maintain a relatively constant minimum temperature, which can be characterized as a "purposive" mental activity. A thermostat consists of nothing but a set of mechanical elements: (a) an element that responds to ambient temperature, (b) an element that has a set point, (c) an element that compares the ambient temperature to the set point, and (d) an element that generates an output (e.g., to turn on the furnace) if the ambient temperature is below the set point. If the apparently purposive behavior of an inanimate, mechanical device like a thermostat could be explained without appealing to anything so literally mental as a purpose, then presumably so also could the behavior of an animate, sentient organism. By embracing a mechanistic orientation these early behaviorists argued they could conform to accepted principles of scientific activity and talk only about publicly observable data and relations, thereby avoiding many of the problems with earlier forms of psychology.

As a result of this general mechanistic orientation, many early behaviorists offered explanations of behavior that involved a kind of input-output framework, with some kind of stimulus energy as the input and some kind of observable behavior as the output. Causation came to be invested almost entirely in the antecedent condition, perhaps as mediated by internal structures.

Even though this whole enterprise had many adherents, all was not well. For example, one important implication of this approach is that a sequence of behavior necessarily consists of smaller independent motor units that are connected together in some sort of sequence, like beads on a chain. Many questioned this implication, and indeed, there was physiological evidence that clearly disputed it. For example, we previously considered how we type the word "the." If the early behaviorist account of typing was correct, then we would be striking the "t" in one and only one way, which in turn would generate neural signals that cause us in turn to strike the "h" in one and only one way, which in turn would generate neural signals that cause us in turn to strike the "e" in one and only one way. A similar explanation would apply in the case of skilled pianists giving a concert—they strike each piano key separately and in one and only one way based on the key just struck. The problem was that physiological investigations showed that the behavior occurs faster than the neural signals in question can even be transmitted, say, from finger up to brain and back to finger. In addition, behavior was more flexible than would ordinarily be suggested by a strict mechanical model and its commitment to antecedent causation. Clearly, then, a mechanical conception appealing to antecedent causation cannot be accurate as a general conception of behavior (Lashley, 1951).

An alternative to the mechanistic approach of early behaviorists arose during the second quarter of the 20th century. During this period, some researchers and theorists reinstated their commitment to causal mental phenomena and talked about "purposive" properties of behavior. One important researcher, Tolman (1932), even talked about a "purposive behaviorism." Although Tolman insisted he was a behaviorist, he freely used terms like "cognitive maps" as well as "purpose." Whether such terms referred to causal entities in a mental domain was hotly debated. Perhaps because of the practices of ordinary language, the general appeal to mental phenomena in the analysis of purpose, intention, and belief has survived in traditional psychology, where the terms are often cast as an underlying mental state with a content. The appeal to an underlying mental state with a content as a cause of subsequent behavior is typically reflected in such statements as "Person A took an umbrella because she believed that it was going to rain." The belief is therefore something in another domain (e.g, the mental domain) that is formed prior to behavior and is held to be necessary to explain the behavior. Further, the explanation may well incorporate other beliefs, such as the accompanying belief that deploying an umbrella will keep one dry when it rains.

As evident in this chapter, for behavior analysts an explanation of behavior involves identifying the contingencies controlling that behavior. We take an umbrella when the weather forecast indicates rain and the consequence of taking an umbrella is to stay dry. The conception of operant behavior with its attendant emphasis on the consequences of behavior allows us to take a consistent, natural science approach to the analysis of behavior, even when the analyses appeal to such seeming mental concepts as purpose, intention, and belief. If there is no such mental domain, then that is not what the terms can be appealing to. Rather, they are appealing to contingencies. At issue is whether they do so effectively enough.

Summary and Conclusions

In conclusion, an analysis of the ways in which such terms as purpose, intention, and belief are actually used reveals that at heart they reflect the manner in which a given class of behavior is functionally related to its consequences. The terms need not be taken as pertaining to events in other domains, which observable behavior is said to index. Behavior that is said to be purposive is operant behavior and may be analyzed in terms of contingencies. Behavior that is said to show intention is often operant or behavior in which our self-tacts exert some measure of discriminative control. The term belief reflects a disposition or tendency to engage in some form of behavior. Unfortunately, cultural usage prevalent in traditional psychology has mischievously elevated the terms purpose, intention, and belief to a status that induces us to see them as causes in a supposed mental domain. As a result, we may fail to recognize the variables and relations in the behavioral domain of which our behavior actually is a function.

References

Lashley, K. (1951). The problem of serial order in behavior. In L. A. Jeffress (Ed.), *Cerebral mechanisms in behavior* (pp. 112-146). New York: Wiley.

Tolman, E.C. (1932). *Purposive behavior in animals and men.* New York: Century.

Key Terms and Concepts

purpose
intention
chain of responses
self-tacts
disposition
lying
belief

Study Questions

1. What are two important ways that behavior is related to environmental circumstances, such that the term "purposive" meaningfully characterizes the behavior?
2. Why are dispositions better understood as effects, rather than causes?
3. Briefly describe the behavioral account of lying.
4. Briefly describe why behavior analysts do not embrace mechanical accounts of behavior.
5. According to the chapter, what does it mean to say that our behavior is intentional?
6. According to the chapter, how can we believe something that isn't true?
7. Why is a mechanical conception not accurate as a general conception of behavior?

Chapter 11

Personality and Individual Differences

An important part of any attempt to understand human behavior is the study of personality and individual differences. After all, each of us has had different experiences that result in our being different persons with different repertoires. Behavior analysts agree that the study of our personality is relevant to questions about who we are and why we respond in particular ways in particular situations. To be sure, the answers that behavior analysts give to such questions differ from those that traditional psychology gives, but the questions themselves are still meaningful. This chapter examines how behavior analysts approach personality and individual differences. We look first at what behavior analysts say about personality. Then, we look at what behavior analysts say about individual differences in the areas of traits, intelligence, and creativity.

Personality

Personality is traditionally defined as the study of the thoughts, feelings, and behaviors that mark us as individuals, such that we tend to behave consistently across time and place. Traditional approaches to the study of personality have often focused on some underlying component of our psychological functioning. There are literally dozens of approaches to personality. We look now at one of the best known approaches, that of Sigmund Freud (1856–1939).

Freud was trained as a medical doctor. Perhaps in today's world he would be called a neurologist. He trained with the best physicians in Europe and often synthesized their points of view into his own unique ideas. In the course of his medical practice, he saw patients whose symptoms didn't seem to have a physiological basis that he could readily identify. As a result, he developed an elaborate theory of personality structure and dynamics that involved mental or psychic phenomena. Freud's approach is often called psychodynamic because of this emphasis on experiences and development.

Freud believed that as biological creatures, we possessed certain instincts or drives. Foremost among them was the instinct or drive for sexual expression. We were typically not even aware of these drives and how they affected us. As a result, Freud termed these mental phenomena unconscious. Unconscious motivation stemming from these drives played a very important role in Freud's thinking.

Freud also believed our personality contained three components: id, super-ego, and ego. The id was present at birth, and was the site of the psychic energy that fueled our instincts. The super-ego is often thought of as the conscience, in the sense that it reflects the prevailing standards of the culture in which we lived. The super-ego is generally acquired as a child. The id and super-ego are opposites. The id wants to gratify its drives immediately, without regard to other consequences. The super-ego acts as a check against the demands of the id. In Freudian theory, problems arise if either the id or the super-ego predominates. If the id predominates, organized culture would be at risk. If the super-ego predominates, we would be shackling if not denying our heritage as biological creatures. The ego is a sort of overall referee or administrator that ideally develops during our lives to balance the demands of the id against the restraints imposed by the super-ego.

We then progress through a series of developmental stages that involve the ways we adjust to our sexual drives and instincts. If the ego has played a healthy, constructive role in our development, we will be mature individuals with legitimate interests and sexual outlets. If the ego has not played a healthy role, we may be fixated in a developmental stage and fall short of mature interests and sexual outlets. For example, our egos may rely on short-term solutions to defend against problems, instead of resolving the ongoing tension between the id and super-ego. Again, we may not even be aware of all the drama that is deep within our personality structure, as it is unconscious.

When psychological problems develop in our lives, for example, because of anxiety or depression, we may need to seek professional help from a psychotherapist. Freud's approach was called psychoanalysis, and the therapist a psychoanalyst, because a client's psychological problems had to be analyzed at the level of the functioning of the underlying personality structure. The process could take several years, and typically involved deep conversations between analyst and client. The analyst would look for hidden meanings in what the client said or had dreamed, and then try to bring up the psychological problems from the unconscious level to the conscious level so that the ego would deal with them effectively.

For Freud, to understand the human condition we needed to understand the complex interplay between our natural biological heritage, personality structure, and life experiences. Prominent among these experiences were our sexual experiences, especially as children. How do behavior analysts view Freudian theory? First, Freud was a strict determinist, in that he believed all our thoughts, feelings, and behaviors were caused. Even words or events that were appeared neutral to an observer carried hidden and significant meaning in the context of an individual's personality functioning. Behavior analysts agree with a deterministic orientation, but look to contingencies in the environment as causes of our thoughts, feelings, and behavior, rather than mental phenomena of a personality structure. Second, Freud talked a great deal in terms of drives or instincts fueled by psychic energy. Behavior analysts acknowledge that certain events, variables, and relations function as reinforcers in our lives. Patterns of behavior organized around these reinforcers are often said to reflect drives or instincts, which seems to be what Freud had identified in his approach. Again, however, behavior analysts do not subscribe to the idea that these various mental forces cause behavior. Third, Freud hypothesized a very elaborate personality structure with a very elaborate set of properties to explain behavior. Behavior analysts do not find it useful to appeal to the mental apparatus of a personality structure such as Freud hypothesized. It may well be that humans have different reinforcers at different points in their development. Similarly, it may well be that as adults, humans have different patterns of behavior, both healthy and constructive on the one hand

and unhealthy and troublesome on the other hand. However, for behavior analysts such differences reflect differences in contingencies during their lives, rather than a personality structure in a supposed mental domain.

Behavior Analysis and Traits

Often discussions of personality and individual differences focus on traits. Traits are generally held to be internal characteristics, expressed in behavior, on which people vary. A trait approach does not seek to divide individuals into types, but rather seeks to identify some number of descriptive terms that can be used to capture a person's individuality.

Much research and theorizing in traditional psychology have sought to develop a systematic approach that identifies some minimum number of traits and a means of measuring them, such as via paper and pencil test or a rating scale. Beginning in the 1930s, the personality theorist Gordon Allport (Allport & Odbert, 1936) conceived of traits at three levels. In decreasing order of importance, the levels are cardinal, central, and secondary. He believed that traits are encoded in the nervous system and give behavior a certain consistency across time and place. The personality theorist Raymond Cattell (1965) saw traits as factors, lying on a continuum. He originally thought there were 16 such factors, and his later work suggested some additional possibilities. Examples include how people ranged on the continuum from cool to warm, from concrete to abstract thinking, from affected by feelings to stable, and from submissive to dominant. The personality theorist Hans Eysenck (1992) saw traits as lying on three fundamental continua: from emotionally stable to unstable, from introverted to extroverted, and from insensitivity and uncooperativeness to interpersonal warmth and helpfulness. Recent trait approaches have focused on five traits, suggested by the acronym OCEAN (McCrae & Costa, 1997). One trait is openness, as in receptivity to feelings, ideas, and values. A second is conscientiousness, as in dependability. A third is extroversion, as in outgoing. A fourth is agreeableness, as in altruism, compliance, and tender-mindedness. A fifth and final trait is neuroticism, as in being anxious and insecure.

Behavior analysts begin their analysis of such individual differences as traits by asking what the word *trait* means, in contrast to the traditional approach. For behavior analysts, a trait may be understood as a dispositional term. That is, a trait is a descriptive term that reflects an observed tendency to interact with the world in a particular way. Behavior analysts have no problem with using trait in a descriptive sense. However, in many cases we are interested in why people behave in a particular way. When we ask about why people behave, we are asking about the causes of behavior. For behavior analysts, answers to questions about the causes of behavior are to be found in contingencies. A trait may therefore be understood an effect of the contingencies that cause behavior, rather than a cause.

Suppose we are interested in understanding why our mathematics scores on standardized tests are higher than our verbal scores. Behavior analysts argue that we may usefully begin by examining the contingencies we have experienced during our lifetime. Presumably, we have experienced more or stronger contingencies connected with mathematics than verbal activities. The experiences can come at different points in our lives, in different settings, with both nonsocial and social contingencies. Teachers, relatives, and peers interact differently with us as we mature, or even after. Behavior analysts do not find it helpful to think that we might have a mathematics trait from another domain of which our higher mathematics scores are merely an expression.

This view of traits differs markedly from the traditional position, in which traits are taken for granted to be causes. Historically, the principal concern with traits was how to measure them, so that talk of traits was scientifically legitimate, rather than their causal status. One early way was to measure the shape and contour of the skull, in a practice known as *phrenology*. The reasoning went that if there was a lump or bump at some particular locus on the skull, and if the person happened to be particularly good at some activity—say mathematics, then the trait must be located at an enlarged portion of the brain beneath the lump. Indeed, if the entire circumference of the skull was much larger than customarily found within a population, then the person must have broadly superior intellectual skills.

A more modern way to measure traits is to use paper and pencil tests. People are asked questions about their behavioral tendencies, likes, skills, and so on, and the answers are then tabulated in a way to reveal statistical consistencies among the answers. Answers that are grouped or clustered together are said to indicate some common underlying trait. For example, suppose someone is described using such traits as determined, stable, responsible, and attentive. This cluster of traits is then consolidated into a single trait, perhaps that of conscientiousness.

In contrast to this approach to understanding human behavior, behavior analysts look first to the history of interaction with the environment. To be sure, one person's body or nervous system may differ in a number of ways from another's, with the result that a given stimulus may well evoke a reaction with a different topography, intensity, or duration in one person than in another. Nevertheless, we still understand the person's behavior by understanding how the person interacts with the environment. For behavior analysts, to conceive of the behavior as being caused by some entity like a trait that is somewhere else, in some other realm of existence, doesn't contribute to an understanding of the person's behavior.

Trait approaches may well describe a person's repertoire, or even allow us to correlate one aspect of that repertoire with another. However, trait approaches leave largely unanswered such critical questions as the origin or source of traits, whether traits change over one's lifetime, and how traits relate to situational determinants of behavior. If traits arise from interactions with the environment, the environment is ultimately responsible for our behavior. If traits change over one's lifetime, then the factors that cause the change are ultimately responsible for our behavior. If situational factors determine behavior, then analyses of the situation will prove useful. To be sure, behavior can be predicted on the basis of traits, but the predictions are basically correlations and predictions are from effect-to-effect, not from cause-to-effect. As a result, traits do not promote the control of a given form of behavior, so that it occurs more or less often. For behavior analysts, always at issue are questions about the causes of behavior, to be answered by understanding contingencies.

Intelligence Testing

We now turn to the study of individual differences through *intelligence tests*. Intelligence tests grew out of several concerns that existed in Western culture during the late 1800s and early 1900s. One was the general impact of evolutionary thinking. According to a popular view, physical traits like height and weight were assumed to be distributed through a population, with a few having very little of the trait, most having an intermediate amount, and a few having a great deal. The particular shape of the distribution resembles a bell, and is often called a bell curve or normal distribution. The argument was that so-called mental characteristics like intelligence must be similarly distributed. A few people had very little intelligence and were said to be strongly challenged in the struggle for survival. Most people had an intermediate amount and got by. A few had a great deal and were said to be favored.

A second concern was the attempt in France to identify schoolchildren who were not thriving in the standard educational environment. Presumably, these children would benefit from remedial help. There were probably many reasons why they weren't thriving, but some subscribed to the thesis in the prior paragraph: They didn't have enough of the underlying trait, but perhaps with remedial instruction they could be helped. In the early 1900s, the Frenchmen Alfred Binet and Theophile Simon developed a diagnostic test for identifying children who would benefit from remedial instruction. In the second decade of the 20th century, such figures as Lewis Terman of Stanford University imported and modified the test for use in the US. The test became known as the Stanford-Binet test, and is common in much of the US educational system. Shortly after the test appeared in the US, two other uses emerged for it. One was to test the Army recruits during the mobilization brought about by WW I. The stated aim was to make the Army more efficient by assigning those recruits possessing a high amount of intelligence to technically demanding jobs, and those possessing a low amount of intelligence to menial jobs. A second use was to screen immigrants to determine whether they were "feeble minded." The stated aim was to ensure the "mental stock" of the US population was not reduced by allowing mentally defective individuals to enter the country.

Intelligence testing seemed to have both practical and theoretical implications. As we have seen, its practical implications concerned education and training. How could the results of the tests be used to enhance instruction? Its theoretical implications concerned an account of individual differences. Did the intelligence of individuals in one supposed racial group differ from that of individuals in another? Did the intelligence of males differ from that of females? Of course, these arguments are just one aspect of the larger issue, namely, the supposed genetic or biological basis of intelligence, derived from one interpretation of evolutionary thinking.

For purposes of comparison, let's consider the early approach of Hippocrates to personality theory. Hippocrates talked in terms of a balance between the 4 "humors": blood, phlegm, black bile, yellow bile. With regard to supposed gender differences relating to intelligence, one question is whether we should assume that women must be routinely out of intellectual balance because of their blood loss during their menstrual periods? Should we always assume that women must therefore be emotionally unstable and constitutionally incapable of being intellectually rigorous? Should we always distrust women to perform an intellectually demanding job? Should we always select men who are not so "disadvantaged," and pay them more? For many years, traditional psychology thought the answers to such questions were all yes. Accordingly, women were often marginalized in society. We can now see that the appeal to such inner causes constitutes mentalism. We do well to remind ourselves that to be a behavior analyst is to be opposed to mentalism, so behavior analysts argue emphatically that the answers to such questions are all no.

We have only to look at much of contemporary psychology to see these ideas persist. Consider contemporary cognitive neuroscience, which seeks to localize specific modular "cognitive abilities" in certain regions of the brain. Speech centers are postulated to be over here, in this hemisphere or lobe; face recognition centers are over there; spatial imagery centers are up here; creative thought is down there; logic and analytic ability are in between and slightly to the left; poetry is up and to the right; memories below them in the amygdala or hippocampus; executive functions are in the prefrontal cortex; and so on. Faux (2002) has whimsically described these efforts as "chasing ghosts with Geiger counters," and has argued that the factual basis for such claims is clearly suspect. Again, to be concerned with such questions is the height of mentalism, and to be a behavior analyst is to be opposed to mentalism.

To be sure, no one disputes that certain bodily activities are accomplished by some structures and not others—around 90 percent of us use our right hands rather than left to sign our names. We certainly have systems of cells in our brains and elsewhere that are active when we sign our names. People who experience strokes or other forms of brain injuries may not be able to perform certain classes of responses, such as those on intelligence tests, by virtue of the localized damage they sustain. The point is that we (our nervous systems) are changed by the contingencies we experience, and we (our nervous systems) store these changes. Well, we (our nervous systems) must store them somewhere. If these stored changes are selectively altered or otherwise disrupted, the behavior in which this underlying physiology participates may well be selectively altered or disrupted. We can "knock out" genes on lab animals and inhibit protein synthesis, so that the experiences don't actually "change" the nervous system. The result is that there is no change to be "stored." However, all of this is a long way from the mentalistic storage and retrieval metaphors and other modular assumptions taken so uncritically from folk psychology and uncritically institutionalized in contemporary traditional psychology in discussions of intelligence.

In addition, although most biological males have probably never looked at their chromosomes through a very strong microscope, a reasonable assumption is that the 23rd pair in the cells of their bodies has an XY configuration, and that this configuration differs from the XX configuration of someone who is biologically female. A further reasonable assumption is that the resulting balance of male and female sexual hormones in the bodies of biological males means their hypothalamuses and no doubt other regions of their brains differ from those of biological females. Such differences presumably mean that on average, biological males will react in different ways to some stimuli than biological females.

Again, none of this implies that there actually is an underlying "cognitive ability" that resides in one or another brain region, and that the supposed ability is genetically determined. For behavior analysts the source of talk about this supposed cognitive ability is the inherent mentalism of folk psychology, and this appeal to the causal mental concepts of folk psychology is quite unreasonable. As Skinner (1974) put it, "The behavioral account ... sets the task for the physiologist. Mentalism, on the other hand, has done a great disservice by leading physiologists on false trails in search of the neural correlates of images, memories, consciousness, and so on" (p. 217).

On the basis of the mentalism of folk psychology, intelligence is taken to be a mental power or ability. One unfortunate implication of a mentalistic view of intelligence is that it is acceptable to treat others prejudicially because they are not worthy of any other kind of treatment. If they aren't smart enough, it must be because they lack the genetic or other mental characteristics to ever be smart enough. Accordingly, why bother to invest in them by educating them, or giving them decent jobs, housing, or medical care?

For behavior analysts, intelligence so conceived is yet another fanciful explanatory fiction that is cherished for irrelevant and extraneous reasons. Our verbal practices lead us to say first that persons do things intelligently. Next we say that persons do something that shows intelligence. Finally, we say that persons have intelligence. What started as an adverb becomes a noun, and people go off looking for the thing in another domain that the noun is said to represent.

An alternative is to view questions about intelligence as questions about stimulus control and organizations of repertoires. To be sure, people do differ, just as other organisms differ. Contingencies give rise to structure within and between aspects of repertoires. However, for behavior analysts there is no justification for inferring that any resulting structure within and between repertoires is the result of an inner causal entity in another domain. Certainly some life experiences add or detract in specific or generalized ways to the development of stimulus control and the organization of repertoires, but culturally based mentalistic assumptions about the presence or absence of some causal trait only interfere with helping people. Behavior analysts do understand that repertoires obviously differ among individuals and that the repertoires of some individuals are deficient. No doubt that on average the repertoires of those in the higher socio-economic classes, or who earn higher annual incomes, are more sophisticated than those in lower classes or who earn lower incomes. Nonetheless, behavior analysts advocate socially helpful interventions to prevent deficient repertoires in the first place or rehabilitate them if they already exist. Again, it seems unlikely that these sorts of interventions will be as robust as they need to be, if we continue to appeal to traditional, mentalistic notions of intelligence.

Creativity

A further example of individual differences to which we turn is *creativity*. It may not be immediately obvious how a scientific approach to behavior can accommodate creativity. Isn't a scientific approach to behavior concerned with a deterministic system. Isn't creativity by its very nature thought to be something that is inconsistent with a deterministic system? In a deterministic system, doesn't everything occur because it has been caused by some set of antecedent conditions? Doesn't creativity mean something is independent of constraint or boundaries? How are such questions to be answered?

Behavior analysts proceed by asking, What does it mean for behavior to be creative? In an important sense, creative behavior is novel. In other words, creative behavior is behavior that hasn't occurred before. Do we mean then that any behavior that is variable when compared with prior forms of behavior should be regarded as creative? After all, if behavior is variable, one instance differs in one or more respects when compared with prior forms of the behavior.

An interesting possibility is that behavior is inherently variable, at least, within limits. At one level, such a statement must surely be true. For example, suppose we sign our names several times in rapid succession. A microscopic analysis of those signatures would presumably reveal that they all aren't exactly the same. We might have pressed harder, made certain loops and lines larger or smaller, or even made the whole signature larger or smaller one time than another. The differences might not be detectable to the naked eye, but they might be easily detectable with suitable measuring equipment. We say "within limits" to indicate that our signatures are not so variable as to prevent them from being recognized as our signatures, instead of, say, the opening words of our national anthem.

Admittedly, the example of repeatedly signing our name is rather mundane. Nevertheless, it does raise a conceptually provocative point. Given that reinforcement contingencies exist, we say they cause instances of a class of behavior to be repeated. How can we reconcile the idea about reinforcement contingencies causing the recurrence of a class of behavior with the idea that behavior is inherently variable? Suppose one property defines the class. However, responses in the class will necessarily have other properties. For example, a rat's lever press must have sufficient force to operate a lever, and this property defines the class. But the response also necessarily has a certain duration, location on the lever, and so on. A response with the one property may satisfy the contingency and produce reinforcement, but what about the other properties of the response? They may be incidental at the time the response is first reinforced, in that reinforcement does not depend on their presence. Nevertheless, they are part of the package that is selected when the response is reinforced. If the contingency of reinforcement was fixed and immutable, specifying one and only one property, the other properties would be always be irrelevant. However, the reinforcement contingency might change in some way over time. If the contingency changes over time, reinforcement might well depend on one or more of the previously incidental properties. Thus, it would be advantageous for behavior to be docile and flexible, rather than stereotyped and fixed, so that different properties of the behavior make it available for selection by changed contingencies.

Is it meaningful to say that if our signatures differ, we have engaged in creative behavior? Well, maybe yes, but also maybe no. A more reasonable position is that variability is a necessary condition for creativity, but not a sufficient condition. By this statement we mean that we would not consider behavior to be creative if it didn't differ in one or more respects from prior forms of the behavior (the necessary condition), but maybe we shouldn't automatically consider behavior creative just because it does differ from prior forms of the behavior (the sufficient condition).

It is relatively easy to think of several ways behavior we call novel or creative might develop. One way is through stimulus generalization. Suppose a rat that has been trained to press a lever when a 1000 Hz tone is present. Many studies of stimulus generalization have shown that if we then turn on a 900 Hz tone, the rat will also press the lever, although perhaps a bit more slowly than when the 1000 Hz tone was present. The lever presses in the presence of the 900 Hz tone are novel, in the sense that they have never occurred before and never been reinforced

Another way is through a principle called multiple control. That is, behavior is often subject to multiple contingencies that combine to affect the response. The result is a novel, never previously observed form of behavior, because of a novel, never previously observed combination of contingencies that have produced it. Moore (2008) mentions an example of a young child who upon seeing a fuzzy caterpillar described it as a "worm with thread." In this example, one contingency is responsible for the child's responding to the worm-like shape of the caterpillar. Another contingency is responsible for the child's responding to the hair-like bristles that project from the caterpillar's body. The verbal response is novel in the sense that it constitutes an unconventional combination of these two sources of control.

A third way is to recognize that often the behavior called novel is carried out in stages, in a sequence extended over time. There can be variations in each stage, or various stages can be reorganized, with the result that the overall form of behavior is novel. Suppose a hungry rat has been trained according to the following procedure: When a light is on, pulling a chain produces a tone, and when the tone is on, pressing a lever produces food. The rat will learn readily to conform to the prevailing procedure. Now suppose we reverse the sequence, so that when the tone is on, pressing a lever produces the light, and when the light is on, pulling the chain produces food. We would find the rat readily responds in the reversed sequence. We can call this reversed responding novel or creative, in the sense that it has never occurred in this sequence before, but the important thing is that the behavior is just a function of the contingencies.

Analyzed as above, creative behavior doesn't mean uncaused. Rather, it may only mean the set of factors that caused the behavior in question hasn't come together before. For behavior analysts, an important possibility is that one can cause creativity in an interesting sense, by bringing together a set of causal circumstances in novel ways. For example, porpoises have been trained to emit a series of jumps, flips, and turns that differed from any previously observed (Pryor, Haag, & O'Reilly, 1969). The porpoises were simply required to respond in a way that they had not responded before. The resulting behavior was quite creative. Similarly, rats and pigeons have been trained to emit a sequence of responses on two response devices that differs from some number of immediately prior sequences (Bryant & Church, 1974; Page & Neuringer, 1985). Again, the subjects were emitting creative behavior, in the form of creative sequences. In addition, humans have learned to type numbers at a computer keyboard that are as "random" as those produced by the computer's random number generator (Neuringer, 1986). A string of random numbers is also a creative response. Important to recognize is that the novel, creative behavior in each case was actually promoted by environmental contingencies.

One way to make sense out of such cases is to understand that behavior at one time becomes part of the environment that can determine behavior at some future time. For example, a subject can easily be trained to make one of two responses on one trial, and then the opposite response on the next trial. In this case, given that one response is made at time (T), that response enters into the determination of the next response, such that a different response is made at time (T + 1). Novel behavior is defined by its relation to one or more instances of prior behavior. In the case of responding in a sequence of randomly varying responses (i.e., responding on the left but not the right of two response devices) or typing a sequence of random numbers, the responses are novel in the sense that the environment requires that any given response differ in some specified way from some number of prior responses, not just one, and the number is usually fairly large.

Creative works of authors or composers often follow such strategies. They write out a series of words or musical notes, and then vary a word or note in the series, resulting in a different composition. Baroque music of Johann Sebastian Bach is said to possess a certain style, as is the writing of John Updike. Any particular composition is called creative or novel, but not so novel that it doesn't have certain identifiable similarities when compared with previous works by the same composer or author. Indeed, the similarities are what define an author's or composer's "style," or indeed a piece being of a certain genre.

Creativity is sometimes talked about using terms such as *divergent thinking*, for example, in problem solving tasks. A well-known problem solving task concerns two strings hanging from the ceiling. The strings are far enough apart that a subject can't reach one without letting go of the other. The room also contains a table, on which there are some tools. The task is for the subject to get hold of two strings simultaneously. The solution would be to use an item in an unconventional way. One of the tools could be tied to one of the strings. This string could be set swinging, like a pendulum, and the subject could hold onto the stationary string and catch the swinging string when it comes sufficiently near. Subjects who have difficulty solving the problem are said to display functional fixedness, which is defined as sticking to a particular mode of action and failing to consider alternative uses for the items. They may not see that the tool can be used as a weight to set one string in motion, thereby bringing it near enough to the stationary string to grasp.

For behavior analysts, the key to understanding all these matters is that they are matters of stimulus control. Subjects who solve such problems have had histories that involve shifting the stimulus control associated with the tools. If one of the tools is a hammer, then clearly a hammer can be used to pound nails. But a hammer also has weight, and if one has experience with weights on strings, and using items in an unconventional way, the alternative stimulus control will develop and the solution will be readily arrived at.

Summary and Conclusions

We have argued that traits may be understood as dispositional terms. Importantly, dispositional terms are descriptive, rather than causal. If we are interested in the causes of behavior, we need to understand the contingencies. Intelligence is commonly assumed to be a trait that is normally distributed in a population, but this assumption warrants reconsideration. Intelligence simply identifies the effectiveness of a repertoire as brought about by contingencies, rather than by some underlying mental ability. Other differences between individuals, such as those pertaining to personality and creativity, may also be understood as caused by differences between the contingencies in their lives.

In closing, we can note that obviously there are certain singular, unique cases of behavior. For example, there are estimates of over 30,000 tragic deaths by suicide in the US each year. In wartime, soldiers have been known to engage in heroic acts of altruism and throw themselves on grenades, to save fellow soldiers. Clearly individuals don't take their own lives or soldiers don't throw themselves on grenades because doing so in the past has been reinforced. In these cases, we can look to the various combinations of factors that combined in some unique way to produce some unique effect. Each factor was independent, but when combined, the net result was the act. For suicide, perhaps individuals have a history of escaping from troubles in certain ways, or acting out by saying "I'll show them!" or "I'll make them remember me!" In military training, individuals are rigorously trained to support their comrades in arms. The complex combination of factors then results in the singular, unique act.

A science of behavior needs to deal with the specific, individual case (sometimes called the "idiographic") as well as the general, collective case (sometimes called the "nomothetic"). Each of us has specific, individual circumstances in our lives that influence us: We have friends, work at jobs, live in particular places. In addition, each of us has general features of our lives that are the same: We eat food, drink water, breathe air, have parents, and so on. Behavior analysis offers a meaningful framework for knitting together the various factors that make humans the unique creatures we are, at all levels. The significant feature of this framework is the contingencies to which we are exposed during our lifetimes. Individual differences are an important part of that story, but the naturalistic story offered in behavior analysis is very different from the mentalistic story offered in traditional psychology.

References

Allport, G.W. & Odbert, H.S. (1936). Trait-names: A psycho-lexical study. *Psychological Monographs, 47*.
Bryant, D., & Church, R. M. (1974). The determinants of random choice. *Animal Learning & Behavior, 2*, 245-248.
Cattell, R.B. (1965). *The scientific analysis of personality*. Baltimore: Penguin Books.
Eysenck, H.J. (1992). Four ways five factors are not basic. *Personality and Individual Differences, 13*, 667-673.
Faux, S. (2002). Cognitive neuroscience from a behavioral perspective: Chasing ghosts with Geiger counters. *The Behavior Analyst, 25*, 161-173.
McCrae, R.R., & Costa, P.T. (1997). Personality trait structure as a human universal. *American Psychologist, 52*, 509-516.
Moore, J. (2008). *Conceptual foundations of radical behaviorism*. Cornwall-on-Hudson, NY: Sloan.
Neuringer, A. (1986). Can people behavior "randomly"? The role of feedback. *Journal of Experimental Psychology: General, 115*, 62-75.
Page, S., & Neuringer, A. (1985). Variability is an operant. *Journal of Experimental Psychology: Animal Behavior Processes, 11*, 429-452.
Pryor, K., Haag, R., & O'Reilly, J. (1969). The creative porpoise: Training for novel behavior. *Journal of the Experimental Analysis of Behavior, 12*, 653-661.
Skinner, B. F. (1974). *About behaviorism*. New York: Knopf.

Key Terms and Concepts

Id
super-ego
ego
trait
phrenology
intelligence tests
personality
creativity
divergent thinking

Study Questions

1. What experiences in his medical practice led Freud to propose his elaborate theory of personality structure and dynamics that involved mental or psychic phenomena?
2. What was the foremost biological drive or instinct in Freud's psychodynamic approach to personality?
3. What were the two concerns that lay behind the development of intelligence tests during the late 1800s and early 1900s?
4. What was one practical and one theoretical implication of early intelligence testing?
5. Briefly describe the traditional view of intelligence as presented in the chapter.
6. Briefly describe the behavior analytic view of intelligence as presented in the chapter.
7. What have much research and theorizing on trait approaches to personality sought to develop?
8. In one or two sentences summarize any of the traditional approaches to personality mentioned in the chapter: Allport, Cattell, Eysenck, OCEAN.
9. What questions do traits leave unanswered?
10. For behavior analysts, what does it mean for behavior to be creative?
11. What are three ways behavior we call novel or creative might develop?
12. How can researchers examine novel or creative behavior in the laboratory?
13. For behavior analysts, what is the key to understanding novel, creative behavior as divergent thinking?

Chapter 12

Attitudes, Attributions, and Situations

The study of attitudes is often thought to be an important if not indispensable part of traditional psychology, especially in the field of social psychology. In traditional psychology, an attitude is ordinarily considered to be an internalized entity in a domain that differs from the domain in which behavior actually takes place. It causes or mediates our evaluative reactions to classes of events, objects, or persons, and hence our subsequent behavior with respect to those classes. Attitudes themselves are not directly observable, but rather only inferred. The three components of attitudes are traditionally said to be feelings, beliefs, and behavior, for example, as measured by checklists on surveys or as inferred from overt behavior.

Although of longstanding interest in traditional psychology, attitudes became increasingly important during WW II, when US government officials sought to induce people to respond more favorably to the country's war effort. For example, government officials thought that if they could change people's attitudes about supporting the war effort, people would buy more War Bonds and better conserve essential resources like gasoline and rubber tires. Attitudes have remained of central importance to American psychologists ever since. In the private sector, many companies routinely employ social psychologists with training in attitude formation and persuasive attempts. These social psychologists devise marketing and advertising campaigns that seek to create positive consumer attitudes about the company's products and thereby increase sales.

The present chapter examines what behavior analysts have to say about attitudes and related topics, and then contrasts the behavior analytic view with the traditional view. According to traditional psychology, attitudes are mental phenomena. As we have seen throughout this book, behavior analysts do not subscribe to the mentalism of traditional psychology. For behavior analysts, the important question is what is at issue when we speak of attitudes. If we do not accept talk of a mental domain as useful, is there a better or more effective way to understand what talk of attitudes is actually about, such that this talk can help us better understand why we behave as we do?

Accordingly, in this chapter, we examine the relation between what we might say about our behavior and then what we actually do, particularly with regard to a topic in traditional psychology called attribution. Traditional psychologists are often concerned with how much of our behavior is caused by supposedly internalized attitudes versus situational determinants, so we examine that topic as well. We close the chapter by examining some unfortunate by-products created by an endorsement of such supposedly internalized causal factors as attitudes. We call these by-products the pernicious social -isms.

Behavior Analysis and Attitudes

As with many topics in traditional psychology, behavior analysts ask, What is meant by the term "attitude"? In what respects does a consideration of attitudes help us explain and understand a person's behavior?

For behavior analysts, an *attitude* is at heart another dispositional term. It summarizes the probability of certain kinds of actions in certain kinds of circumstances. As with other dispositional terms, it is a useful descriptive term. Thus, for behavior analysts, to say a person has an attitude is to summarize that the person is disposed to make certain kinds of evaluative statements in conversation or in writing, or to indicate agreement with certain kinds of evaluative statements on surveys. To account for why persons are disposed to make such statements or engage in such forms of behavior, behavior analysts typically appeal to the contingencies the persons have experienced. The extent to which the past experiences summarized by the term attitude actually do influence behavior is an empirical question. The past experiences might well influence current or future behavior if there are no strong determinants in the current environment to promote alternative forms of behavior. As with traits, any prediction based on an attitude is a prediction from effect to effect, rather than cause to effect.

So understood, the term attitude does not identify a cause of behavior in another domain. Thus, there is no problem with saying that a person has an attitude, provided we recognize that we are describing some aspect of the person's behavior. We are not saying the person literally has some entity that is in another domain inside the person and causes or mediates observed behavior, regardless of whether we call it an attitude or something else.

Verbal behavior is often said to reveal attitudes, and indeed, sometimes there is a high positive correlation between what we say and what we do. Our verbal community often punishes our saying one thing and then our doing something else. It follows that as a result of such contingencies we learn to answer in reasonably accurate ways when we are asked, as we often are, what we like or dislike or any number of other possibilities. Our answers are then said to reveal our attitudes. Again, for behavior analysts, our ability to respond verbally in these cases implies that both our verbal and nonverbal behavior are caused by the contingencies we experience. It does not imply that we have some internal entity called an attitude that causes both our verbal and nonverbal behavior.

To be sure, there is not always a high positive correlation between what we say and what we do, or even what we do on two separate occasions. In other words, our behavior is sometimes variable. What then can we say about the variability we might observe in our behavior? Behavior analysts suggest that we can better understand any variability in our behavior by better understanding the history of our interactions with past environments and the nature of the current environment. For example, the variability between past and current behavior may reflect some difference, however subtle, between the past and current environment. One notable possibility is that some outcome or object that we favored in the past, and about which we would say we have a positive attitude, is much delayed or even probabilistic in the current environment. As a result, the degree to which we favor this outcome or object is much reduced. We may then appear to behave in ways that differ from our attitude. As we can see, what differs is the environment. As noted earlier in this book, this approach may be contrasted with that of traditional views, which argued that the variability in behavior was an inherent property of some inner entity or process.

Implicit Attitude Measurement

An important concern in traditional psychology is how to measure an attitude. Perhaps the most common way is self-report through a questionnaire or survey. However, the results of research using questionnaires and surveys have sometimes been challenged because participants may give biased, socially desirable answers, even though participants may deny their answers are biased. A procedure designed to overcome this possible limitation involves presenting a pair of verbal stimuli to participants in a discrete trials format. Here, we call one stimulus the target, meaning the object of the attitude, and the other a descriptor or attribute, meaning the nature of the attitude. On some trials, the attribute is conventionally favorable or positive, and on other trials less favorable or perhaps even negative. The participants are then asked to indicate whether the relation between target and attribute is consistent or inconsistent, and their response latencies are measured. Independent evidence indicates that participants typically answer with short latencies in this general sort of task when the relation between stimuli is conventionally viewed as consistent, and with longer latencies when the relation is conventionally viewed as inconsistent. Of particular interest in the present procedure is the pattern of short latency responses, which is taken to indicate a consistent relation between target and attribute and, importantly, to indicate a participant's implicit attitude toward the target. That is, short latencies indicating a consistent relation between the target and a conventionally favorable attribute are taken to reveal a positive attitude toward the target. Similarly, short latencies indicating a consistent relation between target and a conventionally unfavorable attribute are taken to reveal a negative attitude toward the target. One version of this procedure is called the Implicit Association Test, or IAT (e.g., Greenwald, McGhee, & Schwartz, 1998). Another, slightly different version of this procedure is called the Implicit Relational Assessment Procedure, or IRAP (e.g., Cullen, Barnes-Holmes, D., Barnes-Holmes, Y., & Stewart, 2009).

Let us consider some specific examples of how this procedure works. Suppose participants are presented with a stimulus pair consisting of the target "young person" and the attribute "energetic." Participants are asked to make one response if they view the relation as consistent, and another if inconsistent. In light of the conventionally favorable status of the word "energetic," a short latency to indicate that the relation is consistent is taken to reveal that the participant has a favorable evaluation, and by extension a positive attitude, toward young persons. Similarly, suppose the stimulus pair consists of "old person" and "tired." As before, in light of the conventionally less favorable status of the word "tired," a short latency to indicate that the relation is consistent is taken to indicate that the participant has a less favorable evaluation, or perhaps by extension even negative attitude, toward old persons. Now suppose the stimulus pair consists of "young person" and "tired," or "old person" and "energetic." Here, longer latencies to indicate that the relation is inconsistent are taken to mean that the attributes don't particularly apply to the targets. Research using such procedures has examined attitudes toward quite a long list of targets: racial categories, sexual orientation, age, drug use, meat-eating vs vegetarian diets, to name a few.

Traditional psychologists might argue that this procedure prevents participants from manipulating their responses in socially desirable ways, and that the latencies expertly reveal an unconscious but nevertheless genuine attitude, as an unobservable mental or cognitive evaluation of the target that can be expected to mediate other behavior. In contrast, behavior analysts suggest that the procedure might well reveal an evaluative orientation toward the target that is free from the possible influence of social factors, if only those called "experimental demand." However, latencies are behavioral processes, not mental or cognitive. According to a behavior analytic interpretation, participants respond in such procedures based on the events, variables, and relations they have experienced during their lifetimes. In a sense, participants may covertly "observe" their own emotional responses to the target and attribute, and respond accordingly. It takes longer to respond when responses to the target and attribute are inconsistent than consistent simply because participants are covertly doing more. Participants have experienced contingencies in their lives when positive or negative covert emotional responses are associated with certain forms of overt behavior. Presumably, these experiences play out in the social circumstances of their lives, as when others ask them how they feel in specific situations and then how they have acted in the past, how they are currently acting, or how they expect to act in the future. The others then supply reinforcing consequences for consistent answers. The present procedure may be understood as a continuation of these same experiences, even if many of the components of the processes are covert and participants respond during the incipient or inchoate stages of the processes. Note that participants need not be able to report they are responding covertly, any more than they need to be able to report they are responding overtly. The important consideration is that the implicit measurement procedures described above measure what the subject is doing as a result of contingencies to which they have been exposed, rather than a mental or cognitive process.

Behavior Analysis and Attribution

Consider next another central topic in traditional social psychology called *attribution theory*. As rendered in traditional social psychology, attribution theory is an aspect of "person perception" and "social cognition." Attribution theory is concerned with the rules or principles people are presumed to follow when they seek to make inferences about the causes of a person's behavior. Heider (1958) proposed that people attribute observed behavior to either internal or external causes, but not both. The internal causes are such things as attitudes, intelligence, expectancies, traits, and various other sorts of personality variables. When one appeals to such causes in an explanation of behavior, one is said to make an *internal* or *dispositional attribution*. When one appeals to external causes, presumably to such environmental factors as reinforcement, one is said to make an *external* or *situational attribution*.

Attribution theory may be summarized in terms of the following implicit principles or processes according to which people are inferred to make internal or external attributions (cf. Kelley, 1967). The first is the *consistency question*: Does the person act in the same way in repeated exposures to the same situation? Here, let us stipulate that the answer is yes, there is high consistency across situations, for it would be difficult to infer anything about the causes of behavior if the behavior is so variable that we cannot make any sense of it. The second is the *distinctiveness question*: Does the person act similarly in similar situations? Here, the person either does or does not act similarly in similar situations. If the person does not act similarly, then the current observation has high distinctiveness. If the person does act similarly, then the current observation has low distinctiveness. The third is the *consensus question*: Are others in the observed situation acting the same as the observed person? Here, others either are or are not acting in the same way as the observed person. If others are acting in the same way, then the current observation has high consensus. If others are not acting in the same way, then the current observation has low consensus. Note that the adjectives high and low here with regard to distinctiveness and consensus do not indicate evaluations of good and bad. Rather, they are merely descriptive, relative terms. In any case, social psychologists argue that when there is high consistency, high distinctiveness, and high consensus, we tend to make external attributions. In contrast, when there is high consistency, low distinctiveness, and low consensus, we tend to make internal attributions. Once a person has started to make one sort of attribution, either internal or external, then one tends to discount the other possibility.

At first blush, the process may seem to start at a neutral starting point, midway between internal and external attributions. However, it turns out that people have a bias toward making certain kinds of attributions in certain cases. For example, researchers and theorists have found that people are biased toward making internal attributions about the behavior of others. This bias is called the *fundamental attribution error*. Researchers and theorists have also found that people are biased toward making external attributions about their own behavior. Taken together, these two biases are often called the *actor-observer difference*.

An important concern in traditional psychology is whether in a particular case there is adequate justification for making an internal attribution and attributing behavior to an inner cause, not whether an inner cause as implied by an internal attribution in fact exists. In this regard, Bem and Allen (1974) and Mischel (1999) among others have noted a state of affairs we can call the *consistency paradox*. The consistency paradox is that we routinely make internal attributions, say by explaining behavior in terms of an attitude, even though studies have found that behavior is not always consistent with the attitude. The problem is that if the notion of an internal attribution is to make any sense, our behavior should be consistent across time (morning, afternoon, evening, Monday or Tuesday or whenever) and place (at home, work, or school), because the internal attribution has presumably identified some causal factor that is part of our psychological make-up. As such, it should always be present to cause behavior. However, as we noted previously, observed behavior does not correlate very highly with any proposed dispositional factor. Nevertheless, we do seem to paradoxically persist in making internal attributions, despite the lack of justification for them. Why? At present, many traditional social psychologists and personality theorists have sought to explain the consistency paradox by talking in terms of an interaction between internal and external factors.

Behavior analysts approach this problem entirely differently. For behavior analysts, persons making internal attributions reflect the influence of the social reinforcement for acting in accord with mentalistic explanatory patterns of folk psychology in Western culture. Internal attributions don't identify genuine inner or mental causes of behavior. The causes of behavior are in the contingencies, rather than in supposed inner or mental entities. Repertoires may be well or poorly organized, but their organization reflects whether the contingencies are well or poorly organized. Their organization does not require an appeal to the inner causes of internal attributions. An analysis of contingencies always puts the matter in good order.

Attitudes From a Traditional Point of View

According to traditional psychology, attitudes involve three components: feelings, beliefs, and behavior. Attitudes are a canonical example of entities from the mental domain that are held to mediate the relation between stimulus and response. Because attitudes are held to mediate those relations, they are thought to be indispensable to psychological theorizing. According to traditional psychology, then, if we can change people's attitudes, for example, by changing how they feel or what they believe about something, we can change their behavior. If we know people's attitudes about something, for example, by the way they report on a paper and pencil survey how they feel or what they believe about something, then from the standpoint of traditional psychology we can better understand what causes them to behave in particular ways.

For traditional psychology, attitudes develop from the influence of the experiences we have at various points in our lives: parents, siblings, peers, media, and so on. They may be conscious or unconscious. The supposed effects of those sources of influence are studied by examining the effects of persuasive attempts. Thus, to study how attitudes develop in the first place or are changed after developing, traditional psychologists commonly examine the influence of four broad classes of factors: the source of a persuasive attempt, the nature of the message that is encountered in the persuasive attempt, the nature of the audience that is the target of the persuasive attempt, and the medium in which the persuasive attempt is transmitted.

To examine the influence of the source, traditional psychologists might examine whether a communicator with high credibility is more effective at changing attitudes than a communicator with low credibility. To examine the influence of the message, they might examine whether the message that presents only one side of an argument is more effective than a message that presents both sides. To examine the influence of the audience, they might examine whether an audience who already has an attitude about some particular topic is more susceptible to a persuasive attempt on that topic than an audience who does not have a pre-existing attitude. To examine the influence of the medium, they might examine whether a written persuasive attempt is more influential than an oral persuasive attempt.

Empirically, research suggests that like many other dispositional factors, attitudes do not correlate very highly with actual, observed behavior. In fact, traditional psychologists have spent a great deal of time and effort trying to figure out why behavior and attitudes are not more closely correlated.

For example, suppose traditional psychologists administer a paper-and-pencil survey that asks about feelings and beliefs, in an effort to measure attitudes. They then find that answers from the paper-and-pencil survey don't correlate very highly with actual, observed behavior. Traditional psychologists might then say something like the following:

1. Perhaps "real" attitudes are not expressed, or they are only selectively expressed, although traditional psychologists may not describe the reasons why they are not expressed.
2. There is less discrepancy between predictions based on attitudes and actual observed behavior if predictions are narrowly based on specific instances related to the subject of the attitude, rather than to the general class of subjects of the attitude. For example, individuals may say they don't like baseball, from which we infer they have a negative attitude toward the game in general. However, suppose we learn that these individuals have decided to attend a baseball game, an action that is discrepant in light of their expressed negative attitude. Closer examination of their actual behavior reveals that what they don't like is a specific team; they may well go to a game if another team is playing.
3. Behavior shows primacy, recency, and frequency effects. For example, an individual might express an attitude. But then the individual might encounter some new form of information. If the individual encounters that information at an early stage (*primacy effect*), the individual might behavior different than if the information is encountered at a later stage, right before the attitude is evaluated (*recency effect*). Information encountered repeatedly might be more effective than information encountered only rarely (*frequency effect*). All of this information might result in behavior at variance with an expressed attitude.

Interestingly, these various steps imply that situational variables promote a better explanation of behavior than internal entities called attitudes, even though traditional psychologists take it for granted that such internal entities are indispensable to an explanation.

In light of all these problems, why does the study of attitudes continue to play such a central role in traditional psychology? The answer seems to be because of the entrenched influence of mentalistic language in our culture. As with many topics in traditional psychology, such psychological terms as attitudes are assumed to refer to things that actually exist in a separate mental domain. Interestingly, just exactly how these things get translated into overt behavior remains unspecified. Traditional psychologists often assume that if inferences can be made about these mental things, then we can somehow better understand human behavior. If that actually were the case, of course, we would presumably see uniformly high correlations between expressed attitudes and behavior. That we don't see such high correlations suggests that whatever the value of speaking of attitudes, that value is not what traditional psychologists say it is.

Internal Attributions and the Pernicious Social -isms

We can make a further important point about internal attributions. The further point is that because internal attributions are commonly accepted to correctly map our psychological functioning, they easily become a license or justification for treating people differently based on the supposed inner entities that are taken to cause their behavior. For behavior analysts, this general orientation then becomes the basis for such pernicious social -isms as racism and sexism. Here is the relation as behavior analysts see it:

1. Members of group A socially reinforce each other's practices of regarding as normative one or more of their own characteristics, such as skin color, hair style, gender, age, place of residence, ethnic heritage, social customs/conventions, sexual orientation, facial features, language, or religion.
2. The members of group A then regard themselves to be superior to, not just different from, the members of group B, whose characteristics differ.
3. The members of group A then make disparaging internal attributions about the causes of the behavior of members of the group B.
4. The members of group A infer that the disparaging internal attributions accurately reflect an inferior underlying mental characteristics of the members of group B.
5. The members of group A assume that because these inferred and inferior underlying characteristics are mental they are immutable, such that their expression in the behavior of the disparaged group B can't be prevented or modified so why even try.
6. Finally, the members of group A invoke the disparaging internal attributions as justification for engaging in discriminatory actions with respect to members of group B, such as denying reinforcers or delivering punishing/aversive stimuli.

In reality, the discriminatory actions are based on the social reinforcement inherent in (a) the stereotyping process correlated with making the disparaging internal attributions and (b) the maintenance of power relationships pertaining to control over the delivery of consequences. All of this is a consequence of mentalism and a concern with supposed inner causes from another domain.

Further analysis suggests that disparaged group B might try to exert *countercontrol* in either of two ways. Countercontrol is group B's pushback to group A's push of discriminatory actions. One way group B might try to exert countercontrol is to argue that the mental causes of their behavior, although perhaps different from those of group A, really are good enough; therefore, group B shouldn't be disparaged. The argument is beside the point, and it is discouraging to see group B resort to it because it concedes the premise of mental causes. Question is never raised as to why make the internal attributions about mental causes of anyone's behavior in the first place, disparaging or not.

A second way disparaged group B might try to exert countercontrol is by making equally uncomplimentary internal attributions about the disparagers in group A. Of course, this kind of tit-for-tat retaliation does not solve the problem. Indeed, it may even perpetuate the problem by again conceding the premise. As before, question is never raised as to why group A should make the internal attributions about mental causes of the behavior of group B in the first place, disparaging or not. Behavior analysts argue that all this is just another indication of the mentalism of folk psychology. Indeed, consider the finding in our culture that there exists a bias toward making external attributions about oneself and internal attributions about others. To accept this bias without trying to understand what causes it is ironically an example of the mentalism of internal attributions: The bias toward the behavior of making internal attributions is itself attributed to some biasing causal entity or process inside the individual. In other words, the fundamental attribution error is itself an example of the mentalistic bias of folk psychology in our culture.

Summary and Conclusions

From a behavioral point of view, attitudes can be legitimate descriptive terms for an understanding of behavior, or for understanding the relation between one form of behavior (e.g., verbal) and another (e.g., motor). However, they are another form of disposition, rather than an entity that exists in some mental domain that causes or mediates observable behavior. The cause of the behavior under consideration lies in the contingencies. Traditional psychology is often interested in determining whether behavior is a function of internal attitudes or the situation, in a process called attribution theory, but this interest is simply further evidence of mentalism. The supposedly internalized attitudes are mentalistic causal entities. We always need to look to the contingencies that prevail in the situation to understand behavior.

In any case, it seems society will continue to have trouble if it follows the practices of traditional psychology and legitimizes attributions that internal factors like attitudes cause behavior. The whole history of social oppression follows making attributions about the supposed internal characteristics of other groups. Hitler's murder of Jews, Gypsies, and Slavic peoples in Europe during the 1930s and 1940s is surely sufficient historical illustration. Events in such well known global flashpoints as Southwest Asia, the Balkans, Central Africa, and the broader Middle East region are surely more recent examples. The principal problem is the institutionalized mentalism of inner causes. Behavior analysts do not adopt this traditional framework, and offer an approach for alleviating the problem.

References

Bem, D., & Allen, A. (1974). On predicting some of the people some of the time: The search for cross-situational consistencies. *Psychological Review, 81*, 506-520.

Cullen, C., Barnes-Holmes, D., Barnes-Holmes, Y., & Stewart, I. (2009). The Implicit Relational Assessment Procedure (IRAP) and the malleability of ageist attitudes. *The Psychological Record, 59*, 591-620.

Greenwald, A. G., McGhee, D. E., & Schwartz, J. L. K. (1998). Measuring individual differences in implicit cognition: The Implicit Association Test. *Journal of Personality and Social Psychology, 74*, 1464–1480.
Heider, F. (1958). *The psychology of interpersonal relations*. New York: Wiley.
Kelley, H. H. (1967). Attribution theory in social psychology. In D. Levine (Ed.), *Nebraska symposium on motivation: Vol. 15* (pp. 192-238). Lincoln, NE: University of Nebraska Press.
Mischel. W. (1999). *Introduction to personality (6th ed.)*. Fort Worth, TX: Harcourt Brace.

Key Terms and Concepts

attitude
primacy effects
recency effects
frequency effects
attribution theory
internal attribution
external attribution
Kelley's consistency question
Kelley's distinctiveness question
Kelley's consensus question
consistency paradox
fundamental attribution error
actor-observer difference
countercontrol

Study Questions

1. For behavior analysts, what does it mean to say a person has an attitude?
2. Are predictions based on attitudes made from cause-to-effect or effect-to-effect?
3. Why might there be a high positive correlation between verbal behavior said to reveal an attitude and nonverbal behavior?
4. How do behavior analysts explain the apparent variability of our behavior, when there isn't a high positive correlation between what we say and what we do, or even what we do on two separate occasions?
5. According to traditional psychology, what three components are involved in attitudes?
6. What four broad classes of factors do traditional psychologists commonly examine in order to study how attitudes develop in the first place or are changed after developing?
7. What are three things traditional psychologists might say when they find that answers from the paper-and-pencil survey said to measure attitudes don't correlate very highly with actual, observed behavior?
8. Briefly describe what Heider (1958) said about how people make attributions.
9. Briefly describe what Kelley (1967) said about how people make attributions.
10. Briefly describe what is mean by the actor-observer difference.
11. What is the consistency paradox, and how do traditional social psychologists and personality theorists explain it? How do behavior analysts explain it?

12. How might internal attributions be responsible for discriminatory behavior?
13. Briefly describe two ways one group might try to exert countercontrol against the discriminatory behavior of another group.

Chapter 13

Feelings, Emotions, Moods, and Motives

A moment's reflection will readily illustrate that our feelings and emotions are uniquely our own experiences. Clearly, other persons can readily observe that we are smiling and laughing. However, they are not in contact with the conditions inside our skin that we call feeling happy. Other persons can readily observe that our skin is flushed. However, they are not in contact with the conditions inside our skin that we call feeling excited. Other persons can observe that our eyelids are drooping. However, they are not in contact with the conditions inside our skin that we call feeling tired.

At the same time, feelings and emotions provide special challenges when we seek to include them in a scientific account of behavior. One of the most important of these challenges concerns their causal status. For instance, we ordinarily talk of causes as preceding effects. Feelings and emotions typically precede publicly observable behavior. If we want to understand who we are and what we do, exactly how is it useful to take these unique and personal phenomena we call our feelings and emotions into account? To continue with our examples above, does our feeling of happiness cause us to smile and laugh? Does our feeling of excitement cause our skin to be flushed? Does our feeling of tiredness cause our eyelids to droop? Our everyday language often conceives of our feelings and emotions as causes of our behavior in a relatively straightforward and uncontroversial way. For example, most people agree that it is meaningful and appropriate to say we eat because we feel hungry. However, as we have seen in prior chapters, behavior analysts are often cautious about assuming our everyday language usefully contributes to a scientific explanation of behavior. This chapter examines how behavior analysts approach questions about the relation between our behavior, on the one hand, and our feelings and emotions, on the other.

Feelings From a Behavioral Point of View

For behavior analysts, what we feel are conditions of our bodies. These conditions come about when we gain or lose contact with significant environmental events, variables, and relations during our lives. We sense these conditions with our interoceptive nervous system.

We earlier asked whether our feeling of happiness causes us to smile and laugh. Behavior analysts find it more useful to say that both our feeling of happiness and our behavior of smiling and laughing are caused by the same thing, namely, some environmental event, variable, or relation linked to the onset of a positive reinforcer or the avoidance or termination of a negative reinforcer. For example, in regard to positive reinforcement, maybe we just found out our favorite sports team won an important game. Maybe we were just reunited with a loved one from whom we had been separated. In regard to negative reinforcement, maybe we just found out that we had avoided a loss in an investment by selling stock before it decreased in value. Maybe we had remembered to check the weather report for rain, and brought an umbrella to keep us dry when it did rain. In such cases, behavior analysts argue that our smiles, our laughter, and the feelings we call happiness are all a function of environmental events, variables, and relations with which we are in contact.

Does our feeling of hunger cause us to eat? As before, behavior analysts find it more useful to say both our feeling of hunger and our behavior of eating are caused by the same thing, namely, not having eaten for an extended period of time.

For behavior analysts, then, a causal analysis of behavior necessarily addresses the full range of the environmental circumstances and events associated with the behavior, rather than simply the feelings and emotions that may have preceded the behavior. Behavior analysts regard accounts that cite feelings and emotions as causes are actually incomplete because the accounts haven't gone back far enough to identify the environmental circumstances and events that caused the feelings and emotions in the first place. In short, to understand the relation between our behavior, on the one hand, and our feelings and emotions, on the other hand, it is useful to understand that environmental events, variables, and relations cause our behavior as well as our feelings and emotions.

Traditional Accounts of Feelings

The approach that behavior analysts take to feelings and emotions differs significantly from traditional psychology. Traditional psychology often stops at the level of the internal feelings. It assigns some causal power to them, and does not go back far enough to identify the circumstances and events in the environment caused the feeling in the first place. The result is that feelings and other internal phenomena such as emotions are held to be independent entities that cause behavior. Much attention is devoted to them, instead of to the circumstances that cause both the feeling and the behavior.

For example, a century ago, a popular idea was that the feeling caused behavior. If we saw a bear, we would become afraid, and the fear would in turn cause us to run. An early American psychologist, William James (1890), proposed an alternative that reversed the sequence: We see the bear, run, and then are afraid, where our behavior of running causes us to become fearful. For behavior analysts, neither of these accounts is satisfactory. It is more appropriate to say that the bear causes *both* our fear and our running.

Traditional approaches compound the problem of how to understand the relation between behavior and our internal phenomena when a great many of the supposed internal phenomena that are taken to cause behavior are simply conceptual entities. We often take for granted that the internal phenomena are "things" that are unobservable but can nonetheless be inferred to have some independent causal existence because we have names for them. For example, we might say we are anxious about an upcoming test in a class. We might then say we have "anxiety" about the test. We then infer that anxiety is some internal conceptual entity we possess that causes the internal respondents we experience, such as elevated heart rate and sweating.

Similarly, we might say we should "use caution" when crossing the street. Using caution presumably means we should look both ways before crossing the street. We then infer that caution is some internal conceptual entity we possess that causes our looking both ways.

In each case above, we have generalized and attributed "thingness" to some named internal condition—anxiety or caution—and then designated it as an unobserved but nonetheless causal entity. The generalization is based on our common linguistic practices of converting (a) adjectives or adverbs that describe into (b) nouns that are causes. For behavior analysts, it is more useful to recognize that we clearly do have feelings, and that both the feelings and any behavior with which they are correlated are caused by circumstances and events in our lives. The feelings are not independent phenomena that cause behavior. To regard feelings and other entities supposedly inside us as phenomena that cause behavior is mentalism, and behavior analysts offer an alternative to mentalism.

Feelings and the Mind-Body Problem

Many discussions of the causal role of feelings and emotions occur in the context of the longstanding philosophical problem called the *mind-body problem*. As the name suggests, this question concerns the relation between the mind, viewed as a distinct entity in a mental domain, and the body, viewed as a distinct entity in a physical domain. In traditional accounts, the two domains differ qualitatively, although some accounts have proposed an interaction between the two. For instance, in Chapter 2 we examined how the famous French philosopher René Descartes conceived of the interaction.

Suppose we accept the premise that the two domains of mind and body really do differ qualitatively. Two important questions about the relation between mind and body would then follow. The first question is, How can something physical, like touching a hot stove, even cause something held to be mental, like the pain of a burn? In turn, the second question is, How can something held to be mental, like the pain of a burn, cause something physical, like moving our hand away? Despite such accounts as Descartes', many have wondered over the years how the two domains can be regarded as qualitatively different if events in one domain can cause events in the other. Indeed, if events in one domain do cause events in the other, the existence of this causal relation would seem to suggest that the events are in fact in the same domain, not different domains.

Our point here is that for behavior analysts, the major concern with supposed answers to the mind-body problem is an assumption of dualism or at least the mentalism of two domains. In the alternative view of behavior analysts, the relation is straightforward: The hot stove causes both the conditioned in our burned finger sensed as pain and the withdrawal. Further, the sensation is not something that happens in a mental domain as opposed to physical domain. It is simply part of the one world in which we live and behave. We can now continue our discussion by further examining the causal status of feelings and emotions.

The Causal Status of Feelings and Emotions

As we have seen, for behavior analysts, when we have a feeling or emotion, what we feel is an internal condition of our bodies. That condition is in turn caused by circumstances and events in the environment. All of this takes place in the same domain as observable behavior. Nothing from another domain, such as a mental, non-physical, or "psychological" domain, is involved.

But can the internal condition itself be considered causal, apart from the circumstances and events in the environment that caused the condition? To answer this question meaningfully, it is useful to elaborate. Let's consider three examples. First, suppose we have a toothache, and we take a pain reliever. The pain was caused by something, say the toxic by-products of bacteria in the tissue surrounding the tooth or in the tooth itself. This state of affairs is commonly called an infection. The toxic by-products stimulated nerve and other cells, resulting in a condition commonly called inflammation. The pain reliever may have blocked our contact with the inflamed tissue. Now suppose the pain reliever wears off. Presumably, contact with the inflamed tissue will resume, and the pain will resume. Initially, the pain reliever blocked contact with the inflamed tissue and resulted in the elimination of the pain. In the vocabulary of behavior analysis we call this negative reinforcement. However, for the pain to be eliminated in a meaningful way, we need to eliminate the source of the pain—the infection or inflammation that caused the pain in the first place. For example, we might take an antibiotic to kill the bacteria, whose toxic by-products have caused the inflammation. In any case, something needs to change the original condition, not just block contact with it. A pain reliever is surely valuable in the sense that it makes us more comfortable during a therapeutic process associated with an antibiotic, but it doesn't eliminate the source of the pain. Although the pain appears to be causal, we can see that we need to go back far enough in the chain of events to meaningfully affect the source of the pain.

Second, suppose we have a pain caused by a cramp in a leg muscle. We might stretch our leg to relieve the pain. The cramp is a sudden contraction that might be caused by overuse, dehydration, or more complex problems like potassium depletion, compression of blood vessels, or irregular nerve conduction. Let's further suppose that stretching the muscle does relieve the pain. What we have done is change the physiological conditions that have caused the cramp. For instance, we may have altered the physiological environment of the muscle, or eliminated the compression. The contraction is surely inside the skin, and the remedy is brought about by taking steps that affect conditions inside the skin. We may not be able to immediately correct the overuse, but what we can do is take steps that ultimately change the firing of the neurons in the muscle. Importantly, the necessary changes take place in the one domain in which behavior takes place, not somewhere separate from the physical world. In any case, we can again see that we need to take some action that affects the source of the pain.

Third, suppose someone is feeling anxious or depressed. The person might then take some anti-anxiety or anti-depressive medication. From the standpoint of behavior analysis, the medication may block contact with the physiological conditions felt as anxiety or depression. However, it is useful to look at what caused the physiological conditions in the first place. Anti-anxiety or anti-depressive medications don't cure the physiological condition. Rather, the medications just affect the way we make contact with the physiological condition. After we take medications, our feelings may appear to have gone away, and maybe in a sense they have gone away for several hours—we are no longer in contact with the internal condition that gave rise to the feelings. As before, however, the medications haven't cured the problem. They have only blocked contact with the internal condition that is felt. Of course, over time maybe the problem that caused us to feel anxious or depressed has been resolved. If we were anxious or depressed about troublesome interpersonal relations, maybe those relations have been repaired. The medications have made us more comfortable in the process. As before, it is most useful for us to take action that affects the source of the feeling.

Sometimes behavior analysts are said to view feelings and emotions as unimportant side-effects that can be ignored because they aren't publicly observable. On the basis of the review here, we can say that feelings and emotions are clearly important in behavior analysis. Anyone who has experienced the pain of a toothache would not regard it as unimportant. Nevertheless, we need to understand that feelings and emotions are not independent entities that exist in another domain and that initiate our behavior. Rather, they are physical conditions caused by events, variables, and relations in our lives. Moreover, if we want to resolve problems caused by feelings and emotions, we do well to address these events, variables, and relations. Treating feelings and emotions as independent entities from another domain is not likely to allow us to address them effectively.

Other Minds

How is it then that we judge others are in pain, if we are not in contact with their internal condition? This question raises another long-standing philosophical puzzle, referred to as the puzzle of *other minds*. Suppose we observe others moaning and groaning, or holding some area of their body that is inflamed. We feel sympathy for them. Why are we sympathetic? Presumably, we do not sympathize with other persons just because they are moaning and groaning. Similarly, we do not sympathize with those who have a toothache just because they are holding their jaws. Most would answer we sympathize with them because they are in pain. Why then do we do so, when we can't literally feel what they are feeling?

As with other philosophical puzzles, there are several ways of answering such questions. One of the most reasonable is based on the process of generalization. We note that we are humans with a body and various sensory systems. We know that when we have been struck in some area, or we have inflamed tissue, or we have a core body temperature of 104 degrees Fahrenheit, we feel pretty bad. We look at others, who also have a body and various sensory systems. There is no reason to suppose they differ from us. If we would be in pain after having been similarly struck, or with similarly inflamed tissue, or with a similar fever, we conclude that they are in pain as well. Through the process of generalization from us to them we sympathize with them.

Persons commonly called malingerers or hypochondriacs exploit these possibilities by evoking sympathy for themselves. In the past, such individuals have found that others will pay attention to them, or that they will be excused from difficult tasks, if they engage in conventionally accepted overt pain behavior, often in exaggerated form to be sure it is noticed. They may whine, limp, or act in ways consistent with being sick or injured. However, their behavior is caused by social circumstances in their lives, rather than by some internal pathological condition. Thus, engaging in overt pain behavior does not mean someone is actually in pain.

Moods, Emotions, and Motives

We noted earlier in this book that traditional psychology views many psychological terms from the standpoint of the S – O – R formulation of mediational neobehaviorism. In this formulation, psychological terms represent mental entities that mediate the relation between S and R, as the O in the S – O – R sequence. Traditional psychology suggests we possess these internal mediating entities as part of our intrinsic psychological make-up. Different stimulus events in the environment will produce different responses, depending on the state of our internal, mediating entities. *Moods*, *emotions*, and *motives* are common examples of such mental entities. As before, behavior analysts question why traditional psychologists pay such little attention to the circumstances and events in the environment that caused the moods, emotions, and motives in the first place.

For behavior analysts, the terms mood and emotion are typically concerned with either or both of two things. First, they are concerned with the changes in the probability that certain classes of responses will be evoked when individuals experience certain classes of environmental events, variables, and relations. Second, the terms are concerned with the internal conditions brought about by those environmental events, variables, and relations. The classes of events, variables, and relations involve elicitation, reinforcement, punishment, or extinction. Some of our responses to these events, variables, and relations are respondents, whereas others are operants. Appeals to internal entities from another domain that mediate the relation between environment and behavior, so prevalent in traditional psychology, are misleading.

The literature of traditional social psychology contains many experiments reporting how behavior varies with respect to what is called mood or emotion, at least in the culture in which the experiments are carried out. As one example, social psychologists have argued that the happier or more guilty an individual feels, the more likely is the individual to engage in altruistic behavior.

Behavior analysts certainly don't disagree with the empirical findings, at least in terms of the percentage of individuals in a population who might be expected to behave in particular ways after they have experienced particular events, variables, or relations. Nevertheless, behavior analysts point out two things with respect to the traditional perspective. First, it is important to go back far enough in the causal chain of events to identify what caused someone to feel happy or guilty in the first place. Otherwise, we are simply trying to make a psychology out of intermediate stages in a causal chain. Consider some research by the social psychologists Isen and Levin (1972). In this research, the experimenters made their participants feel happy in two ways: (a) giving them cookies unexpectedly and (b) allowing them to unexpectedly find some money. The experimenters then found that the participants were more likely to engage in altruistic behavior. For example, the experimenters found that participants who had been given cookies unexpectedly were more likely than others not given cookies to agree with a request to help out in the experiment. Similarly, the experimenters found that participants who had found money were more likely than others who had not found money to help pick up a folder of papers that appeared to have been dropped accidentally. In such cases, we would not want to say that the mood or emotion is the cause of the altruistic behavior because the mood or emotion had been caused by the cookies or the found money. Thus, we can more appropriately say that the circumstances and events in the environment—the cookies and the found money—caused *both* the mood or emotion and the altruistic behavior.

Second, we haven't examined how previous events in the lifetime of the participants in such experiments may have contributed to the results, and how the participants may have come into contact with various culturally expected patterns of behavior in light of those events. For example, if we have unexpectedly found money, we might smile. If we have smiled in the past, others might have smiled at us in return. On average, we have found that interactions with others in the culture who were smiling produces more positive consequences than interactions with others who were frowning. Thus, it may well be that a feeling of happiness is significantly related to subsequent behavior, but there are straightforward reasons for understanding why the feeling is so related. These reasons don't involve any appeal to happiness as an independent causal or mediating entity from another domain. For a large number of people, when one good thing has happened, no doubt several other good things have also happened. The effect reported in the experiments of social psychology is merely correlational, rather than causal.

What then about motives? For behavior analysts, the topic of motivation is concerned with the behavioral relevance of (a) consequences or (b) antecedents related to those consequences in the contingencies in our lives. The term motive is not taken to refer to some initiating causal force inside us. Some motives pertain to life-maintaining processes. Often the word *drive* is used in these cases, although behavior analysts find they can usually analyze behavior without invoking the term drive, perhaps because of its mechanical connotations. A useful alternative term for drive is *establishing operation*, in the sense that certain experiences may establish certain consequences as reinforcers (Michael, 1982). For example, suppose that we ordinarily enjoy eating turkey on the Thanksgiving holiday. If we avoid eating turkey for several months before the holiday, the probability that we pay attention to turkey recipes, and the probability that we will actually go out and buy a turkey instead of some other meal, presumably increases as we near the holiday. The deprivation of turkey increases—establishes—its relevance in our lives. Worth noting is that several days after Thanksgiving, when we have eaten a great deal of turkey in various left-over forms, turkey becomes less relevant in our lives. We are not interested in more recipes for turkey, and we are not inclined to go out and purchase turkey for our next meal.

Of course, we have many motives in our lives because we have many reinforcers. Some motives are social. For example, in the case of humans, we affiliate with others, often seeking their recognition and approval. We are said to have self-esteem in cases when we have well-developed repertoires that are richly reinforced, for example, via the approval and recognition of others. These descriptions pertain to the effects of social reinforcers in our lives. Further, one history of interaction with the environment may lead us to depend on external forms of stimulation for guidance, in which case we are described as externally motivated. Another history of interaction with the environment may lead us to generate stimuli that guide our behavior, perhaps through verbal processes, in which case we are described as internally motivated and self-reliant. Much of traditional social psychology and personality theory is concerned with social motivation in the sense of social reinforcers.

In short, behavior analysts find it useful to say we are more or less motivated when increases or decreases in our behavior are related to variations in the contingencies we experience in our environment, particularly as those contingencies involve certain classes of reinforcers. In this regard, we say our motivation is increased or decreased when deprivation or satiation increases or decreases the effectiveness of those reinforcers. Motives are not taken to be powers or forces in a mental domain that cause behavior.

The Feelings of Reinforcers

A final matter we can address concerns the feelings of reinforcers. To be sure, positive reinforcers typically feel good or pleasant. Should we say that positive reinforcers increase behavior *because* they feel good or pleasant? For behavior analysts, the answer is no. One learning theorist of the past, Edward Thorndike (1874-1949), believed consequences influenced behavior because they produced a feeling of satisfaction that stamped in some hypothetical connection between stimulus and response. Behavior analysts argue somewhat differently. For behavior analysts, reinforcers strengthen behavior and typically feel good or pleasant for a common reason, to be found in our evolutionary history. The point can be emphasized by asking ourselves, If we want to identify the feeling as causing an increase in behavior, isn't there something that caused the feeling? For behavior analysts, the answer is yes—the reinforcer. We always need to be sure we go back far enough in the sequence of events to secure a meaningful analysis. We call a consequence a reinforcer because of its effect on behavior, not because of the feelings or sensations it generates. Thus, although a reinforcer may well contain sugar and taste sweet, we call something a reinforcer because it supports behavior, not because it tastes sweet.

Summary and Conclusions

Feelings and emotions arise when we initiate or terminate contact with significant and meaningful circumstances and events in our lives. Moreover, it is the initiation or termination of the contact that causes both (a) our feelings and emotions and (b) the behavior with which the feelings and emotions are correlated. Reinforcers may well produce pleasant feelings and punishers may well produce unpleasant feelings, but the feelings themselves are not considered causal beyond the circumstances that produced them.

In some cases we are influenced by primary biological processes, such as hunger and thirst. In other cases we are influenced by social factors in our lives, such as affiliation with and recognition by others. Sometimes the feelings generated by environmental circumstances and events are taken as causal, simply because the feelings often precede behavior. From the viewpoint of behavior analysis, to do so is misleading. Feelings, emotions, moods, and motives are terms that are concerned with the domain in which behavior takes place. They identify aspects of the contingencies we experience. It is useful to understand how circumstances and events in the environment caused the feelings, emotions, moods, and motives, as well as any behavior to which these phenomena might be related.

References

Isen, A.M., & Levin, P. F. (1972). The effect of feeling good on helping: Cookies and kindness. *Journal of Personality and Social Psychology, 21*, 384-388.

James, W. (1890). *The principles of psychology*: New York: Holt.

Michael, J. (1982). Distinguishing between discriminative and motivational functions of stimuli. *Journal of the Experimental Analysis of Behavior, 37*, 149-155.

Key Terms and Concepts

eelings
emotions
mind-body problem
other minds
moods
emotions
motives
drive
establishing operation

Study Questions

1. For behavior analysts, what causes feelings?
2. What do behavior analysts say about the causal relation that involves seeing a bear, feeling afraid, and running?
3. Briefly describe why behavior analysts do not regard feelings as independent entities inside us that cause behavior.

4. What are two important questions about the relation between mind and body that follow from the premise that the mind and body differ qualitatively?
5. What do behavior analysts say about the value of pain relievers?
6. How does the process of generalization allow us to solve the problem of other minds?
7. For behavior analysts, to what do the terms mood and emotion refer?
8. Why do behavior analysts argue it is important to go back far enough in the causal chain of events to identify the relation between some emotion and behavior?
9. How do behavior analysts explain why we are more likely to engage in altruistic behavior if we are in a good mood?
10. For behavior analysts, what does it mean to say an organism is motivated?
11. For behavior analysts, do reinforcers strengthen behavior because of the pleasant feelings they generate?

Chapter 14

Applied Behavior Analysis, Abnormal Behavior, and Therapy

The scientific principles of behavior analysis give rise to applications outside the laboratory that seek to improve the quality of life for all individuals. The general term that behavior analysts employ for the application of behavior analytic principles to resolve problems associated with socially significant behavior is *applied behavior analysis*. A related but not identical term from the early days of behaviorally oriented forms of psychology is *behavior modification*. Behavior analysts prefer "applied behavior analysis" to the older term "behavior modification" because the former makes explicit a process of preliminary assessment of the behavior of interest, accompanied by a reciprocity between the person who delivers professional services and the person who receives them. The latter may imply an intervener from outside the situation who steps in to "do things" to the targeted recipient through a series of questionable assumptions about the causes of the behavior, where those assumptions have not been empirically supported. This chapter introduces some features of applied behavior analysis, and ultimately of clinical behavior analysis, which is the application of behavior analytic principles in formal clinical settings.

The range of human experience is obviously quite broad. Some individuals are well adjusted and enjoy highly meaningful and fulfilling lives. However, others face special challenges such as birth defects like Down syndrome or developmental disorders like autism. Still others experience problems in living, such as guilt, depression, anxiety, or substance abuse, which limit their potential. The sources of life problems are as varied as the individuals who are affected by them.

Despite the daunting variety of problems that develop in people's lives, a preliminary behavioral assessment can usefully sort these life-problems into two broad categories. On the one hand, many individuals have problems in their lives when, for whatever reason, they do not engage in some activity often enough, to their detriment or disadvantage. Individuals who are unable to read are obviously at a disadvantage in contemporary society. The inability to read is not necessarily an instance of abnormal behavior, though it may cause stress in the individual's life and be related to problems in other ways. In other cases, individuals may act in ways that are called shy and withdrawn. These individuals may then fail to develop significant interpersonal friendships. They may report pronounced feelings of worthlessness and despair, and they may rarely get dressed or even get out of bed in the morning.

Other individuals have problems in their lives when, for whatever reason, they engage in too much of an activity, and the excess in behavior is maladaptive. For example, they may engage in repetitive, ritualistic behavior like excessively washing their hands or excessively cleaning their house, beyond all considerations related to cleanliness. Their hands may become chapped and the skin dry and cracked because of the excessive washing, or they may spend so much time cleaning their houses that they can do little else. In extreme cases, individuals may have bizarre ideas called delusions about themselves and how the world works. They may constantly hear voices telling them to sell all their possessions and move to a desert island to prepare for the end of the world.

Individuals may also engage in behavior that is not necessarily bizarre or extreme, but that still interferes with a meaningful life. Suppose they frequently interrupt others or finish other persons' sentences during a conversation. Such individuals may be judged as self-centered and not willing to reciprocate in a friendship. It is likely that this tendency is quite annoying to others, and its occurring at a high rate interferes with developing appropriate and meaningful interpersonal relations.

A reasonable first step in any of these cases is to specify, if only descriptively, just what exactly is the nature of the behavior that is causing the problem. Is the individual doing too little or too much of some behavior, and is the deficit or excess causing trouble in the person's life? Is some behavior interfering with the individual's realizing his or her potential or maximizing his or her quality of life? The next step is to identify the circumstances in the individual's life that are related to the behavior in question. This part of the assessment is concerned with analyzing the circumstances that may be functionally related to the individual's current level of behavior. If the behavior is deficient, what circumstances have resulted in such a low rate? If the behavior is excessive, what circumstances have resulted in such a high rate? If the behavior is interfering with the individual's quality of life, why and how is that the case?

The possibilities for improvement typically involve changing the life circumstances in some way so as to substitute adaptive for interfering patterns of behavior. As necessary, the possibilities may also include direct attempt to increase deficient patterns of behavior and decrease excessive patterns of behavior. Suppose the individual had experiences in the past that promoted the maladaptive patterns. Perhaps some earlier forms of behavior were ineffective or were even punished, and the individual then developed alternative patterns that proved to be equally troublesome. The applied behavior analyst needs to understand what those experiences were, and whether those experiences have carried over to the present. The applied behavior analyst then needs to assess whether engaging in a different pattern of behavior will be helpful to the individual. For example, the applied behavior analyst might arrange different consequences for the behavior in question. The aim of arranging different consequences would be to strengthen adaptive patterns of the person's behavior, not just decrease the maladaptive patterns, so that the adaptive behavior occurs at a more suitable rate.

Some Representative Behavior-Analytic Interventions

As seen above, behavior analysts are very much committed to nonmentalistic views of the causes of an individual's abnormal behavior. In turn, behavior analysts are committed to nonmentalistic views of how to strengthen more appropriate behavior. These views are very different from traditional mentalistic views, and we have more to say about how behavior analytic views compare with traditional views later in this chapter. For now, let's examine some classic behavior-analytic interventions from the literature, and note their principal features.

One of the classic articles about behavior analytic interventions is Ayllon and Michael (1959). In this article, the authors reported the results of a project in which they instructed nurses and ward attendants at an in-patient psychiatric institution about behavioral principles such as contingencies of reinforcement. Many of the residents of the institution had been classified with schizophrenia or developmental disabilities and engaged in a startling range of maladaptive behavior. One such resident, Helen (a pseudonym), engaged in "psychotic talk" about 90 percent of the time. This talk superficially concerned such things as her child and men she claimed were constantly pursuing her. On several occasions other residents had actually beaten her in efforts to quiet her. One staff psychiatrist believed that Helen's problem was caused by her belief that she could free herself of her troubles by verbally pushing them onto someone else. Not surprisingly, the psychiatrist's belief had not given rise to any effective interventions that would help Helen. In addition, the authors found out that the nurses and ward attendants would often listen sympathetically to her in an effort to get to the root of her problems. The authors then suggested to the nurses and ward attendants that her psychotic talk might be a form of operant behavior that occurred at its observed high rate because of a particular form of reinforcement: the social attention she received on the ward, such as from the nurses. The nurses may have meant well, but the attention they paid to Helen when she engaged in psychotic talk was actually the root of the problem. Her problem was not necessarily something inside her. The authors suggested that as an alternative, the nurses not pay attention to her psychotic talk but rather only to her sensible talk. The nurses then did so. After the nurses did so for a time, Ayllon and Michael (1959) found that Helen engaged in nonpsychotic talk much more, as much as 75 percebt of the time. Why did it not occur 100 percebt of the time? Ayllon and Michael speculated that the long history of psychotic talk, plus intermittent visits by others such as social workers who had not received the same instruction as the nurses and who did reinforce Helen's psychotic talk by paying attention to her, might have inadvertently contributed to its occurrence. In any event, after the intervention she was not attacked by other residents and was only rarely challenged verbally. Clearly the intervention helped improve the quality of her life, as well as others on her ward.

Another classic article is Wolf, Risley, and Mees (1964). This article concerned Dickie, a three and a half year old boy with autism who displayed a wide variety of other behavioral problems. When he was an infant, he had developed cataracts. After surgery, he was supposed to wear glasses. However, he often threw them around the room rather than wear them. Dickie was very socially withdrawn for a number of reasons, and his inability to see very well was clearly one. The authors first established ice cream as a reinforcer, then followed a shaping procedure. They used positive reinforcement to get Dickie to first carry the glasses, then put them up to his face, then put them over his head, then over his head with the ear pieces actually on his ears, and so on. The process took only about 30 min. To be sure, this situation was a contrived rather than natural one, as most typically developing children wear glasses because they see better by doing so, rather than because someone gives them ice cream for doing so. To help Dickie make the transition to the natural benefits for wearing glasses, he was presented with interesting objects to look at, such as a ring or a clicker. Later he was told to put on his glasses so he could go for a walk, ride in an automobile, or play outdoors. If he removed the glasses, the activity was terminated. The outcome was that he was soon wearing his glasses for more than 12 hours a day. Again, the intervention clearly improved the quality of his life.

Applied behavior analysis is therefore concerned with a series of questions, answers to which are ultimately intended to be of therapeutic benefit to clients (Moore & Cooper, 2003). First, What is the nature of the problem—for instance, is it a deficit or an excess in socially significant behavior? Second, What are the goals of behavior change—for instance, to increase deficient behavior or reduce excessive behavior? Third, What kinds of behavior are of interest, given the totality of the client's life circumstances? Fourth, What events, variables, and relations affect the behavior of interest? Fifth, What are the relevant principles and procedures for change, based on current best practices? Answers to these questions lead in turn to the following questions. Sixth, What are the procedure's overall effects? Seventh, What are the components of the procedure and their effects? Eighth, How do the components produce their effects? Ninth, How can the procedure be improved? Tenth, are the procedures acceptable to, and within the skill sets of the persons involved?

Clinical Behavior Analysis

Behavior analytic interventions have proved especially successful in addressing problems in special education. Thus, a common misperception is that behavior analytic interventions are suitable only for individuals from special populations, like those with developmental disabilities, or for individuals who have specific problems, like biting their fingernails or phobias about snakes or spiders. The misperception continues that behavior analytic interventions are not suitable for the majority of so-called "mental" disorders found in the *Diagnostic and Statistical Manual* (5th Ed.) *(DSM-V)*, such as anxiety disorders or mood disorders or personality disorders. The majority of mental disorders are held to be disorders of "higher-functioning." They are held to involve something internal and mental that is faulty, like the personality structure or brain function or maladaptive cognition. When the causes are thus assumed to be buried within the individual, often in another domain, behavior analysis has not been seen as relevant.

This view has recently been changing, however, as evidenced by the rapid growth in the field of clinical behavior analysis (Kohlenberg, Tsai, & Dougher, 1993). Clinical behavior analysts focus on the complex problems of outpatient adults, just as does traditional psychotherapy. For example, clients may seek help to establish intimate interpersonal relationships, to alleviate socially-induced anxiety connected with public speaking, or to resolve depression initially brought about by job loss but which now extends to all phases of their lives. Importantly, clinical behavior analysts use basic, behavioral concepts to bring about change as a function of the therapeutic relation between client and therapist. More specifically, clinical behavior analysts focus on client behavior, and then on what the therapist does with respect to that behavior. Of particular importance is providing verbal consequences to strengthen adaptive verbal behavior on the part of the client, while at the same time not engaging in actions that would maintain maladaptive behavior, even if inadvertently.

Interventions in clinical behavior analysis typically focus on verbal processes. A key strategy is to discern, within a therapy session, occurrences of the problems that clients describe as occurring in their lives outside of the therapy session. This strategy allows therapists to take advantage of their direct access to clients' verbal behavior during the therapy session. Therapists are therefore in a good position to change relevant client verbal repertoires. For example, clients may speak metaphorically or in a disguised way about their problems. Therapists may see this form of verbal behavior as an effort to be forthcoming, but at the same time to avoid punishment for disclosing that they actually have the problems. In addition, clients may operate under some inappropriate assumptions about how the world works or how others see them, which leads the clients to engage in some kind of verbally regulated or rule-governed interpersonal behavior. The trouble is that both the assumptions and rules are incorrect, which means their interpersonal behavior is going to be ineffective. Finally, an emphasis on verbal processes allows therapists to assess whether clients have large networks of verbally induced problems, in the sense that clients have convinced themselves that because they behave in some particular way in one setting, they should behave similarly in other settings, or else they will be even unhappier than they already are.

Clinical behavior analysts need to be highly skilled in assessing the sources of control and function of their clients' verbal behavior, in order to properly understand any problematic circumstances of their clients' lives. If helpful verbal processes can be brought to bear on those problematic circumstances, clinical behavior analysts hold that their clients' lives will be better integrated and their clients will ultimately function better.

Callaghan, Summers, and Weidman (2003) outline a case history of clinical behavior analysis that we may use as an illustration. The client was a 30 year old Caucasian male who reported being very sad and distressed. The client sought therapy so that he might develop the skills to form and maintain close interpersonal relations and bring about a stability that was lacking in his life. At the time of intake, he lacked an understanding of why he was unable to maintain good relationships, and wondered if he was doomed to go through life single.

The client had 23 treatment sessions with the therapist. Of principal interest was the clinically relevant behavior of the client, and then the therapist's response to that behavior. One class of clinically relevant behavior in which the client engaged was related to talking about his problems. A second class was related to talking about what would constitute an improvement in his life. A third class was related to talking about the origins of his problems, and then the changes in his behavior that would contribute to his improvement. In general, the therapist supported (i.e., verbally reinforced) talk related to the second and third classes, about improvements and changes to bring about improvements. Other talk was simply acknowledged. Callaghan, Summers, and Weidman (2003) provided a very brief albeit hypothetical exchange between client and therapist to illustrate the pattern of verbal interaction that might take place:

1. Therapist: Tell me how you feel coming in here today.
2. Client: Well, to be honest, I was nervous. Sometimes I feel worried about how things will go, but I am really glad I am here.
3. Therapist: That's great. I am glad you are here, too. I look forward to talking with you.
4. Client: Whatever, you always say that. [becomes quiet] I don't know what I am doing talking so much.
5. Therapist: Now you seem to be withdrawing from me. That makes it hard for me to give you want you might need from me right now. What do you think you want from me as we are talking right now?

In this exchange, we can see that in #2, the client is talking in a way related to improvement. In #3, the therapist supports this talk. In #4, the client reverts to problematic behavior. In #5, the therapist doesn't support the talk in #4, but rather invites the client to talk about the variables and relations that might be responsible for improvement. An additional part of the process would be the client's reporting behavior outside the therapy session that was related to problems, and then outside behavior that was related to improvements. The therapist would respond as before, supporting improvements.

Callaghan, Summers, and Weidman (2003) reported that based on the client's self reports as well as the observation of his behavior during the sessions, the client improved a great deal during his treatment. These improvements occurred within therapy sessions, and they generalized to relationships the client had or developed with others outside the therapy sessions. Overall, the client was able to better identify the kinds of relationships he wanted with others, and what he brought to those relationships. He developed a much more effective prosocial repertoire that included emotionally relating to others, noticing and responding to his impact on others, asserting personal needs, and engaging in more effective interpersonal skills. At the conclusion of therapy, the client no longer engaged in the problem behaviors in evidence at the beginning of therapy, and his score on a standardized test measuring depression was much lower. Our point here is that an understanding of behavioral processes can produce therapeutic improvement even when the client is not from a special population, but rather is experiencing the ordinary problems of living.

Comparison to Traditional Views

The behavior-analytic approach differs greatly from traditional views. Traditional views have tended to locate the source of the problem inside the individual in some sense. For example, early theories saw individuals' problems as caused by evil spirits or the Devil. Later theories saw the problems as caused by problems with the personality structure—we saw earlier that Sigmund Freud proposed a well-known theory about how the dynamics of the personality structure brought about troubled behavior, and other personality theorists have had their own theories. Some theories have proposed that the problems are caused by a malfunction of the body, for instance, related to genetics or the central nervous system. The malfunction has never actually been observed, but rather has simply been inferred on the basis of observed behavior.

These traditional, largely mentalistic views of abnormal behavior were heavily influenced by early workers who came from the field of medicine. They brought with them a set of analytic concepts appropriate to medical practice. The result is called the "medical model" approach.

The medical model is

1. A general orientation to the problem of abnormality in which:
    (a) unusual behaviors (bizarre, extreme, disturbing) are viewed as symptoms
    (b) of an underlying pathology
    (c) caused by an underlying internal, physiological, or neurological entity, state, or condition (e.g., chemical imbalance, brain injury, physiological deficit)

2. In the same way that:
    (a) unusual medical conditions (cough, fever, sore throat) are viewed as symptoms
    (b) of an underlying medical pathology (cold, flu, pneumonia)
    (c) caused by an underlying medical entity or condition (bacteria, virus)

3. In each case, the task of the specialist is to infer the nature of the underlying pathology and the underlying cause on the basis of the evidence provided by the symptoms.

As analytic techniques advanced, workers soon realized that perhaps they had overgeneralized: Not every impairment could be traced to irregularly functioning bodily tissue. Nevertheless, the general form of reasoning that underlay the medical model remained strong: Impairments are caused by something inside the person. If irregularly functioning bodily tissue could not be identified, workers then reasoned that something else inside the individual was malfunctioning and must be the cause. The result was a proliferation of a wide variety of internal acts, states, mechanisms, processes, entities, or structures that were assumed to cause the abnormal behavior, analogous to the way internal medical entities caused medical problems. As before, the abnormal behavior was viewed as a symptom of these inner causes. Even the language of medicine was transferred. The person was mentally ill, or had a mental illness. The person had to go to a mental hospital. Terms consistent with disease states came to be used: disorder, episodes, remission, recovery, relapse, and recurrence. Representative inner causes were a weak ego, an inadequate personality, defective moral control, or a faulty cognitive perception. The causes themselves resided in another domain, separate from that of the observed symptoms or maladaptive patterns of behavior. Sometimes the causes were assumed to be linked to physiology, albeit indirectly. For example, consider the term neurosis, common in everyday language although no longer part of the technical diagnostic vocabulary. Etymologically, the term is composed of neur-, as in the root of neuron, and -osis, as in pathological condition. Early uses of the term neurosis were traceable to an assumption that behavioral problems must be caused by pathological weaknesses in the nervous system. When those weaknesses could not be readily identified, usage gravitated toward the current sense of abnormal behavior characterized by anxiety and problems in the personality structure.

Traditional therapies often assume inner entities are the cause of the client's problems. The common mode of intervention is talking: The therapist talks with a client in an effort to resolve the client's problems. Depending on the form of the therapy, the talk will focus on such things as the client's childhood experiences assumed to have symbolic or sexual significance (Freudian psychoanalysis), the client's failure to achieve a genuine self-identity with one's own goals and values (Rogerian therapy), the client's inability to integrate feelings with behavior (Gestalt therapy), or the client's irrational and self-defeating belief systems or ideas (various forms of cognitive-behavioral therapy, such as Albert Ellis' Rational Emotive Behavioral Therapy). The assumption is that the abnormal inner entities, whether they are personality components or faulty beliefs and ideas, are the source of the problems and may be corrected through talk.

Of particular importance is achieving *insight*. Insight means conscious awareness of one's circumstances and problems. Although the various forms of therapy treat insight in slightly different ways, a common theme is that some inner agent directs or controls an individual's behavior. Individuals may be more or less aware of this inner agent, how it operates, and what is important to it. The therapist may need to make inferences about the characteristics of the inner agent, and then assist the clients in coming to a realization of their problems. Once clients became aware or gained insight into their problems through talking, therapeutic benefit was assumed to follow automatically.

Thus, we have it that on the basis of medical model approaches, treatment interventions had to be directed at something internal. According to this traditional orientation, failure to direct the treatment intervention at something internal meant that the intervention was not being directed at the root cause of the problem. If the intervention was not directed at the root cause, then the problem would simply resurface in another observable manifestation. The resurfacing was called *symptom substitution*. This phrase means that if the root cause—something inside that was defective—hadn't been fixed, a different or substitute symptom would simply appear, as a different or substitute manifestation of the person's internal problem.

For example, suppose a woman had obsessive-compulsive tendencies that seriously compromised her lifestyle. Maybe she washed her hands so many times per day that the skin on her hands was raw, cracked, and bleeding. An interpretation based on Freudian psychoanalytic theory might say that at some earlier point in her life, her id—the component of the personality that represents sexual energy and drive, was dominant and she had some sexual experience. Her super-ego—the component of the personality that represents the moral standards of conduct in her society or her "conscience," reacted and she now feels guilty and ashamed about that experience. Perhaps it would be appropriate to say she feels metaphorically "dirty." To overcome the feeling of being dirty, she now metaphorically and symbolically washes her hands to remove the feelings of guilt. If she doesn't wash her hands for some period of time, she starts to feel anxious. Washing her hands multiple times per day is one way her ego—the component of the personality that seeks to adjust to the often conflicting demands of the id and super-ego so that a realistic lifestyle can be achieved, brings some measure of control to her life, albeit perhaps only metaphorically and at some considerable cost.

The Freudian point of view accepts symptom substitution. From the Freudian point of view, if a therapeutic intervention was designed to simply get her to stop washing her hands, the problem with her dysfunctional personality structure would still be there. Thus, if she washed her hands excessively, and a therapist took steps to stop her washing her hands, she would just substitute something else, like cleaning her house excessively. Whatever mechanism the ego adopted to defend against anxiety might appear to work in the short term, but not in the long term because the real problem concerned her personality structure. If the therapeutic intervention does target her personality structure and does strengthen her ego by making her aware of her problems, then the assumption is that any problems she has will more or less take care of themselves. Even if her behavioral symptoms do not immediately subside, the logic of the intervention is that she will ultimately be in a better position to deal with them, through having gained insight.

As alluring as this interpretation sounds, we should point out that there is no evidence in the literature for the phenomenon called symptom substitution, at least as that phenomenon is understood in traditional psychology. Perhaps an intervention that does not allow a client to make contact with a rate of reinforcement sufficient to maintain a more adaptive repertoire will fail, resulting in the appearance of a new and possibly ineffective form of behavior, but that process differs significantly from symptom substitution. Therefore, it is unclear that targeting something inferred to be the problem, like her personality structure, to the exclusion of anything else, like the environmental circumstances related to her behavior, is going to be effective. To be sure, it is entirely appropriate for a therapeutic intervention to target the root cause of a problem. From the viewpoint of behavior analysis, the root cause is the interaction with the environment. Therefore, the therapeutic intervention needs to target the interaction between behavior and its surrounding environmental circumstances, not some unobservable internal entity. In light of the importance of language in human behavior, at least some part of the therapeutic intervention may well involve talking about the problem. However, some of the intervention will also involve taking direct steps to reduce the troublesome behavior itself. The intervention with the environment may address the motivation for the response, or seek to create alternative forms of behavior that are incompatible with the troubling behavior.

Why Do Forms of Traditional Therapy Work When They Do?

Many discussions of traditional forms of therapy have sought to determine whether traditional forms of therapy work, and if so, which form is better for specific problems. It is important to note that each traditional form of therapy is derived from its own core assumptions about development, motivation, the nature of personality, and the nature of the abnormal behavior. Interestingly, each traditional form of therapy assumes it has privileged insight into those factors. If a given form of traditional therapy actually did have privileged insight, we would think that by this time, it would have emerged as the most generally effective form of therapy. Interestingly, the data suggest that for the most part, the various forms of traditional therapy all work about the same.

Behavior analysts accept that traditional forms of therapy may work. The question of interest for behavior analysts is, Why do forms of traditional therapy work when they do? If the reasons why they work can be more clearly identified, then the techniques according to which traditional forms of therapy achieve their therapeutic benefits can be refined so that they work even better or more often.

It may be that some clients have a history that enables them to respond in a healthy, constructive way on the basis of talking. They may have had interactions with parents, siblings, peers, or others prior to the time that the problem developed that allow them to profit from talk. The talk provides various forms of discriminative stimulation that promotes the development of adaptive behavior and the shedding of maladaptive behavior. They may be able to profit from the discriminative control derived from the self-verbalization involved in what is called "becoming aware" or "gaining insight." However, any therapeutic benefit brought about by talking and insight may be understood from the point of view of contingencies, rather than any mediation brought about by conscious awareness as an intervening process. We saw earlier in this chapter that in clinical behavior analysis, the therapist encourages talk about not only the troublesome behavior, but also the circumstances that cause the troublesome behavior. In this way the client develops self-analytical verbalizations that apply outside of the therapy session.

Given that traditional forms of therapy all work about the same, it follows then that when they do work they are all doing about the same thing. That same thing is presumably a set of nonspecific features of therapy that proves to be beneficial: The therapist (a) establishes an interpersonal relationship of warmth and trust with a client; (b) accepts a client as an individual; (c) empathizes, reassures and supports a client; (d) desensitizes a client's debilitating concerns; and (e) strengthens a client's adaptive responses. Indeed, in a classic article Truax (1966) analyzed interactions between therapist and client in one form of therapy, Rogerian client-centered therapy. This form of therapy is traditionally regarded as non-directive. During this form of therapy, the therapist is supposed to show unconditional positive regard, empathy, and warmth that are not contingent on client behavior. Nevertheless, Truax found significant differential reinforcement effects in the exchanges between therapist and client. One term that is used to characterize the relation represented by the nonspecific features is the "therapeutic alliance" between client and therapist. The specific features of some traditional form of therapy, which that form holds to be essential, seem ironically to be inessential. What matters is what the therapist does with the client. The previous discussion of clinical behavior analysis illustrates this principle.

To be sure, therapists are just as different as clients. Some therapists may well be more effective in dealing with some problems and some clients than with others. However, they are more effective because they do something different about the clients and their problems, not because of their assumptions about the nature of personality or about the causal processes from another domain thought to be associated with the abnormal behavior. These therapists empathize more, they reassure better, or they strengthen more appropriate adaptive responses. Like other changes in behavior, a therapeutic change is brought about by a change in contingencies. That change can occur at many different levels, but it is always a change at the level of the interaction between the individual and the environment.

Who Judges Improvement?

A final matter concerns who judges therapeutic improvement. At least three parties are involved in such a judgment: the client, the therapist, and society. If clients pronounce themselves improved, are they actually improved? Self-reports are notoriously invalid. If therapists report the clients improved, are they actually improved? If the clients don't feel better, are they actually improved? If society reports the clients improved, for example by ceasing insurance payments for therapy after eight or ten sessions, are they actually improved? What if both clients and therapists think further treatment is called for? There are no easy answers to these questions. At present, the best answers seem to be arrived at through reasoned, principled, and deliberate analysis by prudent people who have the best interests of the clients at heart.

Summary and Conclusions

As we have noted, abnormal behavior is of central concern in our culture, as well as to individuals themselves. In many cases, abnormal behavior arises during individuals' lives, as the individuals interact with their environments, especially their social environment. To look for causes of that behavior and to seek therapeutic interventions in some other domain, such as a mental domain in which the "personality" is thought to reside, are not likely to be as effective as they need to be. Medical model approaches look for causes inside the person, in a fashion that is analogous to treating medical illnesses, but its underlying assumptions are suspect. In particular, there is no evidence for symptom substitution. Often traditional interventions seek to produce insight, but there is no assurance that gaining insight will alleviate problems. Even if traditional interventions do appear to be effective, their effectiveness is related to factors other than those identified by the school of therapy the therapist practices. Indeed, to look for causes and seek interventions somewhere else, in some other domain, may only prove troublesome for the individual who is seeking help. Rather, improvement seems to be related to nonspecific factors related to what therapists actually do in their interactions with clients. The effective therapeutic factors referred to above may easily be described in more suitable language of discriminative stimuli, contingencies, reinforcement, and extinction.

References

Ayllon, T., & Michael, J. (1959). The psychiatric nurse as a behavioral engineer. *Journal of the Experimental Analysis of Behavior, 2*, 323-334.

Callaghan, G., Summers, C., & Weidman, M. (2003). The treatment of histrionic and narcissistic personality disorder behaviors: A single subject demonstration of clinical improvement using Functional Analytic Psychotherapy. *Journal of Contemporary Psychotherapy, 33*, 321-339.

Kohlenberg, R., Tsai, M., & Dougher, M. (1993). The dimensions of clinical behavior analysis. *The Behavior Analyst, 16*, 271-284.

Moore, J., & Cooper, J. (2003). Some proposed relations among the domains of behavior analysis. *The Behavior Analyst, 26*, 69-84.

Wolf, M., Risley, T., & Mees, H. (1964). Application of operant conditioning procedures to the behavior problems of an autistic child. *Behavior Research and Therapy, 1*, 305-312.

Truax, C. B. (1966). Reinforcement and nonreinforcement in Rogerian psychotherapy. *Journal of Abnormal Psychology, 71*, 1-9.

Key Terms and Concepts

applied behavior analysis
DSM-V
clinical behavior analysis

insight
medical model
symptom substitution
nonspecific features of therapy

Study Questions

1. How do excesses or deficits in behavior constitute a problem in individuals' lives?
2. Briefly describe how Ayllon and Michael (1959) reduced Helen's psychotic talk.
3. Briefly describe how Wolf, Risley, and Mees (1964) encouraged Dickie to wear his glasses.
4. Briefly describe the series of questions with which applied behavior analysis is typically concerned with, answers to which Moore and Cooper (2003) suggested are ultimately intended to be of therapeutic benefit to clients.
5. Briefly describe the three key assumptions of clinical behavior analysis.
6. Briefly describe how Callaghan, Summers, and Weidman (2003) helped a 30 year old Caucasian male who reported being very sad and distressed.
7. Briefly describe the medical model approach as found in traditional clinical psychology.
8. Briefly describe the importance of insight in traditional clinical psychology.
9. Briefly describe what is meant by symptom substitution.
10. Briefly describe the nonspecific features of therapy.
11. What issues are involved in judging therapeutic improvement?

Chapter 15

Ethics and Morality

The field of ethics is concerned with the study of moral conduct. Our English word "ethics" is derived from the Greek "ethikos," meaning "custom," and indeed much of our cultural system of ethics and morality is derived from customs and traditions that began in ancient Greece. Thus, the study of ethics and morality is concerned with the study of how humans ought to live and with what counts as acceptable conduct. Such conduct is concerned with minimizing if not eliminating evil or harm to others. When we speak of *ethics*, we are speaking of the principles by which we evaluate that conduct. When we speak of *morality*, we are speaking of the conduct itself.

As do other chapters in this book, this chapter reviews and analyses its chosen topics from a behavioral point of view. As we will see, a behavioral point of view clarifies many important points in traditional discussions, and leads to a new and refined understanding of ethics and morality.

What is Good Conduct?

What is good conduct? What does it mean to behave in an ethically and morally acceptable way? Behavior analysts address matters of ethics and morality by emphasizing that the behavior in question is operant behavior. Hence, we speak of behavior as moral when it is reinforced by particular consequences. As the definition in the opening paragraph of this chapter suggests, the consequences are minimizing if not eliminating evil or harm to others. Consideration of these consequences helps us to decide whether we want to call the behavior moral or immoral.

Let us consider some examples. Admittedly, the examples may stretch our imagination, but perhaps they will serve to illustrate the important relations. Suppose we see that an individual is having difficulty swimming. We throw a life preserver in the water, and the individual is then able to make it safely to shore. Why did we throw the life preserver in the water? The reinforcer for our behavior is presumably related to our preventing harm to the individual who was having difficulty swimming. As a result, we typically call our behavior moral.

Now suppose that another individual is also having difficulty swimming, but we don't see this individual. We throw a life preserver in the water, and the individual is again able to make it safely to shore. Why did we throw the life preserver in the water this time? We didn't see the individual, so the reinforcer for our behavior was presumably not related to our preventing harm to the individual. The reinforcer may have been something else, such as finding out whether the life preserver would float. In any event, we typically do not call our behavior moral.

Let us modify and extend the example above. Suppose that an individual who was previously having difficulty swimming already has a life preserver. Now suppose that some miscreant takes the life preserver away. Why did the miscreant take the life preserver away? The reinforcer for the miscreant's behavior was presumably related to causing harm to the individual. As a result, we typically call the miscreant's behavior immoral.

Now suppose that we don't see that an individual is having difficulty swimming, and we take a life preserver away that the individual might use to make it safely to shore. Why did we take the life preserver away? We didn't see that the individual was having difficulty swimming, so the reinforcer for our behavior was presumably not related to our causing harm to the individual. As a result, we do not necessarily call our behavior immoral. The qualifier "necessarily" is added here to recognize that an additional factor is whether it is likely the individual would have some difficulty making it to shore without the life preserver, and we were just negligent in not recognizing the potential for the individual to be in peril.

Of course, what we want to do as a culture is to teach people to behave in morally acceptable ways. The integrity of our society turns on the extent to which we minimize if not eliminate the harm we can do to others, either actually or potentially, through our actions. Many of the consequences identified above are socially mediated, in the sense that as we grow up, we learn from others through their recognition and approval how to behave in morally and ethically acceptable ways. At the pinnacle are individuals who regard the opportunity to engage in moral behavior as their highest calling in life, which it surely is.

The traditional view of morality found in Western culture views matters quite a bit differently. According to this traditional view, humans are free, rational beings. They have reasons for their actions. They choose. They judge. Ideally, they accept responsibility, though in some troublesome cases they evade it. Their actions merit praise or deserve blame. They are autonomous agents. Indeed, most of our legal and religious institutions are based on this view. According to the traditional view, then, an individual's behavior is explained by citing some mental process or entity as the cause of that behavior. Moral behavior comes about as a deliberate choice of behaving individuals, who rationally choose to conform to some accepted code of conduct within the social group of which they are members, such as a religious code of conduct.

For the traditional view, an analysis of the circumstances in which an individual lives is not thought to shed much if any light on why the individual acts in a given way. The traditional view is of concern to behavior analysts because it leads us away from an effective understanding of the environmental circumstances that cause individuals to behave in the ways they do. Behavior analysts might well agree that individuals can act in ways that are regarded as rational, but that behavior is attributable to the circumstances individuals have experienced during their lives, rather than some mental process. What is ultimately at issue is how to teach individuals to behave in moral ways. With its emphasis on autonomous events and entities in another domain, such as the autonomous mental processes of an agent who makes rational choices, the traditional view falls short of understanding how a society can actually create and maintain behavior called moral.

Social Impact as Another Consideration

Let us continue our evaluation of morality by considering the importance of the social impact of the behavior. As the term is used here, "social impact" has a broad meaning. In some cases, it relates to the social effect of the behavior for the immediate social group of which the behaving individual is a member.

In other cases, it relates to the social effect of the behavior for the broader culture of which the behaving individual is a member.

In still other cases, it relates to the social effect of the behavior if everyone in the social group behaved in the way in question, not just the one behaving individual. Thus, some form of behavior might not be evaluated as immoral if it occurred in a setting where it would not have a social consequence. For example, yelling "Fire!" would presumably not be evaluated as immoral if the individual who yelled it was marooned alone on a desert island. However, it might well be evaluated as immoral if the individual was in a crowded movie theater and yelled it as a prank, in the absence of an actual fire, just to see people trample each other in their haste to escape.

Many discussions of ethics and morality seek to establish fixed, absolute standards against which to evaluate behavior. These discussions contrast with discussions about whether ethics and morality are only "situational," and are best limited or relative to particular circumstances. For behavior analysts, some matters of ethics and morality are clearly related to particular customs and conventions. The field of cultural anthropology explicitly studies how different practices have emerged and been strengthened in various cultures, for example, concerning dietary restrictions. These practices may be a function of geographic locale. For example, a culture might impose restrictions against eating a certain food. Perhaps growing that food required an expensive commitment of resources such as water or land that could be better used for some other purpose. Crops or livestock that require vast amounts of water in arid climates are noteworthy examples, as are other restrictions to prevent overuse of available resources. The writings of the cultural anthropologist Marvin Harris (e..g., 1977) provide many other examples.

However, behavior analysts also understand that many other matters of ethics and morality transcend the customs and conventions of particular cultural groups. Do these matters mean that eternal, fixed standards do exist after all? Perhaps a more reasonable way to conceptualize the problem is to say that over the evolutionary history of humans as a species, humans who respond in particular ways to particular circumstances of this lives have benefitted, whereas humans who respond in other ways have not. For example, when their government is harshly coercive, oppressive, and exploitive, most humans tend to rebel sooner or later against the government. The outcome is that even though in the short term humans might suffer a fearful cost of protest, in the long term humans are better off for their protests, for example, because of less aversive control and more stability in the culture. Our conclusion here is that humans have evolved in such a way that enlightened, progressive, and participatory social and political practices ultimately contribute to social stability and group welfare. In this sense they come to be regarded as moral. In contrast, the harsh and punitive social practices of tyrants and despots eventually provoke rebellion. Consequently, the harsh and punitive social practices come to be regarded as immoral.

The "Good"

Sometimes the consequences of behavior make that behavior more likely. These consequences, typically called reinforcers, are often regarded as "good," at least for the individual concerned. To label something as good generally requires a broader context than just the one behaving individual, however. For example, consider a bank robber. Robbing a bank is operant behavior. What reinforces the robber's behavior is presumably the consequence of getting money. Indeed, when one bank robber was asked why he robbed banks, he is alleged to have answered "Because that's where the money is." In the narrowest sense, bank robbers might regard their behavior as good. That it is clearly not good may be seen when the broader context is taken into account, as it must be: Robbing a bank is clearly not reinforcing for the welfare and fabric of the larger social group or culture. Bank robbers are taking something that does not belong to them. Of course, robbing a bank is not actually good for the robber either, as the robber is typically caught and sent to prison.

The point is that an individual may behave in a way that might be said to be good for that individual, but bad for the social group. Something that is good for an individual is often a matter of whether it is helpful or adaptive in the individual's life. If someone says that it is good to eat three sound, nutritious meals a day, with no high calorie snacks in between, then presumably the person will lead a longer, healthier life by following such practices. If someone says that it is good to brush one's teeth regularly, then presumably the person will have fewer dental problems. If someone says that it is good to keep one's home free from pests, then presumably the person will have fewer instances of disease and spoiled food. Those outcomes will presumably be reinforcing.

However, what if individuals use large amounts of an insecticide such as DDT to keep their homes free from pests and disease? In fact, what if everyone used large amounts of DDT? DDT has been shown to damage the environment. What is good for the individual may not necessarily be good or reinforcing for the larger social group.

Similarly, what about individuals who work very hard at developing and manufacturing a product? These individuals may well provide a comfortable home and lifestyle for their families, provide jobs with comfortable incomes for others, and be regarded as a credit to their communities. Their hard work might well be described as good. This outcome is reinforcing for the individuals. However, what if a by-product of their manufacturing work is a large volume of industrial waste? What if their lifestyle involves conspicuous consumption, and generates large amounts of trash and garbage? What if everyone did the same? Is their hard work then good? Many would say not, meaning it is not necessarily reinforcing or good for the larger social group.

Often a practice is regarded as immoral and bad if it is coercive, where by coercive we mean it threatens those targeted by the practice with punishment if they do not conform. To be sure, in a limited sense, coercion can be effective as a form of motivation. However, coercion can ultimately lead to dysfunction—those so coerced will seek to escape from the coercion. Thus, the social effects of coercion are ultimately counterproductive, even though coercion may appear to be effective.

A further point is we should not suppose that just because a practice is not coercive, it will automatically yield moral and good social outcomes. For example, state-sponsored lotteries are not coercive in the present sense—individuals are not threatened with punishment if they do not buy a lottery ticket. However, data suggest state-sponsored lotteries entice individuals who can least afford to play the lottery to do so. Spending their limited money in this way is not good for these individuals. As we have seen, the social effects need to be taken into account when we evaluate whether something is good.

To summarize, then, behavior analysts typically evaluate whether behavior is moral or good on the one hand, or immoral or bad on the other hand, by analyzing the contingencies that cause the behavior and its social effects. Such matters are not about metaphysical categories, but rather always about behavior and the circumstances related to that behavior. The social effects range from reducing the quality of the lives of others to infringing on the self-interest of others for the purpose of exploitation and aggrandizement. Ultimately, concerns about whether something is good or bad can be related to survival: If an individual doesn't survive, then questions about whether a given practice or form of behavior is good or bad for that individual are irrelevant. Similarly, if a society doesn't survive, then questions about whether a given practice or form of behavior is good or bad for that society are irrelevant. A society increases its chances for survival if it teaches its members to take steps to promote its survival. Thus, something is good in the broader social context when it promotes survival in the broader social context. Again, such practices as tyranny and dictatorships cannot be considered good. Tyrants and dictators may seek to justify their practices and behavior by claiming they are promoting survival, but ultimately they are promoting only instability.

The Temporal Context

Many discussions of morals and ethics reflect a concern with the temporal context of behavior. For example, a given form of behavior may have some short-term effects, some intermediate effects, and some long-term effects. In addition, some of those effects may be positive, which is to say reinforcing, and some may be negative, which is to say punishing. Indeed, some instances of behavior may have one kind of short-term effect and the opposite kind of long-term effect. Thus, it is important for us to recognize that outcomes may be assessed on multiple levels.

For example, consider the use of DDT, as mentioned above. Using DDT has the short-term beneficial effect of reducing insects and disease, but the long-term harmful effect of damaging the environment.

Similarly, eating nutritious food is presumably a healthy and reinforcing thing to do in the short term, but eating any food to excess is presumably not reinforcing in the long term, and may even be punishing, as in weight gain and other detrimental effects on health. Moreover, eating a particular kind of food, such as red meat, might be reinforcing in the short term, but red meat sometimes has a high amount of fat and other ingredients that for many persons are harmful in the long term. In fact, even the resources devoted to providing red meat might be used to supply more people with an alternative healthy food source, thereby benefitting the social group in the long term.

The Moral-Ethical Matrix

Overall, behavior analysts find it useful to conceive of matters relating to ethics and morals in terms of a matrix. This matrix establishes a frame of reference for the behavior in question, and for evaluating its effects. Along one dimension of the matrix are levels of the social unit. Three such levels are proposed here, for illustration: the individual, the social group, and the culture. Along the other dimension are levels of time. Again, three such levels are proposed here, for illustration: short term, intermediate term and long term. Typically, an action will impact one or more cells. Matters of ethics and morals relate to comparisons of the impact across various cells in the matrix.

	Individual	*Social group*	*Culture*
Short term			
Intermediate term			
Long term			

Particularly significant are clashes between the cells of the matrix. Suppose a given instance of behavior has a short-term reinforcing effect for the individual. However, what if that instance of behavior has disastrous long-term effects for the social group or culture, even if no one else engaged in the behavior in question? What if that instance of behavior has disastrous long-term effects for the social group or culture, but only if everyone engaged in the behavior in question? How are we to regard these problems?

The famous "Tragedy of the Commons" illustrates how a given action might be reinforcing for a small number of individuals over the short term but problematic for the larger social group over the long term (Hardin, 1968; see also Platt, 1973, for related examples). Suppose a social group consisting of 12 families collectively owns a pasture. Each family owns one animal that grazes on the pasture. The common pasture can comfortably tolerate the 12 animals. The resources will not be overused, the grass will grow back, and so on. The animals can graze there indefinitely. Now suppose that one family puts two animals in the pasture. Its profits double. Those consequences are reinforcing for that family, at least in the short term. If another family added a second animal, similar benefits would accrue to the second family.

However, what are the effects if each of the 12 families puts two animals on the land? In the long term, a tipping point would be reached in which no family could graze any animal on the land because all the grass would be eaten and would not have a chance to grow back. The long-term effects for the social group would be disastrous.

The resolution of such problems is complex. For example, the social group might pass laws formally prohibiting such actions and establish some judiciary authority to punish violations of the laws by imposing a fine. The laws may be regarded as formally codified guidelines or discriminative stimuli. The function of the laws is to regulate behavior of individuals and the group in a way that prevents exploitation and promotes stability.

Moral and Ethical Injunctions

Given this approach, what is the force of such words as "ought," "should," and "obligation"? For behavior analysts, such words refer to the contingencies that govern the behavior in question. Suppose we say that individuals *ought* to or *should* behave in some particular way. What we mean is that if a given outcome is important to these individuals, which is to say reinforcing for them, then behaving in the way the contingencies prescribe will result in that outcome.

Obligation may be similarly analyzed. Suppose we say that individuals are obligated to behave in some particular way. What we mean is that the failure to act in the way the contingencies prescribe will result in a punishing outcome. For example, suppose we say that individuals have an obligation to pay their debts. What we mean is that individuals risk some punishing outcome, like not having debts paid back to them, if they don't pay their own debts.

Summary and Conclusions

In conclusion, we have reviewed matters of ethics and morals from a behavioral point of view. We are concerned with why someone behaves in a given way, and also with the social effects of the behavior. The social effects of the behavior concern the effect on the individual, the social group, and the culture. The effects may be experienced in the short term, the intermediate term, or the long term. Morcal or ethical dilemmas come about when there is conflict among two or more cells of a matrix defining the possible cases.

The unconventional nature of this approach may be seen in its contrast with the prevailing orientation of our culture. Traditionally, our culture holds that individuals are agents who have free will or choice. The traditional position is readily evidenced in our religious and legal institutions. Moral or ethical behavior is thought to come about only because of the exercise of this free choice. If the behavior is compelled, then the behavior, no matter how noble the outcome, is not ordinarily regarded as moral or ethical. Although the traditional approach does have the virtue of taking into account some circumstances responsible for the behavior, it still regards the individual as an autonomous initiator of action, rather than as behaving in a context of relevant factors. Ultimately the position does not allow us to genuinely understand the behavior judged as moral and ethical.

References

Hardin, G. (1968). The tragedy of the commons. *Science, 162*, 1243-1248.
Harris, M. (1977). *Cannibals and Kings: The Origins of Cultures*. New York: Vintage.
Platt, J. (1973). Social traps. *American Psychologist, 28*, 641-651.

Key Terms and Concepts

ethics
morality
ought
should
obligation

Study Questions

1. How do ethics differ from morality?
2. What is the behavioral approach to evaluating the "good"?
3. Briefly describe an approach to the analysis of ethics and morals that involves a matrix in which one dimension pertains to levels of the social unit and the other to levels of time.
4. Briefly describe how the "Tragedy of the Commons" illustrates the analysis of ethical problems in terms of a matrix with levels of the social unit on one dimension and levels of time on the other dimension.
5. Briefly describe an independent example of how reinforcing and punishing consequences might conflict in a moral-ethical matrix that involves levels of the social unit on one dimension and levels of time on the other dimension.
6. Briefly describe the behavioral approach to analyzing uses of the terms ought, should, and obligation.

Chapter 16

Values, Rights, and Responsibilities

Human behavior is clearly influenced by many factors that are extended in space and time. Typically, these factors can be counted, measured, or weighed. For example, people respond to environmental cues like lights or tones that signal the availability of certain material consequences, like food when they are hungry, water when they are thirsty, warmth when they are cold, or safety when they are threatened.

In other cases, human behavior is said to be influenced by other, more abstract factors, not discretely extended in space and time. For example, humans are often said to make value judgments and be guided by them. But what exactly are values and value judgments? According to a traditional argument, values and value judgments are often explicitly held to be the type of things that are not behavioral, or indeed, part of the world of "facts." Facts are extended in space and time and can be counted, measured, or weighed. By definition, values are not held to be extended in space and time. As such, the traditional argument goes, values cannot be counted, measured, or weighed. Because human behavior is held to be influenced by values, and values are held to be not extended in space and time as facts are, the argument is that values cannot be part of a scientific analysis of any human behavior they influence. Indeed, the traditional argument takes it for granted that the analysis of any human behavior that involves scientific principles is always going to be at least incomplete, if not entirely inadequate, precisely because it cannot accommodate such things as values and value judgments. Values and value judgments are assumed to lie in another domain, beyond the domain in which behavior takes place. As a result, the traditional argument goes, human behavior needs to be analyzed in the type of terms found in philosophy or theology, rather than a natural science.

As we will see in this chapter, behavior analysts suggest the premise of the argument is incorrect. Concerns about *values*, *value judgments*, *rights*, and *responsibilities* have everything to do with the domain in which behavior takes place. A scientific analysis of human behavior is indeed possible, including those instances of behavior that are said to be influenced by values, rights, and responsibilities. How then do behavior analysts accommodate these more abstract concerns? We begin by analyzing what is at issue when people speak of values.

Values as Reinforcers

For behavior analysts, the term *value* may be understood as a summary term that identifies the type of reinforcers that are effective for a particular person (Skinner, 1971). In some cases, the reinforcers are material objects. Money, new cars or designer labels on clothes are examples. For instance, some individuals allocate a great deal of time and effort in pursuit of more money, newer cars, fancier jewelry, or more clothes with designer labels. We sometimes disparage these individuals by saying they have materialist values.

In other cases, the reinforcers are activities to which one gains access. Some examples here are recess activities at school, video games, or perhaps even some leisure activity, like engaging in a hobby. Here, we say that someone values playing golf because doing so is reinforcing. In exceptional cases, the activities might involve opportunities to help others, such as working on a community recycling project or in a soup kitchen. Here, we might say that someone has humanitarian values.

In still other cases, the reinforcers are more abstract. Social justice, world peace, freedom from poverty, and freedom from disease are four representative examples. In these cases, we say individuals value social justice when they engage in behavior that promotes equal treatment for all citizens, without regard to the color of their skin, the shape of their eyes, their ethnicity, their sexual orientation, or their religion. We say individuals value world peace when they work for it. We say individuals value prosperity when they advocate it, for example, through particular fiscal or monetary policies. We sometimes applaud these individuals by saying they have idealistic values.

Value judgments are somewhat different. They involve choice between reinforcers and the patterns of behavior they promote at the several different social and temporal contexts at which they influence our lives. We make a value judgment when we forgo some immediate tangible benefit for the sake of some longer term benefit for the larger social group, such as not purchasing an item of convenience because purchasing it contributes to degrading the environment in the long term.

We now need to elaborate on the position that values relate to reinforcers. As we discussed in Chapter 15, money is presumably the reinforcer for robbing a bank. Do we mean that bank robbing is justified, or that bank robbing is good and therefore acceptable because it is based on values? If reinforcers can be said to be what is good, is any kind of operantly reinforced behavior then to be regarded as justifiable, good, and the result of values? Obviously, to say that bank robbing is justifiable because it is reinforced operant behavior and the reinforcers are based on values is nonsense. How then can we reconcile a stance that values and what is good relate to reinforcers, with our obvious distaste for bank robbers?

When we use the term values to identify what is reinforcing, we aren't saying that what is reinforcing should be regarded as good for all persons at all times. We can usefully refer to the frame of reference as presented in Chapter 15 on ethics. Although robbing a bank may well produce reinforcers—money—for the bank robber in the short term, robbing a bank is certainly not justifiable for the robber in the long term—the robber can be caught and sent to prison. Robbing a bank is certainly not justifiable or reinforcing or a value for anybody else in the short term or in any other temporal context. Thus, robbing a bank is something that cannot be condoned because it has a harmful impact on other individuals (account-holders, the social group, the culture), regardless of the temporal context (short term, intermediate term, long term). As before, an assessment of the consequences of behavior in a frame of reference provided by the temporal context of the behavior allows a clearer understanding of what values mean, and of when it is or is not useful to subject behavior to certain contingencies designed to modify its frequency.

Rights

Hand in hand with values are rights. For example, in the Declaration of Independence in 1776, Thomas Jefferson asserted that citizens possess certain "unalienable rights, among them life, liberty, and the pursuit of happiness." These rights may be taken to represent a set of values for Caucasian males of the time. These men were seeking to form a democratic style of government as they envisioned it, even though some of them held slaves. Treatises in political philosophy have linked the emerging position to writings of the English philosopher John Locke as well as others. The issues of slaveholding and women's suffrage may well limit our appreciation of Jefferson and the generality of his assertions. Nevertheless, only a few years after the new US Constitution was adopted, 10 amendments were added. Collectively, these amendments are known as the Bill of Rights. More amendments have been added since. An important question for us is, What does the term rights mean?

For behavior analysts, the term *rights* relates to cases in which a governmental entity or individual A constrains certain practices in which individual B can engage; the constraint then evokes countercontrol from B. The "certain practices" of B that were constrained constitute "rights." As mentioned in Chapter 12, countercontrol is a generic term that roughly means resisting. The resisting can take a form ranging from simple dispute to outright revolt. It is the "push back" to the "push" of constraint. The countercontrol may be understood as negatively reinforced operant behavior. For example, humans have presumably evolved in a way that makes being subjected to tyranny, oppression, and exploitation aversive. Consequently, tyrannical exploitation of citizens by a government will bring about revolt by the citizens who will escape from the old form of government and replace it with a new form of government. History provides numerous examples. American colonists (B) began to revolt against the King George III of England (A) in 1775. French citizens (B) revolted against King Louis XVI and the French aristocracy (A) at the end of the 18th century. Russians (B) revolted against Czar Nicholas II (A) early in the 20th century.

The language of the Declaration of Independence asserted that certain classes of individuals then living in what were to become the United States had an unalienable right to life, liberty, and the pursuit of happiness. Before the Revolutionary War, these individuals had to face sanctions in the legal system without due process. After the War, they no longer had to. Before the War, these individuals had to pay taxes to a government without being represented in the legislative decisions to levy those taxes. After the War, they no longer had to. The principle here is not that A (King George III) can arbitrarily and unilaterally extort resources or privileges from B (American colonists), and then attack B when B does not provide them. That may well happen, but the situation does not appropriately involve A's rights, though monarchs customarily asserted it did. For behavior analysts, the situation does not involve rights because the attack is not a function of aversiveness brought about by any constraint of A's behavior: A has no right to extort anything from B.

Responsibility

Hand in hand with the concept of rights is that of *responsibility*. To what then does responsibility relate, according to the point of view being developed here? In some traditional accounts, such as found in various forms of philosophy, responsibility has a moral connotation derived from a system of rights and values, where those terms are viewed as having nothing to do with behavior. However, as we have seen, the terms rights and values have everything to do with behavior. So also does responsibility.

In a sense that may seem rather trivial, the term responsibility sometimes identifies simply the person who has engaged in a given form of behavior. For example, suppose the doorbell rings, and both *A* and *B* are in the room. Suppose *A* answers the door, rather than *B*. In a descriptive sense, question may be raised as to who was responsible for answering the door. This is a question in the past tense about who did answer the door. The answer is *A*, rather than *B*.

Another sense of responsibility is more involved, and doubtless more significant. Again, suppose the doorbell rings, and both *A* and *B* are in the room. In this case, suppose a competent authority has assigned *A* the task of answering the door, rather than *B*, and *A* has agreed to do so. Here, question may be raised as to who is responsible for answering the door. The question is in the present tense. As before, the answer is *A*, rather than *B*.

The contingency under which *A* answers the door in the second case differs from that of the first case, however. In the second case, recall that a competent authority charged *A* with answering the door, and *A* agreed to do so. Presumably the competent authority can administer one consequence when *A* does carry out the task ("praise") and another consequence when *A* does not ("blame"). Presumably the ability to administer these consequences has some bearing on whether *A* actually does answer the door, beyond the consequence of meeting or avoiding whoever is at the door. Thus, this sense of responsibility is about the relation between two parties: *A* and the competent authority. *A*'s agreement with the competent authority means that *A* *should* answer the door if *A* is to gain the approval or avoid the rebuke of the competent authority. The sense of "should" pertains to *A*'s behavior in relation to any reinforcing or punishing consequences the competent authority administers. Importantly, the context for the behavior involves relations in the environment, rather than some nonbehavioral (i.e., moral) principle according to which *A* is assumed to behave.

Jurisprudence

Our system of laws assumes that individuals have free will and know right from wrong as a moral issue at the time of any action. If the individuals nevertheless break the law, they are deemed responsible for their behavior, and subject to punishment by a governmental authority. Indeed, the notion of responsibility is especially likely to be invoked when contingencies of punishment are involved. Common rationales for punishment range from retribution ("an eye for an eye") to deterrence ("teach them a lesson so they won't do it again"). For example, from a standpoint that assumes free will, an individual could rationally choose to refrain from the punishable behavior, thereby avoiding the pain or inconvenience. Indeed, punishment as retribution is often predicated on an assumption of free will. Apart from questions of free will, if the goal is to reduce the rate of the punished behavior, one legitimate question is whether punishment is actually an effective procedure for doing so, when compared with such other procedures as modifying the underlying reinforcement contingencies.

A second legitimate question concerns the principle of determinism. If behavior is determined, then the individual's behavior in the first place was not the result of free will. Rather, it was the result of various causal factors that existed at the time of the behavior. For behavior analysts these causal factors are related to the environmental circumstances of the individual's life. Could the individual have done otherwise? If not, wouldn't the administration of punishment after the fact be ineffective? Are we ever justified in punishing? Doesn't any administration of punishment risk producing countercontrol, as described earlier in this chapter? These matters are complex. We can point out that a punishing consequence reduces the future probability of behavior, just as a reinforcing consequence increases it. Thus, the delivery of a punishing consequence for breaking the law reduces the probability that the individual will break the law in the future. The punishing consequence becomes part of the life history of the individual who breaks the law, presumably in a way that reduces the probability of the illegal behavior in the future. After all, the individual continues to live after engaging in the punishable behavior. In addition, the law becomes part of the culture, such that others are influenced by the delivery of punishers to the one individual. As such, the delivery of punishers to transgressors can contribute to the discriminative control of the behavior of others.

At least three other considerations are relevant when we contemplate the use of punishment. One is whether punishment is even going to be effective. For example, punishment is not ordinarily administered when an individual is judged to be "insane." However, the concept of insanity comes from legal theory, not behavioral theory. According to a traditional viewpoint, judging whether someone is insane typically turns on whether the individual has the capacity to tell morally and legally right from wrong at the time of the action. If the individual cannot distinguish what is morally and legally right from wrong at the time of the action, the action is not ordinarily punished.

For behavior analysts, it is an empirical question whether punishing the behavior of individuals who are classified as insane is going to deter their actions, in the sense of reducing the future probability of the punished behavior. If an individual's repertoire and life circumstances are so dysfunctional that the punishment will not reduce the future probability of the behavior in question, the action is not punished. This does not mean that some action should not be taken toward the individual. Perhaps the individual should be removed from contact with others in society, for the protection of all.

A second consideration is in cases where punishment is going to be effective. Will another means of reducing the probability of breaking the law be even more effective? Even when punishment is effective, that effectiveness typically comes at a cost. For example, the following are common liabilities of using punishment to control behavior:

1. Punishment is a destructive process, rather than a constructive process. In everyday language, punishment only tells an organism what not to do, rather than what to do.
2. Punishment creates hostility toward individuals who administer punishment. When was the last time we felt warm and friendly thoughts toward the individual who gave us a parking ticket?
3. Punishment justifies aversive interactions and inflicting pain. Punishment then becomes an instrument of exploitation and coercion, rather than education and instruction.
4. Punishment may only create avoidance of situations in which punishment is administered. Any reduction in the punished behavior is only an artifact of avoiding situations in which punishment can be administered, or avoiding engaging in the punished behavior when the agent delivering the punishment is present.
5. Punishment does not ordinarily change behavior in the long term unless supporting reinforcement contingencies are also changed. The punished behavior is present to be punished for a reason. The reason is that it is also being reinforced. If we seek to modify behavior, we do well to also modify the reinforcement contingencies that are simultaneously maintaining the punished behavior.
6. Punishment may evoke emotional stress and anxiety in any situation in which it is administered. As a result, punishment may disrupt many different forms of behavior, including unpunished forms, and be counterproductive in the long term.

A third consideration is the process for determining whether the punishment would be delivered. Consequences are most effective when they are delivered swiftly and with high probability after a response. However, consider the case of a crime that has been committed, and which society wants to punish. First, society needs to be sure the actual criminal has been apprehended. Second, society needs to be sure that due process is followed in a court of law. On the one hand, all of this delays the punishment, and the delay reduces its effectiveness. On the other hand, society cannot make the legitimate conviction of the guilty easier and more immediate without also making the inadvertent conviction of the innocent more likely. Most theories of jurisprudence argue for balancing individual rights against societal rights. Court decisions serve to resolve ambiguous cases by providing discriminative stimuli for future actions by society.

Summary and Conclusions

Values, value judgments, rights, and responsibilities are all behavioral matters. In particular, values concern reinforcers. Things we value are things that are reinforcing to us. Value judgments concern choice between reinforcers or patterns of behavior that particular reinforcers promote. Rights and responsibilities are matters of behaving under the influence of particular forms of social organization. Rights pertain to practices that when constrained evoke countercontrol. Responsibilities pertain to standards of conduct that when met are subject by mutual agreement to certain consequences, and when not met are subject to different consequences. The ability of a government to punish those who break laws needs to be balanced against the possibility of punishing the innocent and disrupting social cohesion. As with ethics, the full social and temporal contexts of social behavior need to be examined to understand whether that social behavior contributes to the welfare of the larger social group.

Reference

Skinner, B. F. (1971). *Beyond freedom and dignity*. New York: Knopf.

Key Terms and Concepts

values
value judgments
rights
responsibilities
materialist values
humanitarian values
idealistic values

Study Questions

1. Briefly describe the traditional distinction between facts and values.
2. For behavior analysts, to what does the term values relate?
3. For behavior analysts, what does it mean to say an individual has materialist values? Humanitarian values? Idealistic values?

4. For behavior analysts, to what does the term rights relate?
5. For behavior analysts, to what does the term responsibilities relate?
6. What is the sense of "should" that relates to behavioral contingencies?
7. According to a traditional viewpoint, what criterion is used to judge whether someone is insane?
8. Briefly describe three relevant considerations when the use of punishment is contemplated.
9. Briefly describe the six liabilities of using punishment to control behavior.

Chapter 17

Education

Education is surely one of the most important resources a culture can make available to its citizens. Unfortunately, many studies have shown that the academic accomplishments of students in the US educational system lag behind those of students in other countries. For behavior analysts, the reason is clear: Many of the educational practices in our culture seem predicated on mentalistic and ultimately counterproductive assumptions about (a) the nature of students' intellectual skills and (b) the processes of teaching and learning as they apply to the classroom. Behavior analysts offer their own viewpoint on these matters. The present chapter examines a behavior analytic viewpoint of education, and then contrasts it with a traditional viewpoint. As we will see, the chapter emphasizes a behavior analytic conception of verbal behavior, as it is central to the educational process.

A Behavior-Analytic View of the Educational Process

For behavior analysts, to teach is to facilitate learning, which is best accomplished by arranging contingencies of reinforcement that efficiently enable individuals to do things they could not do before (Skinner, 1968). In this regard, "The first step in designing instruction is to define the terminal behavior. What is the student to do as the result of having been taught?" (Skinner, 1968, pp. 199-200). Thus, in broad scope we can say that teaching starts with determining a *terminal repertoire* for a student. Determining the terminal repertoire typically involves identifying what skills and abilities the student is supposed to acquire by being exposed to the course of instruction. Once the terminal repertoire has been identified, the *beginning repertoire* of the student is assessed. What can the student currently do? The difference between the beginning and terminal repertoires is then divided into small units. Each unit is designed to move the student progressively along the path from the student's beginning repertoire to the desired terminal repertoire. The student is then exposed to the contingencies of the instructional sequence until the student masters each unit and can ultimately engage in the desired terminal behavior.

As we have seen throughout this book, contingencies involve discriminative stimuli, responses, and reinforcers. Common examples of discriminative stimuli in educational contingencies are textbooks, workbooks, outlines, notes, study guides, and objectives. Often these stimuli lead to further stimuli in the form of test questions. The responses in educational contingencies are typically the answers to the test questions. The test questions range from so-called recognition or recall questions, where the answers involve picking the correct alternative in a multiple choice or matching format, to production questions, where the answers involve filling in the blank or writing one or more paragraphs to an essay question. Reinforcing consequences are then provided for mastering each unit along the way, for example, by answering the associated test questions correctly. For students at lower grade levels, common reinforcing consequences in educational contingencies are gold stars or approval from teachers. For students at higher grade levels, common reinforcing consequences are a numerical score, say 95 points out of 100 or a letter grade correlated with accomplishment. For students in college settings, Michael (1991) identified the following as possible reinforcing consequences: (a) increasing the knowledge of subjects that are "intrinsically interesting," (b) approval from others, (c) short-term advantages such as dealing effectively with challenges in daily life outside the classroom, (d) long-term payoffs such as getting a good job, and (e) a higher course grade.

When we say above in abstract terms that our instructional sequence is designed to establish some terminal repertoire in students, what we mean in practical terms is that our instructional sequence is designed to enable students to answer particular questions correctly or to complete particular assignments accurately. The questions or assignments are so constructed as to require increasingly greater proficiency or skill as the academic term or semester progresses. We next need to ask, What are the properties of the answers according to which greater proficiency or skill are measured?

Contingencies and the Matter of Control

To be concerned with the terminal repertoire in teaching and learning is to be concerned with at least four properties of the behavior that the instructional contingencies promote (Skinner, 1968). The first property is the *topography of the response*. In other words, an answer to a test question or an assignment must be topographically correct. In addition, others must be able to identify the answer as correct when it occurs. A second is the nature of the *stimulus control over the terminal repertoire*. The desired answer must occur on the appropriate occasion. The instructional contingencies may also want to instill generalization of that answer to other, related occasions. A third concerns the *temporal or intensive properties of the response*. When appropriate, the terminal behavior must be properly timed, as in a sense of rhythm. A fourth property concerns the *maintenance of the behavior under infrequent reinforcement*. Here, we seek to have students answer questions correctly and complete assignments accurately even when naturally occurring reinforcers are intermittent. Contingencies can be arranged to generate all of these properties, and the educational process needs to take these properties into account to be effective.

To be sure, these four properties apply in different ways in different levels of teaching. No doubt topography is important in training the vocal skills associated with speaking a second language or typing at a keyboard or tightening a spark plug with a torque wrench. Perhaps with certain populations of individuals with developmental disabilities, the temporal and intensive properties of the final form of the behavior are critical. However, writing a well-organized paragraph and then organizing a series of such paragraphs into a coherent essay are not simple matters of response topography or tempo. We emphasize here the extent to which educators take known learning principles into account as they develop courses of instruction. In particular, what do behavior analysts say about how educators can usefully incorporate verbal processes in their instructional practices?

Verbal Knowledge

We examined the topic of verbal behavior in Chapter 4, and the topic of knowledge in Chapter 8. Suppose we now say that a student "knows something" or "has learned something" in a course. What exactly does such a statement mean? For behavior analysts, such a statement is usually concerned with the first two properties of responding generated by an instructional contingency: (a) the topography of the response and (b) the stimulus control over the responses said to show "knowledge." As we have noted, typically the responses in an educational setting are verbal answers to test questions. For purposes of illustration, consider the case of a student who answers a test question correctly, but who has simply copied it from an unauthorized cheat sheet that has been brought into the classroom. Ordinarily, such a student is not said to "know the answer" in any useful sense. The answer is simply a case of transcription, where the stimulus control over a verbal response is written verbal material present at the time the response is emitted. In such a case, we would probably not want to give the student credit for what appears to be a correct answer. The decision to not give the student credit is based on the assessment of the stimulus control over the student's answer. Given that an evaluation of a student's performance is linked to the assessment of stimulus control, what kinds of stimulus control are relevant to an assessment of verbal knowledge?

Tacts

In many cases, a response said to show knowledge is a tact. As reviewed in Chapter 4, a tact is a verbal response that is under the functional control of an object, event, or situation, or some property of an object, event, or situation. Tacts are fundamental and important elements of any verbal repertoire that educational contingencies seek to establish. For example, educational contingencies in chemistry seek to establish tacts that the proportion of hydrogen to oxygen in water is 2:1, and reflected in the familiar expression H_2O.

In addition, most educational systems seek to go beyond simple tacts and establish concepts. As noted in Chapter 4, concepts are special kinds of tacts. For behavior analysts, *conceptual stimulus control* occurs when there is generalization within a class of stimuli but discrimination between the class of stimuli in question and other classes of stimuli. At issue, of course, is the feature or property or set of features or properties that defines the stimulus class, such that all instances possessing that feature or property are treated as equals and distinguished from other instances that do not possess the feature or property. The stimulus class may be defined with reference to structural or physical features, to functional features, without regard to age, and so on. For example, consider the concept of chair. A chair is a thing we sit on or in, regardless of its size, when it was made, whether it has cushions, whether it has 4 legs or 3, whether it is made of wood or metal or both. Chairs are distinguished from tables, which have different features or properties.

A special kind of concept is an *abstraction*. In an abstraction, only a single feature of an event or object or property of an event or object defines the stimulus class, independently of other variables that are present. Concepts and abstractions are not easily developed because of the difficulty in overcoming control exerted by the other stimuli that are always present. To illustrate, let's consider two key terms from the technical vocabulary of behavior analysis: respondent and operant. Each of these terms is controlled by the features of an environmental relation. In the case of conditioned respondents, the relation is that between CS and US that is responsible for the response to the CS. In the case of operants, the relation is that of the response-reinforcer contingency that is responsible for the behavior. We identify a response as a respondent because of the relevant environmental relation, even though the response may be (a) our feeling of anxiety when we enter a dentist's office, or (b) our salivation to the sights and sounds correlated with a good meal. We identify a response as an operant because of the relevant environmental relation, even though the response may be (a) our pushing a button on a vending machine and getting a bottle of water when we see a panel on the vending machine is illuminated, or (b) our dog's running to the kitchen and getting fed when it hears the sound of a can opener opening its can of dog food.

Beginning students often have difficulty with the concepts of operant and respondent behavior. For instance, beginning students often identify an operant under discriminative stimulus control as a respondent, presumably because their answer is under the control of the temporal sequence of events: A conspicuous stimulus comes on, and the response follows shortly thereafter. The degree to which a response illustrates conceptual stimulus control is usually assessed by presenting a novel question with the same general feature or principle as in the original but with other differences. If the correct answer is given to a novel question, then presumably the response is under the appropriate conceptual stimulus control.

In the examples above, students sometimes mistake the dog's running to the kitchen as a respondent because of its relation to the prior stimulus of the sound of the can opener. The sound of the can opener signals the occasion upon which running will be successful in getting food. It does not elicit running. As a result, the sound of the can opener is a discriminative stimulus in an operant relation, not a conditioned stimulus in a respondent relation.

Intraverbal Control

In other cases, the response said to show knowledge is an intraverbal. An intraverbal is a verbal response that is under the functional control of another verbal stimulus, where the relation between stimulus and response is an arbitrary one established by the verbal community. As we noted in Chapter 4, in some instances, an intraverbal consists in just saying the next word in a previously acquired chain of responses. Reciting the alphabet or the Pledge of Allegiance are common examples. In other instances, an intraverbal consists in saying one word when a related word, for example, from the same class, is provided. Saying "Babe Ruth" to "baseball player" is an example. Crossword puzzles in the newspaper or quiz shows on television often involve intraverbals when one word is given and a correct response is required. In the case of intraverbal responses to test questions, presumably the intraverbal had its source in another form of verbal behavior, such as a tact. It may also have been acquired by hearing someone else say it, or by reading it. One popular instructional technique to generate intraverbals is *fluency training* (Binder, 1996), often using *SAFMEDS* ("<u>S</u>ay it <u>A</u>ll <u>F</u>ast in a <u>M</u>inute <u>E</u>very <u>D</u>ay <u>S</u>huffled"). Fluency is the goal of producing the special combination of accuracy plus speed that characterizes competent performance. SAFMEDS involves repeatedly presenting questions in different orders to students over several days (e.g., via flashcards, via a computer) and then the students' demonstrating fluency, that is, responding very quickly and accurately to the questions. In addition to establishing high rates of accurate responding, fluency training can also strengthen components of responses, allowing smaller units to be recombined into larger.

As also noted in Chapter 4, behavior analysts often distinguish between verbally regulated behavior and contingency shaped behavior. Verbally regulated behavior is operant behavior in which discriminative control or other influence comes from prior verbal stimuli. Often the prior verbal stimuli specify the contingent relation among a setting, a response, and a consequence, in the form of a *rule*. Typically, the rule is emitted as an intraverbal. In contrast, contingency shaped behavior is operant behavior in which discriminative control or other behavioral influence (e.g., through an establishing operation) does not come from prior verbal stimuli, but rather from other environmental stimuli, such as lights and tones.

The reason the distinction is important is that we need to acknowledge possible limitations of programs of instruction that simply teach rules as intraverbals. For example, verbally regulated behavior can be rigid. In a laboratory study of this rigidity, Shimoff, Catania, and Matthews (1981) arranged for college students' responding (pressing down on a telegraph key) to produce points later exchangeable for money. Initially, all participants could produce points by responding slowly. If participants responded too fast, their responding earned fewer points. Importantly, the slow responding had been established for some participants by shaping and for others by demonstration and written instructions. Then, the restriction on rate of responding was relaxed for all participants. After the low-rate restriction was relaxed, all participants could earn more money by responding fast. The responding of participants that had been shaped usually increased, in accordance with the relaxed contingency. However, the responding of participants that had been instructed usually continued at an overall low rate. The instructed responding typically continued to occur at a low rate even though these participants experienced the changed contingency and earned more money on the few occasions when they did respond faster.

In the Shimoff, Catania, and Matthews (1981) study, the responding of the instructed participants was verbally regulated by the instruction or rule they were given. The instruction continued to exert a great deal of control over the rate of responding, even though the instruction no longer applied after the low-rate restriction was relaxed and participants experienced that faster responding earned more points. It follows then that instructions can be very strong discriminative stimuli. Verbally regulated behavior may conform very rapidly to an accurate instruction or verbal rule, which makes the verbal stimulus effective in many cases. However, verbally regulated behavior may also fail to adjust when circumstances change and the original instruction or rule is no longer accurate. In this research, students typically have a lengthy history of following rules before they come to the educational environment. This history often reduces students' sensitivity to the consequences of their behavior in the current setting. These differences may be troublesome, in that students may not always be able to perform as expected across a range of situations simply because they can state a rule. An instructional program, including one developed by behavior analysts, should be aware of the extent to which it promotes intraverbals that will serve as rules, and whether this form of control is appropriate for its objectives. Presumably, one of the objectives of education is to have students be able to adjust their behavior to meet the demands of changing situations. Some forms of verbally regulated behavior may not adjust readily if the situation changes.

Some Traditional Assumptions About Students, the Educational Process, and the Role of the Instructor

We saw in Chapter 11 that according to a traditional assumptions, intelligence is an underlying "mental" characteristic that is normally distributed among the population of students, much as such physical characteristics as height or weight are normally distributed. Further, the characteristic of intelligence is assumed to be responsible for basic intellectual abilities from which overt behavior flows, though many theorists assume the underlying intelligence can influenced to some extent by practice or experience. The exact extent of the influence, and the specific kinds of practice or experience that might enhance or limit intelligence, are of considerable debate.

In addition, a common traditional assumption in educational settings is that students develop according to a maturational unfolding of their abilities. The unfolding is often taken to follow a *stage theory*, according to which students are said to possess a set of *cognitive structures* during each stage. The set of cognitive structures possessed at each stage defines what students can and cannot do. Students progress to the next stage when they have achieved a state of maturational "readiness." If an instructor tries to accelerate their readiness, the effects can be counterproductive for both student and instructor. The instructor is obliged to wait until the student is ready and not intervene except in ways that will draw on the cognitive structures that are presumed to have already emerged.

According to traditional assumptions, education is in large measure a screening process, and the instructor is essentially a gatekeeper. In the screening process, the instructor asks questions, and then measures the quality of students' answers. The quality of the answers is assumed to be normally distributed among the population of students, in a reflection of the way that underlying intellectual abilities are distributed among the students. The job of the instructor is to rank the students, based on the quality of their answers. The instructor picks those students who through their readiness have best shown an ability to provide high quality answers (i.e., those from the higher end of a normal distribution), and turns back those who are not ready (i.e., those from the lower end of a normal distribution). Because the students' underlying abilities are assumed to be normally distributed, the traditional assumption is that students' academic grades should similarly be normally distributed.

Evaluation of traditional educational practices is largely concerned with determining whether instructors are making what are called *type I* or *type II* errors. Instructors make type I errors, also called false positives, when they let students through the gate who should not have been let through. The instructor mistakenly infers students have the right underlying mental abilities, when they really don't. Instructors make type II errors, also called false negatives, when they do not let students through the gate who should in fact have been let through. The instructor mistakenly infers students do not have the right underlying mental abilities, when they really do. Debates about evaluation typically focus on the validity of the evidence for making the correct inferences about students. Accordingly, traditional education is greatly concerned with population statistics, individual differences, probability sampling, etc., to be sure instructors have not made a type I or type II error in their attributions about a student's underlying mental abilities. As the probability of type I errors is reduced, the probability of type II errors is increased, and vice versa. A casual review of recent social history suggests that societal emphasis shifted during the social and cultural changes of the 1960s and 1970s from minimizing type I errors to minimizing type II errors.

Behavior analysts make no internal attributions about students comparable to those of the traditional view. Indeed, behavior analysts regard traditional assumptions, such as those about intelligence from which instructional practices follow, as counterproductive. In this regard, behavior analysts might say that "the student is always right" to emphasize that the student is always responding because of one contingency or another, rather than because of some supposedly faulty mental or cognitive process. If a student does not respond in the desired way, then one thing the instructor can do is look at the contingencies that have been arranged, rather than blame the student's lack of abilities.

Concepts, Collateral Responses, and Equivalence Classes

To be sure, an educated student should also be able to engage in "collateral responses." Collateral responses are those that arise throughout the educational process, even though they may not have been directly instructed. Previously in this chapter we used a student's concrete answers to concrete test questions to illustrate the student's knowledge. A moment's reflection suggests that knowledge often consists of the development and understanding of higher-order concepts and abstract relations, beyond the recitation of names, dates, facts, and figures.

Although written from a traditional mentalistic rather than a behavior-analytic perspective, the widely recognized taxonomy of educational objectives in Bloom et al. (1956) constitutes an analysis of the terminal repertoires that a program of instruction might reasonably seek to instill in a student. This taxonomy includes three overlapping domains of learning: cognitive, affective, and psychomotor. The relations among the repertoires in those domains is highly relevant to the question of collateral responses.

In this chapter, we focus on the domain of so-called cognitive learning. This sort of learning is demonstrated by recall and associated intellectual skills: comprehending information, organizing ideas, analyzing and synthesizing data, applying knowledge, choosing among alternatives in problem-solving, and evaluating ideas or actions. This domain is predominant in the majority of academic courses.

Bloom and colleagues identified six levels within the cognitive domain. These levels are listed below. At the lowest level is the simple recall or recognition of facts. At the highest level are more complex activities, such as analyzing, synthesizing, and evaluating ideas. Examples of verbs that represent the intellectual activity associated each level are also listed.

1. Knowledge: Stating specific facts, ways and means of dealing with specifics (conventions, trends and sequences, classifications and categories, criteria, methodology), universals and abstractions in a field (principles and generalizations, theories and structures). Representative verbs are arrange, define, duplicate, label, list, memorize, name, order, recognize, relate, recall, repeat, reproduce, state.
2. Comprehension: Grasping the significance of instructional materials. Representative verbs are classify, describe, discuss, explain, express, identify, indicate, locate, recognize, report, restate, review, select, translate.
3. Application: Using previously learned information in new and concrete situations to solve problems that have single or best answers. Representative verbs are apply, choose, demonstrate, dramatize, employ, illustrate, interpret, operate, practice, schedule, sketch, solve, use, write.
4. Analysis: Breaking down informational materials into their component parts, examining (and trying to understand the organizational structure of) such information to develop divergent conclusions by identifying motives or causes, making inferences, and/or finding evidence to support generalizations. Representative verbs are analyze, appraise, calculate, categorize, compare, contrast, criticize, differentiate, discriminate, distinguish, examine, experiment, question, test.
5. Synthesis: Creatively or divergently applying prior knowledge and skills to produce a new or original whole. Representative verbs are arrange, assemble, collect, compose, construct, create, design, develop, formulate, manage, organize, plan, prepare, propose, set up, write.
6. Evaluation: Judging the value of material based on personal values/opinions, resulting in an end product, with a given purpose, without real right or wrong answers. Representative verbs are appraise, argue, assess, attach, choose, compare, defend, estimate, judge, predict, rate, core, select, support, value, evaluate.

Let us now consider the application of the classification called "cognitive learning" to the case of an individual who is said to "know the meaning of a term." For example, at the end of an instructional program designed to teach a student the meaning of a term, the student should presumably be able to correctly respond in the various situations below, illustrating the levels in Bloom et al. (1956):

1. Select a definition that fits the term
2. Select a term that fits the definition
3. State a synonym of the term
4. State an antonym of the term
5. Match the term with an appropriate synonym
6. Match the term with an appropriate antonym
7. Choose a picture that represents the term
8. State the principle that fits the term
9. State the similarities between the term in question and a second term
10. State the differences between the term in question and a second term
11. Choose the best meaning of the term when it is used in a sentence

These objectives emphasize that understanding the meaning of a term is cast in more than just the recitation of a definition as an intraverbal. Those who are said to know the meaning of a term can also engage in variety of *collateral responses*.

How would a behavior analyst specify the nature of these collateral responses in terms of contingencies? At issue here is the establishment of *equivalence relations*, as reviewed in Chapter 4, often supplemented by conceptual stimulus control. Consider instruction designed to teach students the distinction mentioned earlier between operants and respondents. Suppose an instructor poses two or three examples during class discussions and asks students to identify by a show of hands whether the example is of operant or respondent behavior. Suppose the instructor then asks students on a quiz question to provide an example of one or the other. Students might well provide a "correct" example, but only because they memorized and recited back one of the examples the instructor used. Many instructors would be satisfied that their students had learned the difference, but the students might not have: The answer might be based on simple intraverbals, rather than on "understanding the concept."

A more useful strategy would be for an instructor to ask the students to identify whether a description of a novel behavioral event (i.e., one that the instructor did not discuss in class) was an instance of operant or respondent behavior. Then, other questions would ask students to describe an instance of their own operant or respondent behavior, and as part of their answer, to identify the discriminative stimulus if they were describing operant behavior or the conditioned stimulus if they were describing respondent behavior. In such alternative situations, the students whose earlier answers were intraverbals might not give a correct answer on their one and only try on the quiz question, because there is no intraverbal basis for the answer. The correct answer is a function of complex conceptual stimulus control, equivalence relations, and collateral responses. Presumably, the worthwhile and enduring educational practices are those that implement the necessary kinds of instructional experiences to establish complex stimulus control beyond intraverbal control.

Behavior-Analytic Assessment

Of particular concern for present purposes is assessing the nature of stimulus control over the response said to show knowledge. In most instances, assessing the nature of stimulus control involves assessing the extent to which (a) thematically related collateral verbal behavior, which goes beyond intraverbals, is part of a student's repertoire; and (b) verbal behavior is discriminative for subsequent nonverbal behavior.

The first matter can be assessed by determining generalization, or perhaps the establishment of equivalence relations. Often it is a simple matter of asking a given question in two or three different ways. Perhaps a student could be taught to identify instances of a concept on the basis of spoken, visual, and written stimuli. The relevant question is whether procedures are in effect in instructional programs that seek to determine whether the response is based on conceptual stimulus control, such that it reflects generalization of an abstract principle.

The second matter can be assessed by setting up situations in which a student's nonverbal behavior is discriminative for verbal, and vice versa. Consider the issue of shaping via differential reinforcement of successive approximations. For example, suppose a student can state the principles of shaping in the classroom but outside the classroom cannot actually teach his or her pet dog to sit or stand on its hind legs on command. Alternatively, suppose a student can shape those repertoires quite well but cannot state the principles of shaping.

The student might first receive instruction on how to state what is involved in shaping a target response, such as teaching a dog to sit on command. As part of this instruction, the student might also compose some verbal material indicating what will be done. Videos of other cases of shaping might also be employed. The student would then have to actually shape sitting on command, as well as another response that was not previously in the animal's repertoire. Finally, the student would have to describe how the process of shaping was actually carried out, and the student would compare the first description with the second. The literature regarding correspondence between "saying" and "doing" is voluminous, but presumably discriminative control by self-descriptive verbal behavior is an important part of the educational process, for generating self-knowledge as well as self-management.

What then about students' grades? A common practice is to establish *educational objectives* for a program of instruction. If the objectives take the form of a progressive sequence, the last set of objectives specifies the terminal repertoire the program is designed to achieve. *Letter or numerical grades* are conventional measures used to indicate what percentage of the required terminal repertoire has been achieved by the end of the instructional period. If a student does not receive a passing grade, the teacher is certifying that the student does not have some minimal percentage of the terminal repertoire. As the grade is progressively higher than minimal, the teacher is certifying that the student has a progressively higher than minimal percentage of the terminal repertoire. The important issue is whether students who complete a course with a given grade actually have a terminal repertoire that is commensurate with that grade.

Summary and Conclusions

For behavior analysts, education involves arranging contingencies that facilitate learning. Typically the learning is verbal, as in answering test questions. Behavior analysts argue that in many cases it is useful to define what is to be learned before the process begins, in terms of the objectives of the educational process. An important outcome of the learning process is not simply a rote, intraverbal response, but rather the development of stimulus control that promotes collateral responses in slightly different but nevertheless appropriate situations. The terms concepts, abstractions, and equivalence classes are relevant to this kind of stimulus control. Behavior analysts avoid making internal attributions about the supposed underlying abilities of students, which means behavior analysts do not see themselves as gatekeepers in the educational process. Rather, they look to the contingencies of the learning situation to understand why learning has or has not taken place. If a student's behavior has not changed, it is incumbent on an instructor to determine why, and then take corrective action insofar as such action is possible.

References

Binder, C. (1996). Behavioral fluency: Evolution of a new paradigm. *The Behavior Analyst, 19*, 163-197.
Bloom, B. S., Englehart, M. D., Furst, E. J., Hill, W. H., & Kratwohl, D. R. (1956). *A taxonomy of educational objectives*. New York: David Mackay.
Michael, J. (1991). A behavioral perspective on college teaching. *The Behavior Analyst, 14*, 229-239.
Shimoff, E., Catania, A. C., & Matthews, B. A. (1981). Uninstructed human responding: Sensitivity of low-rate performance to schedule contingencies. *Journal of the Experimental Analysis of Behavior, 36*, 207-220.
Skinner, B. F. (1968). *The technology of teaching*. New York: Appleton-Century-Crofts.

Key terms and concepts

teaching
terminal repertoire
beginning repertoire
topography of the response
stimulus control over the final repertoire
temporal or intensive properties of the response
maintenance of the behavior under infrequent reinforcement
conceptual stimulus control
abstraction
stage theory
cognitive structures
type I error
type II error
collateral responses
equivalence relations
educational objectives
letter or numerical grades

Study questions

1. For behavior analysts, what is teaching?
2. What is the first step in designing instruction?
3. What are five potential reinforcing consequences that Michael (1991) identified for college students?
4. What are four important elements of the terminal repertoires promoted by educational

contingencies that Skinner (1968) identified?
5. For behavior analysts, what does it mean to say that a student "knows something" or "has learned something" in a course?
6. Briefly describe what behavior analysts mean by fluency training and SAFMEDS.
7. What does the verbal stimulus called a rule often specify?
8. Briefly describe how Shimoff, Catania, and Matthews (1981) studied the effect of rules and instructions on operant behavior.
9. For behavior analysts, when does conceptual stimulus control exist?
10. Why are concepts and abstractions not easily developed?
11. Why might beginning students in behavior analysis have difficulty with the concepts of respondent and operant behavior?
12. Briefly describe the 6 levels of learning in the cognitive domain, according to Bloom et al. (1956)?
13. At the end of an instructional program designed to teach a student the meaning of a term, name any 6 of the 11 things a student should be able to do, according to Bloom et al. (1956)?
14. What is meant by the term collateral responses?
15. How are equivalence relations important in the educational process?
16. For behavior analysts, why is it important that students who complete a course with a given grade actually have a terminal repertoire that is commensurate with that grade?

Chapter 18

Societies and Cultures

A culture may be understood as the total material, social, and behavioral context of a group of people who live and work at a particular time and in a particular place. Of special concern to behavior analysts are cultural practices. For behavior analysts, cultural practices may be viewed as continually evolving, just as other forms of behavior evolve. Hence, the study of behavior is directly relevant to the study and functioning of a culture and its practices.

Three Levels of Selection

We saw in Chapter 3 that the principle of selection may be meaningfully applied to the study of behavior. It is now useful for us to expand our review of the ways in which behavior is selected. Behavior analysts suggest that behavior is selected at three levels: *phylogenic*, *ontogenic*, and *cultural*. Selection at the phylogenic level takes place during the evolutionary history of the species. These instances of behavior are selected through their contribution to survival. The result is a repertoire of innate behavior. Innate behavior by definition is relatively invariant with respect to the environment. If a large proportion of the an organism's repertoire consists of innate behavior, the organism is likely to be in good stead so long as the environment doesn't change in significant ways. However, if the environment does change in significant ways, the organism's relatively inflexible repertoire is likely to be ineffective, and the organism probably won't be able to adapt and survive. Like other species, humans have many forms of innate behavior. For example, we salivate to food, and our hearts race when we are startled by lightning and thunder. The sucking reflex is crucial to an infant's thriving. The blinking reflex protects and maintains the cornea. However, as important as innate behavior is, including to humans, the fact remains that organisms do adapt to changing environments and survive. That is, their behavior changes as a function of the many different events and circumstances they experience during their lifetimes. These behavioral changes highlight the role of selection at the ontogenic level.

Selection of behavior at the ontogenic level takes place during the lifetime of the individual organism. This form of behavior is made possible by a nervous system that changes as the organism interacts with the environment. Worth noting is that the ability of the nervous system to be changed through its interactions with the environment and to bring about concomitant changes in behavior is itself a product of phylogenic selection. Ontogenic selection results in a repertoire of operant behavior, as we saw in Chapter 3. Operant behavior affords a great deal more flexibility to organisms as they interact with the environment. Humans have an extensive repertoire of operant behavior, and we have reviewed the fundamental importance of operant processes throughout this book.

To be sure, an important part of the environment with which we interact as humans is our culture. Selection of behavior at the cultural level takes place at a grander scale, and is the focus of the present chapter. Except for hermits, most humans live in social groups. As they live together, humans have developed certain practices for dealing with various aspects of their lives. For example, we have developed certain practices related to hunting, gathering food, preparing food, disposing of waste, raising offspring, securing shelter from the elements, and so on. In addition, these practices are transmitted throughout the group as group members interact socially. Verbal behavior is an important means for transmitting these practices. The practices, the way they are transmitted in the group, and the overall context in which they develop constitute the culture of the group.

Cultural Practices

We may then view the group as analogous to an individual organism, and the cultural practices of the group as analogous to the operant repertoire of the organism. Just as the environment selects the operant behavior of an individual organism, so also does the environment select the practices of a group, as a part of its culture. In a given environment, if the group engages in practices that allow it to deal effectively with the environmental challenges it faces, the group will survive. Its practices are then perpetuated in future generations of the group, in a process analogous to operant reinforcement. If a group engages in practices that don't contribute to its welfare, the group is at considerable risk. It and its practices may not survive, in a process analogous to operant extinction.

Moore (2008) used an example of hunting to illustrate how cultural practices might evolve. Suppose one hunter in a group learned to approach prey from the west. Although that hunter was sometimes successful, some prey escaped to the east. Now suppose another hunter learned to approach prey from the east. Although that second hunter was also sometimes successful, some of those prey escaped to the west. A moment's reflection indicates that if the two hunters worked together, they could achieve much more than if they worked independently. As a result, a particular form of cooperative hunting might evolve as a cultural practice, through its contribution to group welfare.

Our review of cultural practices applies to a group that lives in a given time, at a given place, and under a given set of environmental circumstances. Let's consider what happens to the group if there are changes in the circumstances of the group's lives. We can start by noting that humans, like other organisms, have evolved in ways that make them especially susceptible to certain features of their environment. For example, consider what we eat. Most of us are aware we are susceptible to the reinforcing influence of sweet tasting foods or food with a high caloric content. For much of our history, humans did not exist in a land of plenty. Under these circumstances, this susceptibility served us well. This susceptibility was presumably the result of phylogenic selection in our evolutionary past. The fruit that tasted sweet provided energy and many nutrients. A diet favoring food items with a high caloric content was adaptive because the items provided a good return when balanced against the cost of obtaining them, particularly when the next meal was uncertain. Thus, organisms whose behavior was susceptible to the strong reinforcing influence of these foods would quite reasonably have an advantage during natural selection and survive.

Now, however, environmental circumstances have changed for many people, such as those who live in the industrialized countries of Europe and North America. Nonetheless, we continue to like and be reinforced by food that tastes sweet or has a high caloric content, just as we did tens or hundreds of thousands of years ago. To get food that tastes sweet, we once had expend energy by climbing trees to pick fruit. We no longer have to do so. We just open a cupboard door and pick something from the shelf that contains large amounts of refined white sugar or high fructose corn syrup. To get food with a high caloric content we just super-size our order of French fried potatoes. The result is that we develop tooth decay and gain weight, and then wonder why. The circumstances of our lives have changed over time. However, the susceptibility of our behavior to its formerly adaptive consequences has not changed, and it no longer serves us well. Of course, we are aware that many people living in many parts of the Earth are at risk from starvation and poverty. For them, food that tastes sweet or that has a high caloric content is certainly not the problem that it is for people of industrialized countries. Indeed, it might well save lives. The point of the present analysis is that different environmental circumstances yield different outcomes.

Humans and other organisms are also especially susceptible to the reinforcing effect of immediate consequences. That is, humans and other organisms seem to have been selected to respond to a great extent based on how quickly things happen in their lives. We are less sensitive to larger scope measures of how things happen, such as overall rate measures. As noted above, a susceptibility to immediate consequences was presumably beneficial as humans evolved during evolutionary time. Often the time at which our next meal or next drink of water would be available was uncertain. It would then be advantageous if a form of behavior was strengthened when it resulted in immediate food or water, and thus predominated over other forms of behavior whose consequences were remote in time. Indeed, there might not even be a next time for the behavior to be strengthened if the food or water were not available in the future to exert a reinforcing influence.

The analogy to Darwinian natural selection suggests that cultural practices have evolved in ways that manifest the disproportionate importance of relatively immediate outcomes, just as have forms of individual behavior. For example, suppose we encourage agricultural practices in the culture that maximize annual harvests. Are we paying sufficient attention to crop rotation and how the soil is affected? Suppose we encourage harvesting fish or wildlife in the culture? Are we paying sufficient attention to whether we are depleting the stock? Suppose we encourage cutting down trees for the immediate use of their wood for lumber in the culture. Are we paying sufficient attention to whether we have planted new trees to replace the ones we cut down? Suppose we routinely inject antibiotics into the animals we raise in our culture, so that they grow larger. Are we paying sufficient attention to whether the antibiotics are inadvertently selecting pathogens that are resistant to the antibiotics? In each of the above cases, and no doubt many others, our susceptibility to securing relatively immediate outcomes has resulted in certain practices that may have a deferred but harmful consequence.

The point is that our environments have now changed. As compared with our ancestral past, many humans now live in a land that offers ready access to food. However, we still have our susceptibility to sweet foods, foods with a high caloric content, and immediate outcomes. As a result, obesity and short-sightedness have become problems. These are not failures, but rather unfortunate by-products of relations that previously contributed to our adaptive success. The important consideration is whether we recognize that our practices need to change as our environment has changed.

A final point in regard to cultural practices concerns the concept of memes. Dawkins (1976) suggested the concept of memes to explain the transmission of cultural practices within a group. Memes are hidden replicators, analogous to genes, only with regard to cultural practices, rather than morphology and individual behavior. Memes have been defined in a variety of ways. Popular definitions typically appeal to the underlying representation of information as found in the beliefs and concepts that prevail in a culture. In the sense memes bear the same relation to minds that genes do to brains. According to this sense, practices spread within a culture because the minds of the members of the group are shaped by the common ways of thinking that have developed in the culture—by memes. Practices differ between cultures because the cultures have different memes. The concept of memes has proved controversial because of its mentalistic connotations: Memes are held to be something from a nonbehavioral domain such as the mental or cognitive that causes behavior. As a rule, behavior analysts are opposed to mentalism, and look askance at memes. Behavior analysts obviously recognize that practices may be similar within a culture but differ between cultures. However, behavior analysts explain the similarities and differences in terms of contingencies. Practices may well be similar within a group because the members of the group experience similar contingencies in their common environment, not because entities called memes from another domain have shaped their minds. Practices may well differ between cultures because those cultures exist in different environments and the contingencies associated with those environments have selected different practices, not because different memes have shaped their minds.

Evolution of a Culture

We can see that groups are continuously faced with evolutionary challenges as their environments change over time, just as individual organisms are continuously faced with evolutionary challenges as their environments change over time. Importantly, given that environments change over time, a critical feature of a culture is that the group continually assesses whether its practices need revision. A group that does not promote concern among its members about whether its ongoing practices are contributing to the welfare of the group, particularly as that welfare is measured over the long term, risks not surviving. Indeed, promoting such a concern would be an important element of educating future generations in the group. If the group does not educate its members to assess its practices, then so much the worse for it. It may not survive. If it does not survive, no one need worry further about its practices, as there will be no group to engage in any of the questionable practices.

A familiar distinction relating to the orientation of cultures is collectivism versus individualism. To put the matter simply, a *collectivist culture* puts the welfare of the group ahead of the welfare of the single individual. Some Asian cultures are often cited as examples of collectivist cultures. An *individualist culture* puts the welfare of the single individual ahead of the welfare of the group. Some industrialized Western European and North American cultures are often cited as examples of individualist cultures.

Our discussion here should not be taken to imply that one orientation is necessarily better than the other. For example, if a culture leaned heavily toward the collectivist orientation, in one set of environmental circumstances that culture might thrive. In another set, that culture might disregard the individual processes and exploit its individual members, ultimately evoking countercontrol and social instability. Alternatively, if a culture leaned heavily toward the individualist orientation, in one set of environmental circumstances that culture might thrive. In another set, individual members might pursue their own selfish agendas, to the exclusion of what others are doing, and that culture might ultimately be in peril when the welfare of the group is disregarded.

The "Tragedy of the Commons," reviewed in Chapter 15, is a suitable example. To review, suppose a group of families share a pasture (a commons) in which animals may graze. Next, suppose that one family disproportionately increases the number of animals it puts into the pasture. That family is obviously better off in the near term with a larger number of grazing animals. However, what happens if other families, seeing the benefit that accrues to the first family, also increase the number of animals they put into the pasture? If they do so, then putting so many grazing animals in the pasture may deplete it to such an extent that soon, no family will be able to graze any animals because there is no grass upon which to graze; it had all been eaten and will not grow back. The result is that all families suffer in the long term. Therefore, it is of immense benefit for the culture to educate it members about the possibilities of such difficulties and institute practices that prevent problems from developing. As we have identified, the culture that doesn't educate its members and promote preventive practices risks not surviving.

Design of a Culture

In an interesting and important sense, a culture is a grand experiment in living. Experiments have participants, and they have independent and dependent variables. The participants in the grand experiment are the members of the culture. The independent variables are the cultural practices and their consequences, as considered over the near and long term. The dependent variable is the welfare if not the very survival of the culture. As we have seen, the practices of a culture arise in response to the demands of the environment. With any luck, the practices contribute to the welfare of the culture. However, if the environment changes, a culture needs to have educated a sufficient number of its members to be alert to whether its practices will continue to serve it well.

An example from contemporary life may illustrate the problem. Let us say that 150 years ago, the use of fossil fuels as an energy source was not especially harmful. The fossil fuels were cheap, readily available, and efficient. They may not have been used extensively, and the otherwise harmful by-products that were a result of their use at a given level could be absorbed by the environment without significant harmful effect, as measured by acid rain, air pollution, and so on. In short, there were obvious near-term benefits associated with fossil fuels as an energy resource.

However, as the population increased, the use of fossil fuels also increased. The harmful by-products increased in the environment, and the ability of the environment to absorb the by-products decreased. Thus, we have acid rain. We have air pollution in the form of smog and particulates. We have the emission of greenhouse gases that lead to global warming and acidification of the oceans. In the near term, the availability of cheap, readily available, and efficient energy may have seemed like a good idea, in that it supported cultural growth and the welfare of group members. In the long term, however, that growth was invoking a hidden environmental cost. The cultural practices that promoted fossil fuels as an energy source were not contributing to the long-term welfare of the culture. If anything, the practices were compromising the long-term welfare of the culture through pollution of the environment. Regrettably, because the immediate near-term outcomes were beneficial, even though the long-term outcomes were not, the practices grew to become strong. The practices need to be re-examined, to determine whether they serve the long-term welfare of the culture.

Democracy

What then is a recommended form of government? On the one hand, clearly some oligarchy or form of tyranny cannot be recommended. History readily shows that tyrants will engage in exploitive practices that are detrimental to the long-term welfare of the culture. On the other hand, government through some form of uninformed plebiscite may not be helpful either, as the risk is great that many practices will have only an immediate, rather than a long-term beneficial outcome.

The ancient Greek philosopher Plato proposed one form of government in his book *The Republic*. In this book, certain individuals were trained to govern the others. Various other books have written about utopias, or ideal communities. Skinner (1948) wrote about his version of such a community in a book called *Walden Two*. This community was based on behavioral principles, and incorporated some features of the *Republic*, namely the possibility that some would be trained to contribute by governing based on the contingencies established by the community.

The possibilities for utopian governments in modern life are remote, and perhaps justifiably so. Rather, most relatively stable forms of government in recent times appear to involve representative or parliamentary democracy. Why have democracies largely survived and been more stable than other forms of government? The most reasonable answer is that they maximize countercontrol through diversification. That is, democracies arrange a system of contingencies that interlock the behavior of those who govern and the behavior of those who are governed. In other words, successful forms of government employ vast systems of checks and balances. The individuals who govern are elected and serve with the consent of the governed. If they engage in questionable behavior, they are recalled, prosecuted legally, or at least not re-elected. If they attempt to tyrannize, they are removed from power, forcefully and sometimes at great cost, but removed nonetheless. If they promote policies that contribute to the long-term welfare of the group as a whole, they are re-elected.

We have seen that the behavior of organisms is strongly influenced by near-term relations, even when behavior more responsive to long-term relations would be better. Governments are no different, even democratically elected governments. For example, consider governments that engage in deficit spending. Although this practice has the potential to promote long-term growth, governments seem to engage in deficit spending more because of the near term benefit—politicians can deliver immediate benefits to their constituents. These politicians are then more likely to be re-elected. As a result, politicians compete with each other to have a central authority like the federal government pay for various kinds of projects in their districts. However, this practice also has long term liabilities. Fist, there can be inflation. Second, sooner or later, the money that is borrowed has to be re-paid, with interest. By way of summary, the following conclusions seem appropriate. When it comes to governing, the political left clearly understands the effects of positive reinforcers rather than aversive stimuli, though less so the importance of contingencies. The political right clearly understands the importance of contingencies, though less so contingencies involving positive reinforcers than aversive stimuli. The dysfunction that is seen at various current levels of government is not surprising.

Summary and Conclusions

What is relevant to the social contingencies involved in making government work is making the underlying contingencies contribute to the welfare of the culture. To be sure, the checks and balances afforded by countercontrol need to be in place. Citizens need to participate in the processes according to which their governments carry out the business of governing. In particular, citizens need to become informed about threats to the culture, and then to elect leaders who are sufficiently informed about those threats and who mobilize cultural resources to combat those threats. At present, it appears that the challenges to such processes come from the size of the governmental unit. As the size increases, so also does the remoteness of the contingencies that need to be maintained. As the remoteness of the contingencies increases, their effectiveness decreases. Citizens need to be in direct contact with the positive effects that their governments have in their lives. The fundamental challenge for a government is to ensure this direct contact, and the contingencies with which this contact is correlated, are maintained as the size of the government increases. Just as the appreciation of other concerns in our daily life can be enhanced by taking a behavioral point of view, so also can the appreciation of the processes according to which we view our culture and by which we govern ourselves.

References

Dawkins, R. (1976). *The selfish gene*. Oxford: Oxford University Press.
Moore, J. (2008). *Conceptual foundations of radical behaviorism*. Cornwall-on-Hudson, NY: Sloan.
Skinner, B. F. (1948). *Walden Two*. Indianapolis: Hackett.

Key Terms and Concepts

culture
phylogenic level of selection
ontogenic level of selection
cultural level of selection
collectivist culture
individualist culture
memes

Study Questions

1. Briefly describe what it means for behavior to be selected at the phylogenic, ontogenic, and cultural levels.
2. How are the principles of reinforcement and extinction relevant to the study of cultural practices?
3. Briefly describe how it may have been advantageous during evolutionary time for humans to be selected for a susceptibility to the reinforcing effect of food that tasted sweet or had a high caloric content.
4. Briefly describe how it may have been advantageous during evolutionary time for humans to develop a susceptibility to the immediacy of reinforcers, rather than their overall rate.
5. Briefly describe a situation in which our susceptibility to securing immediate outcomes has resulted in certain practices that may have a deferred but harmful consequence.
6. Briefly describe why it is important for a group to promote concern among its members about whether its ongoing practices are contributing to the welfare of the group, particularly as that welfare is measured over the long term.
7. Who are the participants, and what are the independent and dependent variables in the design of a culture?
8. What is the advantage of forms of government based on representative, participatory democracy?

Chapter 19

Conclusions

We have now explored quite a number of topics from a behavioral point of view. We began by arguing that behavior analysis is an empirical science of behavior. In this regard, behavior analysts call for data-based decisions about whether a clinical treatment program, a business practice, a personnel decision, a government policy, or even just an idea that is translated into action is effective. Ignoring data (or even failing to gather data) when we make decisions risks ineffectiveness and even injustice, for it means that the decision is made on the basis of unrecognized and often irrelevant criteria, such as whim or personal prejudice. Clients may waste time and resources by following recommendations about ineffective rather than empirically supported interventions, employees may be promoted for their friendliness to their boss rather than skills and productivity, and so on. Such decisions often lead to very unfortunate consequences. The point is that those who don't attend to how decisions are made and the consequences of those decisions often end up considerably disadvantaged.

Empiricism is sometimes disparaged in contemporary society. For example, many critics argue that empiricism is restrictive and ignores the unobservable features of human life that make us uniquely human, such as our thoughts and aspirations, or our desires and emotions. Therefore, it cannot possibly be an appropriate orientation for understanding human behavior. Behavior analysts surely agree that people think about the future, aspire to higher things, desire world peace, or feel elated or depressed about their stock market portfolios. Behavior analysts also recognize that some of these terms may relate to events that are unobservable from the vantage point of another person. Behavior analysts ask how such cases might be accommodated in a naturalistic science of behavior, rather than ruled out of consideration. For behavior analysts, nothing needs to be ignored, or even pursued in different disciplines. Rather, these terms relate to natural occurrences as individuals interact with their environment. Of course, when these terms are taken to refer to events in a different domain, say a mental or cognitive domain, which need to be talked about in mental or cognitive terms, then behavior analysts do become concerned about the talk, and question both its source and its usefulness.

Sciences further assume that the world is an orderly place, and that orderly relations may be found in the subject matter a science investigates. As we have seen, behavior analysis is a science of behavior, so behavior analysts quite naturally assume that behavioral events are orderly with respect to environmental circumstances, and that these events are just as orderly as the physical events that physicists study, the chemical events that chemists study, or the biological events that biologists study. However, an assumption that behavior is orderly with respect to environmental circumstances often runs counter to many of the traditions of Western culture, such as those found in politics, religion, and jurisprudence. For example, the traditions of Western culture take it for granted that humans have free will, or that their behavior is so complex that it simply does not lend itself to deterministic analyses. There is no way to conduct an experiment that would prove or disprove these traditions. Rather, we have to rely on the weight of the evidence. Comparable traditions have existed in other sciences. In the area of physics, Aristotle believed that objects accelerate as they fall because they are becoming happier to be reunited with Earth. In the area of anatomy, some believed that objects were alive because they were believed to possess a vital life spirit. Indeed, the root word of spirit comes from breathing, as in respiration. We revisit this usage every time we say individuals are inspired when they do something ingenious, or that they have expired when they die. In the area of medicine, flies and vermin were assumed to generate spontaneously from trash and refuse and cause disease.

The point is that all these explanations have given way to explanations that involve more naturalistic principles. As we learn more and more about behavior, we learn that it is an extraordinarily complex subject matter, with extraordinarily complex causes. Nevertheless, it still surrenders to scientific analyses. That the causes of behavior are complex doesn't mean behavior is uncaused. Rather, it means that we must analyze behavioral events more closely to understand those complex causes.

Humans are sometimes said to have existential crises, to face meaninglessness in their lives, and to be adrift. Clearly there are many ways to conceptualize and speak about such states of affairs. For behavior analysts, what is being talked about is the disconnect between behavior and its consequences. Behavior has meaning when it produces adaptive consequences. The question of meaninglessness is concerned with behavior that lacks adaptive consequences. Events happen and nothing can be done to avoid or escape them. Perhaps an opportunity exists to gain something positive, but nothing we know how to do has the desired positive consequences. Perhaps an opportunity exists to avoid something negative, but nothing we know how to do avoids the negative event.

We need not fear that a natural science approach changes anything about the human condition (Sidman, 2001). Statements about events do not change the events themselves. Unfortunately, however, statements may facilitate or sometimes interfere with our coming to better understand those events. Whether we are aware of it or not, or whether we like it or not, something causes human behavior. Behavior analysts did not invent the causes of behavior, any more than physics invented gravity or biology invented photosynthesis. One role of a science is to clarify the orderliness of the causes with which it is concerned. Ultimately, the question for behavior analysts is similar to asking ourselves whether making a grocery list helps us to remember what to buy at the market, or setting an alarm clock helps us to get up at some desired time in the morning. We act to control our environment by making a grocery list that will guide our purchases at the market, or by setting an alarm that will awaken us at a desired time, and our lives are ultimately better as a result. So would it be in the larger context. We act to manage our behavior in the area of education or global warming or pollution, and our lives can ultimately be better as a result. We can start by discarding appeals to causes of our behavior that supposedly reside in other domains. In place of such causes, we can identify circumstances and events in the environment in which we live. The aim is to live a life free from deprivation and want, and to maximize our potential as humans. We are free when we are not subject to the constraints imposed by negative events in our lives, and can gain the most from positive events. As we noted in Chapter 5, we aren't free when we go to the library but can't read, nor are we free when we go to the seashore but can't swim.

Clearly, a genuinely scientific view of human nature offers exciting and rich possibilities for us to achieve our full potential. We have not yet seen what we can make of ourselves, perhaps because our science of behavior is not yet behavioristic enough. In principle, as our science of behavior does become more behavioristic, we can learn more about making ourselves better readers, writers, citizens, and parents. We can learn more about preventing and rehabilitating inadequate repertoires. We can learn more about conserving our natural resources, maintaining the integrity of the environment, managing population growth, developing our economies in environmentally sustainable ways, preserving the dignity of human capital, and allocating resources to human needs instead of weapons of mass destruction. Given such a rich view of human nature, the prospects for improving the welfare of all members of our society are promising indeed.

B. F. Skinner wrote many books throughout his career. He concluded one of his most controversial books, *Beyond Freedom and Dignity* (1971), with the following paragraph:

> Early versions of environmentalism were inadequate because they could not explain how the environment worked, and much seemed left for autonomous man to do. But environmental contingencies now take over functions once attributed to autonomous man, and certain questions arise. Is man then "abolished"? Certainly not as a species or as an individual achiever. It is the autonomous inner man who is abolished, and that is a step forward. But does man not then become merely a victim or passive observer of what is happening to him? He is indeed controlled by his environment, but we must remember that it is an environment largely of his own making. The evolution of a culture is a gigantic exercise in self-control. It is often said that a scientific view of man leads to a wounded vanity, a sense of hopelessness, and nostalgia. But no theory changes what it is a theory about; man remains what he has always been. And a new theory may change what can be done with its subject matter. A scientific view of man offers exciting possibilities. We have not yet seen what man can make of man. (p. 215)

More noble words have rarely been spoken.

References

Sidman, M. (2001). *Coercion and its fallout* (rev. ed.). Boston: Authors Cooperative.
Skinner, B. F. (1971). *Beyond freedom and dignity*. New York: Knopf.

Name Index

A
Ackroff, J. 82
Allen, A. 112
Allport, G. 99
Aristotle 26, 171
Ayllon, T. 129

B
Bach, J. S. 105
Bacon, F. 78
Bandura, A. 49
Barnes-Holmes, D. 110
Barnes-Holmes, Y. 110
Bem, D. 112
Binder, C. 155
Binet, A. 101
Blakesleee, S. 61
Bloom, B. 158, 159
Bransford, J. 61
Bryant, D. 104

C
Callaghan, G. 131
Catania, A. C. 156
Cattell, R. 99
Cheney, D. L. 34
Church, R. 104
Cooper, J. 129
Costa, P. 99
Cullen, C. 110

D
Dawkins, R. 165
DeNike, L. 59
Descartes, R. 13, 23, 56, 58, 70, 120
Dickie 129
Dolezal, H. 84
Dougher, M. 130

E
Ellis, A. 133
Eysenck, H. 99

F
Faux, S. 101
Foree, D. 86
Franks, J. 61

Freud, S. 59, 97, 98, 132

G
Greenwald, A. 110
Gregory, R. 84

H
Haag, R. 104
Hardin, G. 143
Harris, M. 140
Hefferline, R. 59
Heider, F. 111
Hein, A. 83
Held, R. 83
Helen 129
Hippocrates 101
Hugdahl, K. 61

I
Isen, A. 123

J
James, W. 119
Jefferson, T. 147

NAME INDEX

K
Keenan, B. 59
Kelley, H. 111
Kohlenberg, R. 130

L
Lashley, K. 95
Levin, P. 123
Locke, J. 147
LoLordo, V. 86

M
Maslow, A. 49
Matthews, B. 156
McCrea, R. 99
McGhee, D. 110
Mees, H. 129
Michael, J. 124, 129, 153
Mischel, W. 112
Moore, J. 104, 129, 164

N
Neuringer, A. 104, 105

O
O'Reilly, J. 104
Oakes, W. 60
Odbert, H. 99

P
Page, S. 104
Pavlov, I. 75
Pinker, S. 70
Plato 168
Platt, J. 143
Pryor, K. 104

R
Ramachandran, V. 61
Risley, T. 129
Rogers, C. 49
Rotter, J. 49

S
S. B. 84, 85
Salaman, R. A. 41
Schwartz, J. 110
Seyfarth, R. M. 34
Shimoff, E. 156
Sidman, M. 171
Simon, T. 101
Skinner, B. F. 33, 41, 50, 75, 76, 82, 102, 146, 152, 153, 168, 172
Spielberger, C. 59
Stewart, I. 110
Stratton, G. 84
Summers, C. 131

T
Terman, L. 101
Thaver, F. 60
Thorndike, E. L. 124
Tolman, E. C. 95
Truax, C. 135
Tsai, M. 130

U
Updike, J. 105

W
Wallace, J. 84
Warren, R. 82
Watson, J. B. 14, 58
Weidman, M. 131
Weiskrantz, L. 59
Wolf, M. 129
Wundt, W. 14

Subject Index

A
abstraction 154
abstraction 39
actor-observer difference 112
agency 47, 48
agent 47
Ames room 76
applied behavior analysis 127
attention 85, 86
attitude 108, 109, 110
attribution theory 109, 111
awareness 59, 60

B
beginning repertoire 152
behavior 2
behavior modification 127
behavior analysis 1
belief 93
bell curve 100
Benham disk 81, 88
Bill of Rights 147
blindsight 60

Bloom=s taxonomy 158

C
chain 5, 91, 94
chromosomes 23
classical S - R behaviorism 14
clinical behavior analysis 130
CNS 69
cognition 64, 69
cognitive structures 157
collateral behavior 57
collateral responses 157, 159
collectivist culture 166
communication 35
competence 75
concept 38
conceptual stimulus control 154
conditioned punishers 6
conditioned reinforcers 5
conditioned respondent behavior 9
conditioned respondent seeing 82

conditioned stimulus 9
consciousness 53, 58, 61
consensus question 111
consistency paradox 112
consistency question 111
contingency shaped behavior 155
copy theory 87
countercontrol 115, 147, 168
covert operant behavior 57
cramp 121
creativity 103, 104
cultural level of selection 163
cultural practices 164, 165
culture 164

D
daydreaming 64
DDT 141
Declaration of Independence 147
declarative memory 67
democracy 167

depression 17, 121
design of a culture 167
determinism 98, 148
differential reinforcement of successive approximations 7
discrimination 8
discriminative stimulus 4
disposition 92, 93, 99, 109
distinctiveness question 111
divergent thinking 105
DNA 24
dreaming 86
drive 124
DSM-V 130

E
echoic memory 67
educational objectives 158, 160
ego 98
elicit/elicitation 9
emit/emission 4, 7
emotions 118, 125
epigenetics 26
episodic memory 67
epistemological dualism 76, 77, 78
equivalence relations 159
equivalence relations 40
establishing operation 124
ethics 138, 139, 140
evolution of a culture 166
explanatory fictions 17, 55
external attribution 111
extinction 7

F
feeling of freedom 48, 49
feelings 118, 119, 125
feelings of reinforcers 124, 125
fitness 28
fluency training 155
folk psychology 42, 48, 102

form of behavior 3
free will 19, 20, 21
freedom 48
frequency effects 113
functional characteristics of behavior 3
functional fixedness 105
functionalism 14, 94
fundamental attribution error 112

G
gene 24
generalization 7
generic nature of stimuli and responses 8
gestalt therapy 133
grammar 39

H
habit 4
humors 101

I
iconic memory 67
id 98
idealistic values 146
idiographic 106
immediate consequences 165
implicit association test (IAT) 110
implicit attitude measurement 110
implicit relational assessment procedure (IRAP) 110
individualist culture 166
individuality 46
insight 133
intelligence tests 100
intention 92
interactionism 13
internal attribution 111
interpretation 42
intraverbal 39, 159

introspection 14

J
junk DNA 24
jurisprudence 148
justified true belief 74

K
knowing how 74
knowing that 74
knowledge 73

L
language 35
letter grades 160
lotteries 49
lying 39, 93

M
Mach bands 81
maintenance of the behavior under infrequent reinforcement 153
making a decision 65
managed response 50
managed self 50, 51
managing response 50, 51
managing self 50, 51
mand 37
mapping the human genome 25
material cause 26
materialist values 146
meaning 35
mechanism 94
mediational S - O - R neobehaviorism 14
medical model 132
memes 165, 166
memory 66
mental rotation 83
mentalism 15, 16
mind 13, 14, 15, 69
mind-body problem 120

missing fundamental effect 81, 88
mnemonics 68, 69
moods 122, 123
morality 138, 139, 140
motivative operation 6
motives 122, 123
Müller-Lyer illusion 83, 88
multiple control 104
multiple gene traits 25
mutations 26

N
Necker cube 85, 87
negative punishment 6
negative reinforcement 5
neuroscience 16, 17, 71
nomothetic 106
nonspecific features of therapy 135
novelty 104
numerical grades 160

O
obligation 143
OCEAN 99
ontogenic level of selection 163, 164
operant behavior 4
operant seeing 82
optical illusions 83
other minds 122
ought 143

P
personality 97
phantom limb pain 61
phrenology 100
phylogenic level of selection 163
positive punishment 6
positive reinforcement 5
primacy effects 113
private/covert behavioral events 18, 55

problem solving 65
procedural memory 67
proposition 37
psychoanalysis 98, 133
psychophysics 87
public accompaniments 57
punisher 6
punishment 6, 148, 149
purpose 90

R
random behavior 7
rational emotive therapy 133
reasoning 65
recency effects 113
reference 35, 36
reification 42
reinforcement 5
reinforcer 5
Republic 168
respondent behavior 9
responsibilities 145, 147
rights 145, 147
Rogerian therapy 133
Roman numerals 37
rule 156

S
SAFMEDS 155
saying vs doing 109, 160
selection of behavior 28
selection of bodily characteristics 28
self 46, 50, 51
self-consciousness 54
self-control, self-management 48, 50, 51
self-tacts 92
semantic memory 67
sensory memory 67
sentence 37
shaping 7
short-term memory 68
should 143

single gene traits 24
situational ethics 140
social impact of behavior 140
stage theory 157
Stanford University 101
Stanford-Binet test 101
stimulus control 7
stimulus control over the terminal repertoire 153
stimulus generalization of pain 57
strong free will position 20
Stroop effect 82
structuralism 14, 94
suicide 106
super-ego 98
symptom substitution 133
syntax 40

T
tact 38, 154
teaching 152
temporalBintensive properties of the response 153
tennis 37, 40
terminal repertoire 152
thermostat 94
thinking 57, 64, 69, 93
three-term operant contingency 4
toothache 121
topography of the response 153
Tragedy of the Commons 143, 166
trait 99
transducers 80
type I error 157
type II error 157

U
unconditioned punishers 6
unconditioned reinforcers 5
unconditioned respondent behavior 9

unconditioned stimulus 9
unconscious 59

V
value judgments 145, 146
values 145, 146
variability 103

verbal behavior 33
verbal community 33
verbal episode 33
verbal knowledge 154
verbal reports 55
verbally regulated behavior 41, 155

vervet monkeys 34

W
Walden Two 168
weak free will position 20
white noise 81
working memory 68